The BEAUTY
OF GOD'S
HOLINESS

THOMAS L. TREVETHAN

IVP

InterVarsity Press
Downers Grove, Illinois
Leicester, England

InterVarsity Press
P.O. Box 1400, Downers Grove, IL 60515, USA
38 De Montfort Street, Leicester LE1 7GP, England

© *1995 by Thomas L. Trevethan and InterVarsity Christian Fellowship of the United States of America.*

InterVarsity Press®, U.S.A., is the book-publishing division of InterVarsity Christian Fellowship®, a student movement active on campus at hundreds of universities, colleges and schools of nursing in the United States of America, and a member movement of the International Fellowship of Evangelical Students. For information about local and regional activities, write Public Relations Dept., InterVarsity Christian Fellowship, 6400 Schroeder Rd., P.O. Box 7895, Madison, WI 53707-7895.

Inter-Varsity Press, England, is the book-publishing division of the Universities and Colleges Christian Fellowship (formerly the Inter-Varsity Fellowship), a student movement linking Christian Unions in universities and colleges throughout the United Kingdom and the Republic of Ireland, and a member movement of the International Fellowship of Evangelical Students. For information about local and national activities write to UCCF, 38 De Montfort Street, Leicester LE1 7GP.

All Scripture quotations, unless otherwise indicated, are taken from the HOLY BIBLE, NEW INTERNATIONAL VERSION®. NIV®. Copyright © 1973, 1978, 1984 by International Bible Society. Used by permission of Zondervan Publishing House and Hodder and Stoughton Ltd. All rights reserved.

Cover illustration: J. A. Kraulis/Masterfile
USA ISBN 0-8308-1607-0
UK ISBN 0-85111-678-7

Printed in the United States of America ∞

Library of Congress Cataloging-in-Publication Data

Trevethan, Thomas L., 1944-
   The beauty of God's holiness/Thomas Trevethan.
      p.   cm.
   ISBN 0-8308-1607-0
   1. God—Holiness.   2. God—Meditations.   I. Title.
BT147.T74   1995
231'.4—dc20   *94-45406*
                                                          CIP

British Library Cataloguing in Publication Data

A catalogue record for this book is available from the British Library.

17	16	15	14	13	12	11	10	9	8	7	6	5	4	3	2
09	08	07	06	05	04	03	02	01	00	99	98	97	96	95	

Preface

The seed from which this book grew was planted in 1979, when I read Richard Lovelace's profoundly insightful *Dynamics of Spiritual Life: An Evangelical Theology of Renewal.* Discussing the preconditions of renewal, Lovelace observed,

> *Acceptance of Christ and appropriation of every element in redemption is conditional on awareness of God's holiness and conviction of the depth of our sin.* As Calvin states in the great opening chapter of his *Institutes,* these two factors are essential to that degree of self-knowledge which drives a man to inquire after Christ, and they are deeply interrelated. Men and women cannot know themselves until they know the reality of the God who made them, and once they know the holy God, their own sin appears so grievous that they cannot rest until they have fully appropriated Christ.[1]

This observation seems to me more true now than when I first encountered it, not least because I have lived with its truth as I have haltingly attempted to compose this statement about the holiness of God. The health of the church depends on its embracing the reality of God's holiness. So I write with the prayer that this work will contribute something to the renewal and revival of the people of God.

Sinners have always been averse to serious reflection on the themes taken up in this book. In Old Testament times, the prophets' audiences reacted against preaching about judgment.

> "Do not prophesy," their prophets say,
>> "Do not prophesy about these things;
>> disgrace will not overtake us."
> Should it be said, O house of Jacob:

"Is the Spirit of the LORD angry?

Does he do such things?" (Mic 2:6-7)

In my ministry among university students and faculty I have seen an identical allergic reaction. Small wonder that our culture, having given itself to secularism, relativism and subjectivism, finds distasteful the truth of God's unrivaled majesty, sovereignty, goodness and justice. But it is particularly sad to find the same reaction among professing believers.

Given our penchant toward relativizing accounts of the views we find disagreeable, it is all too easy to dismiss the biblical account of the holiness of God as the quirk of an ancient society or the product of authoritarian personalities. I trust you will join me in resisting this characteristically postmodern impulse. Rather, seek actively to test the truth-value of the claims of this book, especially at those points where your first impulse is to simply dismiss them.

In conversations about these matters, others have often reminded me that holiness is not the whole truth about God. They are right. But that does not give us a mandate to ignore such difficult aspects of the truth in favor of more pleasant ideas associated with God's mercy, patience and love. We would prefer to ignore the truth about God's holiness, and this preference speaks volumes about our own culture-bound outlook. In so doing we domesticate the living God, distorting the truth about his character (a half-truth can, after all, be a whole lie) and lulling ourselves into a self-contented spiritual slumber.

Again, Lovelace points us to the way forward:

God's mercy, patience and love must be fully preached in the church. But they are not *credible* unless they are presented in tension with God's infinite power, complete and sovereign control of the universe, holiness, and righteousness. And where God's righteousness is clearly presented, compassionate warnings of his holy anger against sin must be given, and warnings also of the certainty of divine judgment in endless alienation from God which will be unimaginably worse than the literal descriptions of hell. It is no wonder that the world and the church are not awakened when our leadership is either singing a lullaby concerning these matters or presenting them in a caricature which is so grotesque that it is unbelievable.[2]

Honesty compels me to make one final observation. J. I. Packer begins the foreword to *Knowing God* by saying, "As clowns yearn to play Hamlet, so I have wanted to write a treatise on God."[3] His pithy saying has often caused me to reflect on my own efforts to compose this book. Certainly I play something of a fool to Packer's clown. Is it not arrogance for me to attempt

a project about which a wiser and more gifted person expresses such diffi-
dence? And in addition to the arrogance of even attempting this project, there
lurks the danger of deceiving myself into thinking that in writing about these
realities I have mastered them in my own life.

Packer, again, cites these wise words of C. S. Lewis: "Those like myself
whose imagination exceeds their obedience are subject to a just penalty; we
easily imagine conditions far higher than any we have really reached. If we
describe what we have imagined we may make others, and make ourselves,
believe that we have really been there."[4] So temptations to pride abound on
every side, threatening either to abort this whole project or to distort it in such
a way that it fails to be of any genuine value to God's people. Our world
certainly does not need one more proud utterance by a self-important teacher.
So I have been praying that this text will point beyond itself to the Holy One
whose glory should be our supreme passion.

"Consider therefore the kindness and sternness of God." So the apostle
Paul enjoins us (Rom 11:22). Notice, kindness *and* sternness. To stress kindness without sternness results in the worship of a magnified image of human
tolerance. Sternness without kindness distorts God into a hideous gargoyle.
In either case we are deprived of that true knowledge of God and of ourselves
which leads to life.

With a prayer for the renewal of God's people and the extension of God's
kingdom, I trust that this book will enable you to "behold your God" (Is 40:9
RSV) in the majesty and beauty of his holiness.

1

THE MEANING
OF *HOLY*

*H*OLY IS THE MOST INTIMATELY DIVINE WORD IN THE BIBLE. IT IS THAT IN GOD which marks him off as God. To say that he is holy is to say that he is God. Holiness, in Scripture, is the fundamental attribute of God that conditions and qualifies all other attributes.

Holy apparently comes from a Semitic root that means "to cut." Hence its basic meaning is "to separate" or "to make distinct" (as in "to cut off"). Most fundamentally, as a divine attribute it claims that God is other and set apart from everything else, that he is in a class by himself. God is not just quantitatively greater than us, but qualitatively different in his greatness. He is transcendent, infinitely above or beyond us. The true God is distinct, set apart, from all that he has made as the only truly self-sufficient Being. All his creatures depend on him; he alone exists from within himself.

And the true God is distinct, set apart, from all that is evil. His moral perfection is absolute. His character as expressed in his will forms the absolute standard of moral excellence. God is holy, the absolute point of reference for all that exists and is good. Across the board he is to be contrasted with his creatures. At heart he is a glowing-white center of absolute purity.

Biblical Images of God's Holiness

The foundational significance of holiness is underscored in the biblical passages where God himself is encountered. Consider, for example, Moses' encounter with God in the burning bush (Ex 3). God's first move in revealing himself to Moses is to declare his holiness (Ex 3:5). And this narrative of God's revelation to Moses and Israel reaches its colossal climax by an awesome restatement of the same truth. The flame of holiness that burned in the bush becomes an awesome mountain of fire blazing up into heaven (Ex 19). In what he spoke to Moses and in his mighty deeds, this holy God is declared to be the One who overthrows his enemies and saves his own people. Liberation and judgment are equally aspects of his holiness and together help define his holy character.

Or, again, consider Isaiah's formative encounter with God in the temple (Is 6). The prophet is allowed a glimpse into the reality of heaven, where the seraphim cry to one another, "Holy, holy, holy is the LORD Almighty" (v. 3). In Isaiah's vision this holy God is high and lifted up (unimaginably great and exalted), sitting on a throne (sovereign over all). His glory fills all the earth (he is the uncreated Creator of our wonderful world), and his presence fills Isaiah with a sense of guilt and the need for forgiveness (moral purity). Thus we are given profound insight into the importance and nature of God's holiness.

Finally, consider John's vision of heaven in Revelation 4. Again the heavenly court sums up its unceasing worship: "Holy, holy, holy is the Lord God Almighty, who was, and is, and is to come" (v. 8). In addition to stressing the Holy One's eternity, the vision shows him sitting on a throne, ruling over all his creatures and the course of history (the scroll of 5:1), and he receives worship as the Creator of all things.

In these accounts of seeing and meeting God, the central aspects of his holiness stand out clearly. The Holy One is high and exalted, great beyond our imagining, the uncreated Creator of all that is, the sovereign Lord of all. Further, the Holy One is perfect in goodness, a lover of justice and righteousness whose wrath goes out against all that is evil and whose mercy reaches out to deliver the poor, the helpless and the needy. As such he alone is worthy of the praise of all his creatures. These thoughts are well summarized in Psalm 99:

> The LORD reigns,
>   let the nations tremble;
> he sits enthroned between the cherubim,

let the earth shake.
Great is the LORD in Zion;
    he is exalted over all the nations.
Let them praise your great and awesome name—
    he is holy.

The King is mighty, he loves justice—
    you have established equity;
in Jacob you have done
    what is just and right.
Exalt the LORD our God
    and worship at his footstool;
    he is holy.

Moses and Aaron were among his priests,
    Samuel was among those who called on his name;
they called on the LORD
    and he answered them.
He spoke to them from the pillar of cloud;
    they kept his statutes and the decrees he gave them.

O LORD our God,
    you answered them;
you were to Israel a forgiving God,
    though you punished their misdeeds
Exalt the LORD our God
    and worship at his holy mountain,
    for the LORD our God is holy.

God and the Gods

It is worth reminding ourselves that Israel—and the early church as well—was surrounded by peoples who conceived of the divine reality in a very different way, in a way exactly contradictory to the teaching of the Bible.

The basic difference between Yahweh and the gods of the ancient Near East becomes evident when we compare the following poems. The first comes from Mesopotamia in the late second millennium B.C., while the second is from Psalm 29 in our Old Testament. While they are quite similar in poetic form and both describe an approaching thunderstorm, the two poems present contrasting views of the relationship of the divine to the world.

A storm cloud lying on the horizon,
    its heart inscrutable.
His word, a storm cloud lying on the horizon,
    its heart inscrutable;
the word of great Ani, a storm cloud lying on the horizon,
    its heart inscrutable;
the word of Enlil, a storm cloud lying on the horizon,
    its heart inscrutable;
the word of Enki, a storm cloud lying on the horizon,
    its heart inscrutable;
the word of Asalluhe, a storm cloud lying on the horizon,
    its heart inscrutable;
the word of Enbilulu, a storm cloud lying on the horizon,
    its heart inscrutable;
the word of Mudugsaa, a storm cloud lying on the horizon,
    its heart inscrutable;
the word of Shiddukisharra, a storm cloud lying on the horizon,
    its heart inscrutable;
his word which up above makes the heavens tremble,
his word which down below rocks the earth,
his word wherewith the Anunnaki gods destroy,
his word has no seer (who can foresee it),
    no diviner (who could divine it),
his word is a risen flood-storm,
    it has none who could oppose it.[1]

Ascribe to the LORD, O mighty ones,
    ascribe to the LORD glory and strength.
Ascribe to the LORD the glory due his name;
    worship the LORD in the splendor of his holiness.

The voice of the LORD is over the waters;
    the God of glory thunders,
    the LORD thunders over the mighty waters.
The voice of the LORD is powerful;
    the voice of the LORD is majestic.
The voice of the LORD breaks the cedars;
    the LORD breaks in pieces the cedars of Lebanon
He makes Lebanon skip like a calf,

> Sirion like a young wild ox.
> The voice of the LORD strikes
>   with flashes of lightning.
> The voice of the LORD shakes the desert;
>   the LORD shakes the Desert of Kadesh.
> The voice of the LORD twists the oaks
>   and strips the forests bare.
> And in his temple all cry, "Glory!"
> The LORD sits enthroned over the flood;
>   the LORD is enthroned as King forever.
> The LORD gives strength to his people;
>   the LORD blesses his people with peace. (Ps 29)

For the men and women of the ancient Near East the "divine" was experienced basically as immanent rather than transcendent. The divine spiritual reality was conceived as "indwelling spirit, as power at the center of something that caused it to be and thrive and flourish."[2] Rather than seeing God as using the bush to signal his presence, as Moses did, the ancients were apt to conceive of God as "the power of the bush, the vital force causing it to be and making it thrive and flourish."[3]

This most fundamental difference signals a clash of worldviews, of basic perspectives that took the people who held them in radically different religious and cultural directions. So basic were the differences that when they came into contact, conflict was inevitable.

Worlds Ruled by Magic

Starting with the worldview of the immanent force, the distinctive characteristics of the religions of the ancient Near East are quite understandable. This worldview led inevitably to a plurality of gods that were personifications of the inner power of diverse forces of nature. In a basically agricultural society the principal deities were those that controlled the elements, the change of seasons and the powers of fertility. In some sense the gods actually *were* these natural phenomena.

Because natural forces can be both beneficial and destructive, it was inescapable that the gods embody both cruelty and kindness, evil and good. And because there were so many gods or goddesses, each relating to only a limited aspect of the world, religious life became compartmentalized and chaotic. To make matters worse, natural phenomena often are quite destructive and seem in conflict with one another. So these often cruel gods and goddesses came to be thought of as being in constant conflict and war with one another. This combination of evil and good in the divine and constant chaos and conflict among the gods made the gods inscrutable and quite unknowable in any personal sense. They were powerful to be sure, but because they had no stable character or constancy, the idea of friendship with the gods was quite foreign.

Further, because the divine was bound up with its corresponding natural phenomenon, worship was conceived as a sort of "sympathetic magic." The deity was invoked and its power released by actions that imitated the outer form of the natural phenomenon associated with it. For example, if fertility in the fields and flocks was desired, "holy" sexual acts were performed to release the power of the god. Because agricultural prosperity was highly desirable but completely subject to rather capricious natural forces in ancient Canaan, sacred prostitution was widely practiced.

On the other hand, the presence of the deity was to be found in "striking" events and happenings in the course of nature. So one could trace the ways of gods and goddesses by making lists of these happenings and use the lists to predict future divine acts. What counted as "striking" varied quite widely according to time and place. For some it was powerful or unusual weather conditions that arrested attention. Others charted astronomical phenomena, producing the pseudoscience of astrology. Others studied the relatively minor variations in the appearance of the livers of animals. Still others kept lists of omens, including perhaps the particularly plaintive call of a bird or an unusual string of luck in tossed dice. The goal, in each case, was to trace the ways of the deities within natural phenomena in order to predict the future.

As a result images, cultic drama, incantation and divination became the dominant forms of worship. Another name for all of this is *magic*. Magical worldviews are inevitable when the divine reality is immanent but not transcendent. A whole technology arises to invoke and predict the course of reality. But notice, there is little true rational understanding, just the juxtaposition of random happenings that give a measure of predictability to the affairs of life. This worldview produces astrology, not astronomy; ectiscopy (the inspection of animal livers and other entrails), not medicine; technology, not science. By these means the god or goddess was placated, encouraged, caused to act—in short, manipulated for the benefit of its devotees.

Not surprisingly, a people's convictions about ultimate reality tend to mirror and shape the basic character of their social life. Among the neighbors of ancient Israel this was certainly true. The gods, conceived as immanent powers, came quite naturally to be identified with the fortunes of their people.

The god became the guarantor of the affluence of his people, the power latent in the nation's army and the foundation of the nation's political order. Characteristically the god's social reality was focused in the king, who was thought of as a demigod himself and the mediator of the god's presence. The social result was a highly authoritarian, rigidly stratified regime. The king and his extended family owned all the material resources and ruled absolutely as agents of the deity. The gods became defenders of this rather oppressive status quo.

But notice what happened to the estimate of the god when the king and the nation suffered setback. The god was shown to be deficient, along with his people. Obliteration of the nation would leave the god on the trash heap of history as well.

The Holy One of Israel

The faith of Israel, alone among the peoples of the ancient Near East, started with the conception of a holy, transcendent God. From this perspective all the strange differences that set apart Israelite religion among the faiths of the ancients are understandable.

First, because Yahweh is "high and lifted up," he is in a class by himself. Monotheism flowed directly out of a worldview based on the transcendent reality of God.

Second, because Yahweh was above the natural world and the flow of history, it was possible to conceive of a dramatically different account of his relationship to good and evil. The immanent deities of paganism, because of their essential connection to our fallen world, had to be thought of as embodying both the good and the evil attributes we find around us. They were, like us, fallen persons with a complex and corrupted moral character that included both cruelty and kindness, dishonesty and truthfulness, lust and genuine love. In philosophically sophisticated paganism, moral goodness and virtue became detached from the gods and their superstitious worship.

The Holy One, however, is above and outside our fallen world. As its maker he has permitted it a measure of moral freedom, even the freedom to oppose him. Evil arises as a mystery, to be sure, but it does *not* arise from within the Holy One. Further, goodness is not outside of God. Rather, it is rooted in and measured by his character and his will (which arises from and expresses his character). Finally, as the ruler and sustainer of all of his creatures, the Holy One stands over against evil as its enemy and judge. His worshipers are not forced to choose between loyalty to what they know to be good and loyalty to their Maker. In the end they can be certain of the triumph of good and the defeat of evil because of the authority and power of the Holy One. So it is that the one holy God can logically be conceived of as being good through and through. Evil is no part of his basic character.

Third, because God alone was the maker and ruler of the apparent chaos of conflicting forces of nature, it was possible for the Israelites to trust that there was a stability to his character. The finite deities of paganism were hopelessly fickle, changing whimsically as the circumstances they confronted changed. In this they resembled those circumstances, of course, for they were immanent within the changing moods of nature. Their combination of power and changeableness made them someone to reckon with. But you had to be cautious in approaching them. You could never be sure what sort of mood you might find them in.

Fourth, the combination of stability (self-consistency or faithfulness), goodness and power in the Holy One make it possible to see why a committed relationship (or covenant) and trust were central to Hebrew life in a way they never could have been under notions of an immanent deity. Here is a God who does not change on a whim, nor is it possible for change to be forced on him by overpowering circumstances. He can be counted on. Further, because he is self-consistent in this marvelous way, it is possible to learn his ways and his will. Though he always exceeds our capacity to comprehend him fully, understanding is not out of the question. Finally, because he is good through and through we need fear no evil from him. He has no destructive side waiting to lash out at us. We can draw near and find a friend, a covenant partner, in the Holy One.

The Worldview of Transcendence

Other unique elements follow from these four basic factors. Fifth is that Israelite religious practice was distinct from all others in the ancient world in its rejection of images, magic, divination, necromancy and other black arts, and of any concept of sexuality or fertility in God. Indeed, Hebrew has no word for "goddess." These rejections are absolutely astonishing, for magical practices were widely characteristic of the cultural milieu of Mesopotamia, Egypt and Canaan. By far the greatest number of religious texts unearthed from the environs of Israel were collections of omens used in the practice of divination or magic. And no religious artifact of ancient civilization is more characteristic than the idol.

For two reasons, none of these practices was necessary for Israel. Its God did not change like the weather; he was constant in his transcendent majesty. And this same God spoke in a clear and unambiguous way to his people by the prophets (see Deut 18:9-11). Indeed, magical practices are deeply offensive to God, for they are attempts to manipulate him rather than expressions of trust in his constancy and his spoken word.

Sixth, this basic conviction about the transcendence of God underlay the uniqueness of the Hebrew Bible. Central to the Bible is a tradition of prose narrative and historical reporting quite unlike the "national epics" of surrounding peoples. The epic is a long narrative poem that extols the virtues and accomplishments of legendary ancestral heroes, particularly in their battles with traditional enemies and often with the gods themselves. The recitation of national epics thus promoted national pride and moved people to imitate the character and derring-do of their great ancestors. Scholars have often carelessly spoken of the "national epic" of ancient Israel or conjectured about an oral creation epic and exodus epic upon which biblical writers drew. But what we actually find in the Bible is a deliberate avoidance of epic. As Israeli Bible scholar Shemaryahu Talmon has argued,

> The ancient Hebrew writers purposely nurtured and developed prose narration to take the place of the epic genre which by its content was intimately bound up with the world of paganism, and appears to have had a special standing in the polytheistic cults. The recitation of the epics was tantamount to an enactment of cosmic events in the manner of sympathetic magic. In the process of the total rejection of the polytheistic religions and their ritual expressions in the cult, epic songs and also the epic genre were purged from the repertoire of the Hebrew authors.[4]

Seventh, the sociopolitical shape of Israel's society was also startlingly unique. Yahweh, the Holy One, was Israel's King. For many centuries Israel was without a human king, and only very reluctantly was a limited form of monarchy adopted. Notice how oddly anti-imperial its kingship was to be in contrast to the practice of monarchy among its neighbors (see Deut 17:14-20). Israel's king was to have no advanced military technology ("horses and chariots"), no harem and no accumulation of wealth. He was to be reckoned a "brother" who placed himself under the authority of the law of Yahweh like all other Israelites.

Indeed, the infinite sovereignty of the Holy One over the whole nation greatly reduced the relative importance of all kinds of human authority within the nation. The result was an amazingly egalitarian social vision quite unlike anything in the wider cultural environment of Israel. The king was a vassal king (not an autonomous imperial monarch), as much subject to God's covenant law as any of his subjects. The judge and the offender both stood before the bar of the Holy One's justice. The landlord was only a tenant on land owned by his God (not his human king). Slave and master were alike slaves of the Lord. The father was one of a nation of the sons of God. As Christopher J. H. Wright concludes in his stimulating account of Old Testament ethics,

There is, then, a strong link between Israel's theocentric monotheism (the central arch of her faith) and her tendency towards her own brand of socio-political and economic "egalitarianism." This did not obliterate differentials, but attempted to continue them within the proper limits of functional necessity for the harmony and peace of society. Faith and obedience rendered to an absolute God militated against allowing absolute power or prestige to any human authority. The sociological outworking of this link between covenant faith and socio-political and economic structures . . . resulted in Israelite society exhibiting clear and probably deliberate contrasts with their contemporary neighbours, politically and economically, on a scale which makes them possibly unique in the ancient world.[5]

Eighth, the transcendent Yahweh was not a tribal God bound to the fate of his people, their nation-state or a human king. He was above them. Therefore, God's spokesmen, the prophets, did not endorse the status quo. Rather, they consistently raised a radical critique of Israel and its neighbors in the name of Yahweh. They even predicted the destruction of Israel in the name of Israel's God. In fact, it required an obliteration of Israel as a nation-state and as a culture in the Babylonian captivity to convince the Israelites of the unique and sole glory of their God. Indeed, it is impressive testimony to the basic conception of Yahweh as transcendent that their faith survived such a holocaust.

A Clash of Worldviews

Remembering Israel's captivity in Babylon reminds us that grasping and affirming this radical faith in a transcendent God was no easy task. Surrounded by people who held and practiced a basically different faith, Israel was constantly under pressure to surrender its basic and most important conviction. Often the nation succumbed to this pressure. Conflict was inevitable.

We see this conflict in its most gripping form in Elijah's contest with the 450 priests of Baal on Mt. Carmel (1 Kings 18:17-40). The Baals were Canaanite fertility gods whose worship undoubtedly involved wild orgiastic rites and perhaps even infant sacrifice (see the summary indictment of Israel's defection from God in 2 Kings 17:15-18). Baal worship made its way into the life of Israel by a gradual process of accommodation to the culture of Canaan. But an unparalleled influx of Baalism occurred during the reign of Ahab. He married Jezebel, a princess from neighboring Sidon, who brought her religion and its outward forms with her into the very heart of God's people. Ahab built a temple to Baal in Samaria, worshiped there himself and erected a sacred grove (an Asherah) where private idolatrous rites could be conducted. In sum, Ahab "did more to provoke the LORD, the God of Israel, to anger than did all the kings of Israel before him" (1 Kings 16:33).

In response the Lord raised up Elijah to contest these syncretistic and unfaithful practices. After announcing a three-year drought, Elijah was protected from Jezebel's bloody purge of Yahweh's prophets. Finally he called on Ahab to send the prophets of Baal to meet him at Mt. Carmel for a definitive test to determine the identity of the true and living God. As Elijah said to the people, "How long will you waver between two opinions? If the LORD is God, follow him; but if Baal is God, follow him" (1 Kings 18:21).

Two altars were erected, two bulls were killed and prepared for sacrifice. Each side was to call on its god to ignite the sacrifice. As the priests of Baal began their wild, ecstatic incantations, Elijah looked on. With irony, contempt and humor he taunted them: "Shout louder! . . . Perhaps he is deep in thought, or busy, or traveling. Maybe he is sleeping and must be awakened" (1 Kings 18:27).

Then Elijah stepped forward, prepared his altar and sacrifice and had it drenched with water three times to assure the people who stood watching that this was no magic trick. Simply and briefly he called on the Lord, asking him to vindicate not only Elijah but also his own great name, so that Israel would know who was God indeed. Immediately fire fell from the Lord and consumed the whole altar.

The proper conclusion to this whole episode was made crystal-clear by the prophet Jeremiah, speaking about three hundred years later on the eve of Jerusalem's destruction:

Their idols are like scarecrows in a cucumber field,
    and they cannot speak;
they have to be carried,
    for they cannot walk.
Be not afraid of them,
    for they cannot do evil,
    neither is it in them to do good. . . .
But the LORD is the true God;
    he is the living God and the everlasting King.
At his wrath the earth quakes,
    and the nations cannot endure his indignation. (Jer 10:5, 10 RSV)

You would think that such a display would have settled the issue of "who is

God?" once and for all. The people were impressed momentarily. But the pressure of the surrounding culture and an apostate leadership in the nation made this victory a temporary one. Though a faithful remnant of true Israelites was established and encouraged, Israel's days were numbered. So strong is the natural, fallen human bent toward conformity to the surrounding world. And so "natural" is our inclination to an immanent, manageable god. As W. H. Auden sadly observed, "We would rather be ruined than change."

The Clash Continues

Not surprisingly, the infant Christian church was forced to face the same struggle as it moved out in mission toward the pagan world of late Greco-Roman civilization. Luke records the first skirmishes in what was also to be a centuries-long battle. Recall how the unsophisticated farmers in Derbe and Lystra shouted that Paul and Barnabas were deities (Acts 14:8-18). Appalled, the missionaries tore their clothes and immediately tried to correct this manifestation of "immanentism."

Paul faced a more sophisticated philosophical version of the same view in the great cultural center of Athens (Acts 17:16-33). Again his spirit was "greatly distressed" (v. 16), and he was moved to challenge the great immanentist philosophical system of Stoicism by teaching the truth that "the God who has made the world and everything in it is the Lord of heaven and earth and does not live in temples built by hands" (v. 24).

In Ephesus Paul confronted a more spiritist, mystical and irrational version of the same basic religion; Acts 19 uses biting irony and humor to tell the story. The syncretistic sons of Sceva tried to use the name of Jesus mindlessly. Their attempt to employ what they saw as Paul's powerful technological tool (the name of Jesus) backfired. The unimpressed demon remarked, "Jesus I know, and I know about Paul, but who are you?" (v. 15). Here in Ephesus, as in other places, the power of the Holy One triumphed.

Indeed, despite the intensity (years of official and unofficial persecution) and duration (at least four centuries) of the struggle, and despite the weakness of the young church (it was at first a tiny minority of conscience, often an illegal society), the truth of the Holy One triumphed again and again. Not least this victory over a great and sophisticated pagan civilization was due to the courageous faithfulness of God's people to the basic concept of the holiness of their God.

In our day there are similar challenges to a robust faith in the holiness of God. Many people seek to explain the biblical concept of God as simply the product of ancient times which emerged along the path of a long evolutionary development: Beginning with a very primitive faith in demons, the human race traveled the long, arduous road of increasing refinement until it arrived at either a pure immanent spirit or a purely scientific mechanistic world with no spirits at all. Certainly the biblical faith was an important stage along the way, but it is only that—an inferior, even primitive, stage of development that must be understood as a totally conditioned product of its environment. No modern would want to be locked in the past, infatuated with a primitive idea whose time has passed.

Did Israel Borrow Its Religion?

Such an account of the history of religion, however, is plainly inadequate. The Old Testament conception of holiness leaped onto the stage of human history as a radically strange idea and a true innovation. It was scarcely understood by the masses in Israel and was treated as an extreme oddity by Israel's neighbors. As late as the time of the primitive church, Jews and Christians were reckoned "atheists" because they did not believe in the gods.

There are certain vestiges of past or other religious cultures in the Old Testament writings. To be of any value, God's revelation had to take root in real historical languages and cultures. But these same writings show a marked tendency to divest the terms of their original connotations. Often mythological expressions are used as poetic symbolism without indicating the slightest reverence for the original deities. William Albright's conclusion is worth noting:

> It may confidently be stated that there is no true mythology anywhere in the Hebrew Bible. What we have consists of vestiges—what may be called the "debris" of a past religious culture. There are, however, a great many vestiges from Canaanite religion among the Hebrews. The names of many pagan gods and goddesses continued to be used in Hebrew for religious and nonreligious purposes, just as in English. For instance, when we speak of eating breakfast cereal we certainly do not mean to imply the worship of the goddess Ceres. The word has simply been borrowed and applied to products of that name. . . . If anyone insists that these etymologies prove the mythological character of our beliefs, we should have every right to laugh him out of court, and yet such reasoning is still common among historians of religion.[6]

Likewise, many aspects of Hebrew life and religion showed obvious formal similarities to those of surrounding peoples. But because of Israel's radically different view of God, these similarities were merely formal, external likenesses that upon inspection prove to have radically different significance.

Two instances should suffice to demonstrate that this is so. One is the whole sacrificial apparatus. All the peoples of the ancient Near East offered sacrifices in very similar ways. Altars of similar description in portable shrines or temples of much the same description were the scene of the offerings of the same range of animals, which were slaughtered and manipulated in similar ways. But the significance of the sacrifices turns out to have been quite different at crucial points. In Israel sacrifice never provided something God needed (like food), nor did it "buy off" God. Rather, it functioned to meet humanity's need for restoration to God's fellowship and favor, and it served as a concrete expression of thankfulness for God's initiative of grace. Further, the rite was not magical in any way. In and of itself it never accomplished its purpose apart from the proper spiritual motivation and understanding in the worshiper.

Doubtless many Israelites failed to grasp or live up to the biblical ideal. As they increasingly fell under the influence of Canaanite ideas, defection from God's revealed will in the covenant also increased. Sacrifice and worship in general became steadily more superstitious, magical and self-serving. The prophetic critique of sacrifice arose not as a rejection of sacrifice per se, but as a correction of abuse and a reminder of the *purpose* of sacrifice: the enjoyment of fellowship and communion between the Holy One and his people.

Interestingly, the prophetic movement itself is another instance of formal similarity to other ancient Near Eastern cultures. All kings had their retinue of prophets who plied the trade of predicting the future. Not surprisingly, these "kept" prophets were almost never "prophetic." Rather, they read the proper omens—an admittedly ambiguous and confusing task—basically to conform to the intentions and prejudices of their monarch, who often was viewed as a demigod himself. The contrast with the true prophets of Yahweh couldn't be more striking. They always stood over against the king and the current status quo as messengers of God's covenant. Often they were champions of the rural proletariat, the poor and the powerless. And most striking of all, never was there any trafficking in the occult, wresting the secrets of a hidden future from reluctant deities. Rather, the prophets spoke "the word of the LORD," a message addressed to the mind and heart of his people by the one true King of all. The aim, as in sacrifice, was restoration to a true, living, vital communion with their covenant God.

The transcultural element in Israel's religion thus turns out to be not a few random bits and pieces, but the Hebrews' most fundamental conception of the nature of their God. Evolutionary development and cultural borrowing seem quite inadequate to account for the sorts of differences that separate the biblical tradition from the rest of the ancient Near East. Everything was conditioned by the fact that Israel held radically and tenaciously to the transcendent holiness of God. As a result, its whole worldview was different from that of its neighbors. Would it not be wisest (as well as most faithful) for us to view Israel's faith as the product of knowledge given to the Hebrew people from beyond their ken, as the result of the revealing activity of the Holy One? Certainly you could not be counted as irrational for doing so.

The New Immanentism

Not only does the popular evolutionary view of religion err in its assessment of the character and origin of the biblical faith, but it seems equally mistaken in its view of the end of the evolutionary process. We who proclaim and defend biblical faith in the Holy One find ourselves opposed not so much by the irreligion of our opponents as by their actual religious zeal. Speak about the spiritual force that indwells all things humane, decent and beautiful, and you are met with polite, even friendly interest. Better still if you affirm that this "ground of being" is reached via any number of paths, so that we can all approach it according to our own preferences and insights.

Such is the contemporary religion I call "immanentism." It commands the widest possible assent, ranging on the academic side from Paul Tillich's "God beyond God" and Alfred North Whitehead's "process theology," to pop-culture ideologies like "the Force" of *Star Wars* and various New Age movements.

But the atmosphere in conversation clouds as soon as you mention a God with a determinant character who has set purposes and acts accordingly—a concrete, choosing, commanding, acting God. People become uncomfortable, even angry, as they label these ideas crude, primitive and unscientific.

Now this fashionable immanentism is certainly no new thing. It is arguably among the most ancient of "religious" conceptions, the permanent natural bent of the human mind as it gropes after the divine and shapes its own religion. This religion of the all-pervasive spirit is characteristic of India and the East from beyond the edge of recorded history. It formed the cultural milieu of Israel's environment. The Greeks rose above it only fitfully and incompletely in the philosophies of Plato and Aristotle. By the early Christian era they had relapsed into the great pantheistic synthesis of Stoicism. In more recent times it reemerged philosophically in idealism, particularly in G. W. F. Hegel, under whose influence it was blended into Christian theology. The writings of William Wordsworth, Ralph Waldo Emerson and William Blake were steeped in the same spirit. More recently still we witness the fascination with Eastern religions and various New Age philosophies among secularized and jaded Westerners. Indeed, immanentism is congenial to the modern mind, as its advocates never tire of telling us. But the fact that a boot fits does not prove that it is a new boot, let alone that it will keep your feet dry.

As for most people born and educated under late modernity, the holiness of God was a profoundly difficult concept for me. I was schooled under the tyrannical grip of scientism, and my preliminary skirmish with the biblical God had to do with the problem of "miracle." The idea of a God who broke the laws of nature and interfered in its orderly process seemed deeply repellent. But the wise and patient counsel of two professors at my secular university and C. S. Lewis's masterful *Miracles* helped me acknowledge both the descriptive character of scientific laws and the adequate power of the Creator to do whatever, in his wisdom, he might know to be good. To my chagrin I had no genuinely compelling grounds for rejecting the Holy One's intrusions. Indeed, I had no reason to even label them intrusions.

Then the real battle was joined, for it became clear that such a God not only could, but must, demand my ultimate allegiance. The wonderfully paradoxical and gracious words of Jesus, "Whoever finds his life will lose it, and whoever loses his life for my sake will find it" (Mt 10:39), pressed in on me. I did not hear the promise or see the blessing in them. But the force of the reality of the Holy One weighed on me. Late in the evening in November 1963 I knelt by my bed and bowed to the absolute centrality of the Holy One come to us in Jesus of Nazareth.

Of course that was not the last skirmish. Always I would prefer to be the linchpin of reality. I preferred to pursue my own vocation and career, not responding to the call of the Holy One but talking only to myself about myself. I preferred to get away with petty lies and dishonesties. I preferred to live for the sake of my own fulfillment, according to my own insights and intuitions. But all this fog of personal "selfist" mythology only obscures the beauty of reality. And by the mercy of the Holy One, the fog burns away under the brightness of his light. That light sears and burns on occasion, but it also lights up reality with purpose and joy. By losing my life, as Jesus says, I have found it.

We are told repeatedly that the vast majority of people believe in God. But human beings, particularly modern ones, are reluctant to surrender the concept of an abstract, impersonal deity. The god of immanentism is very comfortable; it does nothing and demands nothing. Like a bottle of aspirin sitting in a medicine cabinet, it can be taken out, dusted off and used at our convenience to assuage our cosmic aches and pains. Such a god will not pursue you, will not interfere in your private affairs. There is no danger that the earth will quake, lightning will flash and the mountains will melt like wax at its approach. There is no question of owing it our absolute allegiance or of standing open before it to give account of ourselves.

Supposing We Really Found God

The Holy One of the Bible is rejected by a shallow modernity (or a traditional paganism—they amount to much the same thing) not because he is spoken of naively as a man. No, the Bible's view of God is hated, at bottom, because it pictures him as King, a warrior king who attacks our selfish little worlds with his demand for repentance and obedience. Or we turn aside from the Bible's view of God because it makes us uncomfortable with its talk of God as Judge before whom great and small will stand to give account. As C. S. Lewis muses,

An "impersonal God"—well and good. A subjective God of beauty, truth and goodness better still. A formless life-force surging through us, a vast power which we can tap, best of all. But God Himself, alive, pulling at the other end of the cord, perhaps approaching at infinite speed, the hunter, king, husband—that is quite another matter. There comes a moment when children who have been playing at burglars hush suddenly: was that a real footstep in the hall? There comes a moment when people who have been dabbling in religion ("Man's search for God!") suddenly draw back. Supposing we really found Him? We never meant it to come to that. Worse still, supposing He had found us? So it is a sort of Rubicon. One goes across, or not. But if one does, there is no manner of security against miracle. One may be in for anything.[7]

I invite you to cross this Rubicon with me and confront the Holy One in all his magnificence.

PART I

THE HOLINESS OF GOD

2

THE MAJESTY
OF GOD

GOD SHRINKERS HAVE BEEN AT WORK IN WESTERN CULTURE, SCALING DOWN THE Holy One to the measure of the human mind and experience. Shut out of his creation by seventeenth-century deism, silenced, as a matter of method, by eighteenth-century rationalism (Immanuel Kant) and scaled down to the dimension of our religious experiences by nineteenth-century romanticism (Friedrich Schleiermacher), the living God who creates and rules and intrudes in the flow of history to rescue and speak was seriously diminished in the understanding of "modern" people. The God of the Bible became an embarrassment, a primitive tribal deity in need of radical updating by humankind come of age.

In our disillusioned twentieth century, people are no longer convinced of the myth of progress. We know that things are not getting steadily better, nor are human beings getting any wiser. And it seems clear that science, despite its vast prestige and the real intellectual progress it has brought, does not tell us all we need to know, or even what we most need to know. Our prodigious technological achievements rise to mock our inability to live together in peace, to care for the helpless, to order our increasingly chaotic lives justly and peacefully. It is we who are the primitives, moral and spiritual dwarfs, caught in the web of our proud self-assertion.

Nevertheless, we have chosen to be heirs of the God-shrinking process. Contemporary secularism forces God to the periphery of life and suggests that he is impotent, or at least not a factor, in most day-to-day life. Humanism continues to promote the increasingly discredited notion that humanity is the measure of all things, even God. Materialism, through the advertising media, assaults us on both conscious and unconscious levels with the perverse notion that life does indeed consist in an abundance of possessions.

We become, consequently, a tribe of thrill-seekers, grabbing for all the gusto we can get, or we fit in and become "organization men," cautiously half-alive, hedging our every bet, drained of adventure and joy. In either case our self-absorption is near total. We live for ourselves under the slogan "Do your own thing." "Blessed are the self-actualized, for theirs is the good life."

We have not given up religion. Indeed, we continue to "improve" on the Bible's view of God. We relegate God to the sphere of inner experience as the means to peace of mind, the great dispenser of warm fuzzies. God is like a giant aspirin: take God three times a day and you will feel no pain. Our Maker is transformed into a means to achieve our ends of success, material comfort and personal peace.

A God of Vast Power

For Christians who profess to believe in the God of the Bible, the situation is rarely so extreme. But each of these intellectual and cultural forces lays claim to our attention and loyalty. The din of our surroundings leads us to accommodation, in both our way of living and in our view of God, a god markedly smaller than the Holy One. We need help to resist the mentality of God-shrinking, to focus and expand our understanding of the greatness of God.

Throughout Scripture the true and living God is beyond our imagining. To help unshackle our minds, it often bids us compare God with things we think of as great. A classic example of this is found is Isaiah 40:12-31. This poetic exaltation of the Holy One is filled with questions designed to jolt us out of familiar habits of thought. The key question, repeated in verses 18 and 25, is, " 'To whom will you compare me? Or who is my equal?' says the Holy One."

Three sorts of things are tried on for size in rapid succession. First, powerful or awe-inspiring phenomena (vv. 12-17): the oceans, mountains, human knowledge and justice, nations, human religious devotion. The outcome of this initial comparison is found in verse 17: compared to God they are all "less than nothing." Next we try powerful kings and political leaders (vv. 21-24). We discover, however, that God is King, that "he sits enthroned above the circle of the earth" (v. 22). His sovereignty is greater than even that of the most powerful human monarch in two ways: his power is greater (v. 23) and his rule is permanent. Unlike all things created, including kings and powerful people, God does not grow weary or old, does not run down and wither away. He does not decline because of the pressure of external events or because of any defect in his own eternal life (v. 28). The Holy One is the everlasting God, the Creator of all (v. 28), and therefore powerful over all, knowing all, present at all places. The Lord is the mighty and eternal King, King of kings and Lord of lords (Rev 19:16). It is he who enthrones human authorities, and it is he who sweeps them away. Again, the conclusion forces itself upon us that there is no comparison between our notion of greatness and power and the greatness and might of this God.

Finally Isaiah bids us compare God to the starry host of heaven in their vastness and splendor (v. 21). Is there a human soul so dead as not to be awed by the majesty of the heavens? Perhaps we do not feel the impulse of the ancients to worship the stars, but we have a clearer conception of the immensity of the cosmos, its teeming galaxies and quasars and black holes which are careening away from each other, its austere and mathematically precise order. But note, the Lord not only made and knows the billions upon billions of the heavenly bodies, he also leads them into their proper place day by day, night by night. He is not "God-of-the-gaps," a useful explanation for what we cannot now explain, who gradually disappears in the face of scientific explanation like Alice's Cheshire Cat. Nor is he a cosmic performer of sideshow magic tricks on a large scale. Rather, he is the living God who causes and sustains the regularities of the cosmos. His glory and greatness are seen in the orderly beauty of the heavens, every bit as much as in the creative intrusions into the cosmos which we label "miracle." The cosmos in its vastness and order is not just a piece of machinery, open to his tinkering. It is his creature, dependent on him at every place along the line.

Notice the conclusion that Isaiah forces on us. What began as an invitation to *compare* God with his creatures ends with the necessity to *contrast* him with all that we know. The one true and living God must be contrasted to his creatures across the board. He is qualitatively different in his greatness. His majesty exceeds our wildest or best thought.

This root idea of God's incomparable greatness is expressed throughout Scripture. For example, in Moses' triumph song, praising God for his deliverance from Egypt, we read,

> Who among the gods is like you, O LORD?
> > Who is like you—
> > > majestic in holiness,
> > > awesome in glory,
> > > working wonders? (Ex 15:11)

One psalmist echoes this question:

> Who is like the LORD our God,
> > the One who sits enthroned on high,
> who stoops down to look
> > on the heavens and the earth? (Ps 113:5)

Another (in Ps 139) asserts that the Lord knows our thoughts before we think them (he does know all) and presses us with questions that make us reckon that his presence is inescapable within his creation (he is present everywhere, seeing everything). Jeremiah proclaims,

> No one is like you, O LORD;
> > you are great,
> > and your name is mighty in power.
> Who should not revere you,
> > O King of the nations?
> > This is your due.
> Among all the wise men of the nations
> > and in all their kingdoms,
> > there is no one like you. (Jer 10:6-7)

In a similar manner, the praise that bursts out in Paul's letters extols the incomparable greatness of the Holy One. For example:

> Oh, the depth of the riches of the wisdom and knowledge of God!
> > How unsearchable his judgments,
> > and his paths beyond our tracing out!
> "Who has known the mind of the Lord?
> > Or who has been his counselor?"
> "Who has ever given to God,
> > that God should repay him?"
> For from him and through him and to him are all things.
> > To him be the glory forever! Amen. (Rom 11:33-36)

Now to him who is able to do immeasurably more than all we ask or imagine, according to his power that is at work within us, to him be glory in the church and in Christ Jesus throughout all generations, for ever and ever! Amen. (Eph 3:20-21)

Indeed, "immeasurably more than all we ask or imagine," with its triple intensifying superlative, is a phrase that aptly and accurately expresses the greatness and the excellence of the Holy One.

The Trap of Vagueness
In the way it speaks about the Lord, Isaiah 40:12-31 not only stretches our thinking about God but also warns us against two traps that threaten our thinking about God. First is the trap of vagueness. Since God is so far beyond our ken, we could easily think of him as a "divine-sort-of something," as "an infinitely extended rice pudding" (in the words of C. S. Lewis).

Some of this vagueness enters our thinking when we misunderstand the traditional description of God as "infinite." It is important to recognize that *infinite* as applied to God is not a spatial concept. What we tend to have in mind when we think of infinity is a very long line of dominoes, the sort you knock down by tipping the first domino into the second, thereby setting off a chain reaction. We could always add one more domino to the very long line, ad infinitum. Such a conception is certain to lead to false conclusions. This spatial image of infinity makes it impossible to answer the child who asks, "Daddy, am I standing on God?" It tends to an antibiblical pantheism.

Against these spatial images we need to think of *infinite* in its literal sense of "not-finite," "not limited." *Infinite* is thus a theological shorthand for speaking about God's incomparable greatness, his being qualitatively greater than all of his creatures. There are no limitations in him due to creatureliness or to sin. He is the great "I AM," the Lord Yahweh, the only being who has life within himself. Nor are there any limitations outside the Holy One, since all outside of him are his creatures. All creation has a true and objective existence; it is not a dream in his mind. But all his creatures depend on him. He alone exists independently. Time and space, two of the limiting, created parameters of our creaturely existence, do not and cannot limit or hinder the Holy One. In the words of Walter Chalmers Smith's great hymn:

> Unresting, unhasting, and silent as light,
> Nor wanting, nor wasting, thou rulest in might;
> Thy justice like mountains high soaring above
> Thy clouds, which are fountains of goodness and love.

> To all, life thou givest, to both great and small;

In all life thou livest, the true life of all;
We blossom and flourish as leaves on the tree,
And wither and perish but naught changeth thee.
("Immortal, Invisible, God Only Wise")

Vagueness also becomes a problem through a misunderstanding of the traditional description of God as immutable or changeless. Again an important biblical truth is involved. The Holy One says, "I the LORD do not change" (Mal 3:6). Indeed, if the Holy One is as great as Scripture claims, this assertion makes perfectly good sense. No forces or circumstances external to God would be powerful enough to alter him against his will. Since he is perfect, improvement (positive change) is impossible. And decline (negative change) seems equally impossible as it entails a loss and lack of perfection. Says the psalmist,

In the beginning you laid the foundations of the earth,
    and the heavens are the work of your hands.
They will perish, but you remain;
    they will all wear out like a garment.
Like clothing you will change them
    and they will be discarded.
But you remain the same,
    and your years will never end. (Ps 102:25-27)

This biblical assertion of the changelessness of the Holy One must not be misunderstood, however, as reducing God to the static changelessness of a perfect statue or a "frozen pose." If God's perfection were of a frozen, static sort, it would be impossible for him to interact with the constant changes of human history. God would have to be remote and abstract, an unmoved Mover, if the change of history were not to taint his frozen perfection. But the holy God is anything but remote and abstract. His holiness is full of vibrancy and vitality. He is the *living* God (Deut 5:26; Josh 3:10; 1 Sam 17:26, 36; 2 Kings 19:4, 16; Ps 42:4; 84:2; Is 37:4, 17; Jer 10:10; 23:36; Dan 6:20, 26; Mt 16:16; 26:63; Acts 14:15; Rom 9:26; 2 Cor 3:3; 6:16; 1 Thess 1:9; 1 Tim 3:15; 4:10; 6:17; Heb 3:12; 4:10; 10:31; Rev 7:2). His transcendence means that he is near, not far (Deut 4:7; Ps 34:18; 75:1; 145:18; Is 50:8; 55:6), because space and time represent no barrier to him. His unchanging greatness does not consist in some frozen perfection.

To understand God's changelessness rightly, we need to see it as a dimension of his faithfulness, his moral and volitional self-consistency. In coming near to sinners, the Lord's life (Ps 90:2; 102:26), character (Mal 3:6; Jas 1:17)

and purpose (Ps 33:11) are never altered. But his relationship with men and women and his treatment of them do change as people's character and behavior change. For him to punish the humble and repentant or to reward the proud and unrepentant would be to betray horrible imperfection and degeneration. Equally, for the Lord to break his promises and drop his plan to judge and to bless sinners would be a disastrous breach of faith. Says the Holy One to his people, "I the LORD do not change. So you, O descendants of Jacob [undeserving as you are], are not destroyed" (Mal 3:6). The Holy One alters his relationship to his creatures *so that* he does not change in himself. For the Holy One to stand aloof from his creatures would be a stark contradiction of his own perfect, living goodness. As Paul says, "If we are faithless, he remains faithful, for he cannot disown himself" (2 Tim 2:13).

This faithful changelessness, this self-consistency of the Holy One, is the reality behind the Old Testament texts that speak of the Lord's "repenting" (see Gen 6:6, 8; 1 Sam 15:11, 35; 2 Sam 24:16; Jer 26:3, 13, 19; Joel 2:13; Amos 7:3, 6; Jon 3:9-10; 4:2). Each of these texts says the Lord changed his treatment of a person or group of people. But in each case the change came about *because* the Lord remained consistent in his character and purpose.

Perhaps this stands out most clearly in 1 Samuel 15. Because Saul has been disobedient, the Lord rejects him as king over the Israelites. In verse 11 the Lord through Samuel says, "I am grieved [KJV 'It repenteth me'] that I have made Saul king, because he has turned away from me and has not carried out my instructions." Later in the same chapter Samuel, again speaking for the Lord, says to Saul, "He who is the Glory of Israel does not lie or change his mind; for he is not a man, that he should change his mind" (v. 29). Here Samuel is not contradicting his earlier words. Rather, he cautions us not to see the Lord's repentance as identical to ours. The repentance of the Holy One does not include remorse for the way the Lord has been acting, as if he had done some evil thing. Evil, or even lack of wisdom, is just not possible for his perfect holiness. Indeed, this biblical description of the Holy One (like all other such analogies drawn from the realm of human personality and relationships) does not invite us to imagine that God feels and responds just as we do. He is not a man expanded to cosmic proportions, "the guy upstairs." His inner life is not the object of our understanding. He is far, far beyond us in his majestic holiness.

The passage gives no suggestion that the Lord is surprised by Saul's disobedience and so must change his mind and develop a contingency plan. When we human beings change our minds and alter our plans, it is because of either a lack of foresight to anticipate everything or a lack of strength to execute everything. But since the Holy One is both all-knowing and all-powerful, he never needs to reverse his plan.[1] Rather than representing a change in plan, divine "repentance" accomplishes the Lord's plan, for "the plans of the LORD stand firm forever, the purposes of his heart through all generations" (Ps 33:11).

Equally clearly, for God not to act in the face of our sin and rebellion would manifest a moral indifference that would contradict his living, perfect goodness. So he, the living God, whose name is holy, who never changes, does act. He changed his relationship to Saul (and to other sinners) so that he himself might not change in his character or his plan for his people. The changelessness of the Holy One, then, guarantees that he will change his relationship to sinners as he works out his faithful plan for human history.

A Personal God

Now that certain common misunderstandings of God's infinity and immutability have been cleared away, we may return to Isaiah and note the two ways he helps us to avoid the trap of vagueness.

First he helps us to see that the Holy One is a *particular* God. God has a name, Yahweh, the name revealed to Moses at the burning bush (Ex 3:13-17). In most English versions this is the name that appears when God is called "LORD." It would help us to see the particularity of the biblical conception of God (and provide a more accurate translation to boot) if we would render this name as "Yahweh."

In the New Testament this particularity of God does not change, for there God is revealed in the life of one particular man, Jesus, and the one name of God is revealed as "Father, Son and Holy Spirit" (Mt 28:19-20).

Isaiah's second defense against vagueness is to speak of the Holy One as a person. Indeed, God is spoken of as "he" some fifteen times in these few lines of chapter 40. To some such an approach to God is hopelessly naive. They mutter under their breath about "primitive anthropomorphisms" (a horrible verbal missile, that phrase) and consider themselves beyond such childish thinking. But consider carefully, for personal language is both our highest and our most accurate language for speaking of God.

All of our language about God is based in analogy. His incomparable greatness demands that this be so. The Holy One inhabits eternity, exists beyond time and space. We are necessarily time- and space-bound. Direct description of God is out of the question for us. If we are to speak of or to him, it must be in the categories of our creaturely existence. We must use "pictures," likenesses and similarities. And to conceive of God as a person means that we apply the highest analogy available to us. All others, whether static or dynamic, and no matter how helpful, are necessarily less exalted.

More important, however, to speak of God in personal terms is also our most accurate speech, not because we create this analogy but because he has created human beings in his image or likeness. The Holy One is the archetype of all true personhood. Our personhood is a real but finite copy of his uncreated Person.

Other sorts of language may be helpful in conceiving aspects of God's character. For example, "the Lord is our rock and our fortress" helpfully pictures his stability, faithfulness and protection. But no language takes us more deeply into the divine nature than the language of persons and personal relationships.

Consider, for example, the Bible's assertion that "God is love." Such a conception of God gives us a thrilling insight into the goodness of the Holy One—an insight into his inner life, if you will. But this love language is analogical, and it remains for us to determine the precise reference of the analogy. Our loves are often selfish, fickle, unwise and immature. These defects surely cannot apply to the Lord.

With any personal language applied to God, we must read away any limitations due to creatureliness or defects due to sin. Further, because of God's greatness, there is doubtless an intensification of personal qualities as they exist in God. So his love is eternal, the expression of a sovereign purpose to do good to his creatures that cannot fail. For Isaiah it is a comfort that God's loving care is greater than ours (see 40:27). He reminds Israel that the Lord never grows weary or faint, and so we may expect him to strengthen us in our weariness and discouragement.

Notice that when we take account of the limitations and intensifications required for speaking of God analogically, to think of the Lord in this way, as a living person, overcomes our tendency to turn his greatness into a vague abstraction.

God Beyond Our Imagining

The second trap Isaiah warns us against, quite explicitly and strongly, is the trap of imagination. With biting irony he describes the worship of a toppling god (a real pushover!) created by the skill of human craftsmen (40:18-20). Even more biting is his description of the man who carves an idol, bows down to it and then uses the wood shavings to build a fire to warm himself and cook his meal. Isaiah's conclusion: "He feeds on ashes, a deluded heart misleads him" (see Is 44:9-20). Such is a crude form of the trap of imagination.

Perhaps it would be more accurate to speak of the trap of *misguided* or *proud* imagination. Imagination includes the ability to synthesize, to create generalizations and abstractions, to pit what might be against what is, to conceive future alternatives. It is the wellspring of human creativity, a source of delight, a vital human capacity. Imagination, like all of God's gifts to his creatures, is a good thing. But like all things human, imagination has been corrupted and twisted. This wonderful capacity can be used to make us delight in falsehood, ugliness and selfishness. Worse still, it can deceive us into preferring our own imagined pictures to reality, so that we set our affections on the unreal and destructive. We imagine ourselves able to adequately and truly represent the Holy One through the work of our limited minds and hands.

Doubtless, few of us crassly worship statues of our own making. But that does not eliminate the danger of idolatry. The essence of idolatry is to conceive of God according to our own pet concepts and mental images. Whether we take the further step of carving a statue is of less consequence. "I like to think of God as being . . ." we say; or we fasten on certain favorite Bible verses or ideas to the exclusion of others less to our liking. For example, many conceive of God's love in basically sentimental terms, apart from his justice and wrath, and they end up shrinking our heavenly Father to a senile, doting grandfather. When we allow ourselves to think of God however we please, we take a seat around the campfire with the deluded ancient craftsman.

These are the great questions that should confront us and trouble us:

□ Are my thoughts of God consistent with what he is really like?

□ Are my thoughts worthy of this great God?

□ Have I sided with the God-shrinkers in order to have my own selfish way rather than bowing down to the Holy One?

Modern Idolatries

What is it that causes us to prefer certain images over others? Our preferences tend to be controlled by a combination of our conscious and unconscious personal psychological needs and the assumptions and values of the social order we find ourselves immersed in. Our way of life, our circle of friends and the wider influences of the communications media shape our convictions far more profoundly than we normally recognize. Thus influenced, we find ourselves first involved and then committed to a way of life. We give ourselves to its maintenance for the sake of personal comfort, to meet our needs and to progress further toward what our social environment identifies as the "good life." The temptation to fit God into our plans and our thinking becomes well nigh irresistible. He becomes one more prop for the American way of life, or for the revolution, or for any other version of the good life we may happen to embrace. In our highly pluralistic and relativistic world, our choices are legion and no one may disapprove or ever evaluate our choices.

Notice, however, that all of these choices tend to be driven by us, our needs, our group, our values. We give ourselves body and soul to a cause of our own choosing. All too often that cause is our own comfort and peace of mind. But even when our values are noble, the net effect is the same. Our ultimate loyalty, our best energy and the bulk of our time are given to something of our choosing, something other than the Holy One. He is displaced from the place of supremacy. He may be great, but something of our choosing is even greater. *God* becomes a three-letter symbol that supports whatever we choose. "Certainly God approves of us. He would never meddle with our truly important concerns. Rather, he will help us get to where we want to go."

We give ourselves to our career, our spouse, our children, our country, our cause—something or someone other than the Holy One—and make the theological adjustments that accord with our basic choice. I think of certain college classmates of mine whose careers have taken off like a rocket. They appear to have it all, everything that money and power can afford. And not unlike the rich fool in Jesus' parable, they are fundamentally empty. It is particularly sad to see professing Christians whose success leaves them poor toward the Holy One and sad that their life has counted for so little in his kingdom. I'm sure you have known folks like this. I think, for example, of former Republican party chair Lee Atwater, who climbed to a position of great power at a young age. Then he was stricken with brain cancer and forced to question the basic loyalties of his life. To his credit he openly repented of his life of unqualified devotion to electoral politics.

Now the idolatrous character of this sort of thing is clear. But those of us whose careers have *not* been wildly successful can see all too much of ourselves in it as well. Our envy and admiration of the lifestyles of the rich and famous speaks volumes about our deepest loyalties, desires and ambitions. Again, it must be said, "A deluded mind misleads us."

Avoiding the trap of imagination demands our dealing with both of these forms of idolatry. To overcome idolatry in our thoughts about God we must stretch ourselves beyond our own pet images, mental or otherwise, to understand God as he really is. At exactly this point, however, we run up against our deepest limitations. As creatures, we simply do not have the power to comprehend our great God. "My thoughts are not your thoughts," he says (Is 55:8). Furthermore, we are *fallen* creatures, sinners whose rebellion against

THE BEAUTY OF GOD'S HOLINESS

our Creator leads us to distort, suppress and smother the truth about God that we might otherwise know (see Rom 1:18).

The Need for Revelation

If we are ever to escape idolatry and attain any truth about God, he must come down to us—he must initiate our knowing and translate his thoughts into terms we can deal with. Our knowledge of the Holy One depends on his initiative and his grace. True knowledge of God—knowledge that corrects our idolatrous imaginations—is available only as a result of divine revelation. As Emil Brunner notes, " 'Canst thou by searching find out God?' To man's proud 'not yet' the Bible replies 'not ever.' "

Isaiah is keenly aware of this problem:

> A voice says, "Cry out."
> And I said, "What shall I cry?"
>
> "All men are like grass,
>   and all their glory is like the flowers of the field.
> The grass withers and the flowers fall,
>   because the breath of the LORD blows on them.
>   Surely the people are grass.
> The grass withers and the flowers fall,
>   but the word of our God stands forever." (Is 40:6-8)

What people may say about God can never be genuine, lasting knowledge of the Holy One. Their words perish, as they themselves will. Fashions in theology change nearly as rapidly as fashions in clothing, not least in our own God-shrinking age. But according to Isaiah's repeated assertion (an assertion endorsed by the Lord Jesus and throughout Scripture), the Holy One *speaks*. That is, he condescends to send verbal messages by human spokespersons (prophets and apostles) to his speaking and understanding creatures so that they will come to know the most essential truths about himself. He selects the truest descriptions and analogies from our finite world and balances them against each other (as we saw in 1 Samuel 15), so that with our finite and fallen minds we may come to understand and know him. God's speech to us has a permanent character; it does not pass away. We can avoid idolatry only by sticking to what he says.

This approach to the knowledge of God is deeply offensive to our proud rationalism. We do not want to hear that knowledge of the Holy One is not and cannot be our achievement or discovery. We resist the notion that knowledge of God is an undeserved gift. But it is clear from his incomparable greatness and our bent to idolatry that if there is to be any knowledge, any true speech about God, any theology, then God himself must first speak to us.

Notice what follows as a necessary consequence. The basic requirement on our side for knowing the Holy One is humility of mind and heart (see Prov 3:34; Is 57:15; 1 Pet 5:5-6). We need to silence our mouths and set aside our agendas to attend to him. It is to the humble that the Lord reveals himself. We overcome our idolatrous imaginations by listening carefully and reverently to God's Word.

Giving God Leftovers

It is harder to counter the more subtle and insidious idolatry that comes when we give our greatest loyalty to someone or something other than the Holy One. Understood in this way, idolatry is the basic root of our sin. We know, cognitively, that God is great beyond our imagining and that we owe our very life to him. We may even be very biblical and orthodox in our thinking about God and still not give him our deepest loyalty, the place of first importance. We find it all too easy to fit the Lord God into our lives, giving him a place and keeping him in that place. So we give him not our best, but the leftovers of our lives.

Such was also the case in the day of the prophet Malachi. Consider his denunciation of his contemporaries:

You will see it with your own eyes and say, "Great is the LORD—even beyond the borders of Israel!"

"A son honors his father, and a servant his master. If I am a father, where is the honor due me? If I am a master, where is the respect due me?" says the LORD Almighty. "It is you, O priests, who show contempt for my name."

"But you ask, 'How have we shown contempt for your name?' "

"You place defiled food on my altar."

"But you ask, 'How have we defiled you?' "

"By saying that the LORD's table is contemptible. When you bring blind animals for sacrifice, is that not wrong? When you sacrifice crippled or diseased animals, is that not wrong? Try offering them to your governor! Would he be pleased with you? Would he accept you?" says the LORD Almighty.

"Now implore God to be gracious to us. With such offerings from your hands, will he accept you?"—says the LORD Almighty.

"Oh, that one of you would shut the temple doors, so that you would not light useless fires on my altar! I am not pleased with you," says the LORD Almighty, "and I will accept no offering from your hands. My name will be great among the nations, from the rising to the setting of the sun. In every place incense and pure offerings will be brought to my name, because my name will be great among the nations," says the LORD Almighty.

"But you profane it by saying of the Lord's table, 'It is defiled,' and of its food, 'It is contemptible.' And you say, 'What a burden!' and you sniff at it contemptuously," says the LORD Almighty.

"When you bring injured, crippled or diseased animals and offer them as sacrifices, should I accept them from your hands?" says the LORD. "Cursed is the cheat who has an acceptable male in his flock and vows to give it, but then sacrifices a blemished animal to the Lord. For I am a great king," says the LORD Almighty, "and my name is to be feared among the nations." (Mal 1:5-14)

These words describe very religious folk who came to public worship and made a show of giving. But secretly they found worship a burden, because they loved their own comfort and luxury most of all. They gave only their leftovers, "the ashes of their hearts," gifts that in fact made a mockery of God's unrivaled greatness.

I am no stranger to this mockery of God. My own first conscious temptation to give leftovers to the Holy One came when I was a college student, not many years after I chose to follow Jesus seriously. The temptation centered on the issue of vocation. A little personal background will clarify something of my struggle. I am the heir of a family of Welsh and Cornish miners, the first generation in my family never to work in a coal mine and the first to be privileged with a university education. My pursuit of engineering was largely motivated by thoughts of upward social mobility and wealth.

Following Jesus carved away at the crassly materialistic dimensions of my motivation. Yet I discovered that I could excel academically and that I deeply enjoyed study and research. I would be fulfilled, I concluded, by pursuing advanced study and a career in university teaching. This I viewed as a magnanimous gesture on my part toward the Lord. Indeed, I went so far as to tell the Holy One that I would teach in a Third World university so as to serve his purpose of world evangelization. But *first* I would pursue the Ph.D.

Then I attended the Urbana Missions Conference in December 1964. As I listened to the story of Indian student worker P. T. Chandapilla, it became clear just how idolatrous my whole process of career decision had been, just how alluring to me was the pride of knowledge and learning, just how arrogantly I was dictating terms to the One I had learned was my Lord and Master. This insight was particularly painful, and the Lord's demand to me was particularly clear: I must renounce the Ph.D., rather as the rich young ruler was called upon to renounce his wealth.

I remember standing on a small bridge in the University of Illinois engineering campus, pouring my heart out to the Lord. I was angry (how dare he make such a capricious demand of me?), ashamed (how could I be so blind in my pride and so full of spiritual-sounding rationalizations?) and fearful (what would my parents and teachers think of this wild, irrational decision I was being driven to?). I was not conscious of the potential for joy and blessing the Holy One was holding out to me. That was to come later, as a genuine surprise, with the long-term dividend of settledness and satisfaction. What I was conscious of most was the weight of his reality pressing in on me in an absolutely undeniable and unescapable fashion. And so I opened my tightly grasping fist and offered my career to him without precondition. I know now to describe that weight of reality as the fair glory of the Holy One.

Thankfully, this was not to be my last encounter with his correction and reduction. But for me it was a sort of spiritual Waterloo, one of those great losses that are pure gain, a wound that brought healing. Sheldon Vanauken describes his own "severe mercy" from the Holy One, and all who genuinely encounter God know something of what he describes.

Halfheartedness curses God's people and makes them revolting to God himself. May God unshackle our lives from ways that make a mockery of his greatness. May he deliver us from the doublethink that views our leftovers as adequate gifts to bring to him. May he transform us from God-shrinkers into persons who are committed in deed and in truth to his incomparable greatness.

3

GOD THE CREATOR

TODAY IT IS OUR CUSTOM TO CALL THE VISIBLE WORLD AROUND US *NATURE*. Often we are treated to rhapsodic praise of the wonders of nature, its vastness, intricacy and grandeur. Sometimes "nature" is even personified as "Mother Nature," that beneficent grand dame who works all things out wondrously and naturally. And we have witnessed a "return to nature" movement, rejecting a sterile man-made environment and glorifying the fertility and beauty of the good earth.

Now this habit of speech may be innocent enough. But often we find ourselves captive to our speech habits and limited by the mental landscape they picture for us. Even people who profess to believe in "God, the Father Almighty, Maker of heaven and earth," use this form of speech almost without fail, constantly referring to the world as *nature* and not as *creature*. I fear that an unfortunate "denaturing" of our understanding sets in, a failure to appreciate what it means to be a creature among God's other creatures, living consciously in communion with our Creator.

Three hundred years ago Robert Boyle, known today as the father of chemistry, wrote a critical essay attacking this habit of speech. Not only is *nature* a vague term, he said, unnecessary and confusing in the pursuit of scientific understanding, but it betrays a notion that is dangerous to robust Christian faith. He concluded that *nature* is "a vulgar notion, a licentious word, and one which is detrimental to a fully based faith in the Creator."[1]

Boyle notes that the Old Testament contains neither the word nor the concept *nature*. Rather, we encounter repeated warnings against the deification of any of God's creatures. The whole world owes its existence, its beauty, its grandeur to its Creator. It has no independent existence, and therefore it constantly pours forth its Maker's praise (Ps 19). To speak of "nature" seems subtly to obscure the Creator from our consciousness. After all, *creature* implies a Creator, but *nature* just is there, existing unto itself in splendid isolation.

So we need to take care that we not become casualties of our own speech. Whatever our verbal habit, we must consciously seek to give our admiration, praises and thanks "directly to God Himself, who is the True and only Creator of the sun, moon, earth and those other creatures that men are wont to call the works of Nature."[2] We do well to engage in thoughtful reflection on the Holy One as the uncreated Creator of all things.

The Uncreated Creator

The Old Testament Scripture begins its teaching about the Creator God by using the image of a builder or a craftsman. For example,

Where were you when I laid the earth's foundation?
Tell me, if you have understanding.
Who marked off its dimensions? Surely you know!
Who stretched a measuring line across it?
On what were its footings set,
or who laid its cornerstone—
while the morning stars sang together,
and all the angels shouted for joy? (Job 38:4-7)

The Hebrew verb *create (bārā')*, which is most intimately associated with the Lord's work of creation, means "to craft," "to give order and meaningful shape." But throughout the creation account the concept of craftsmanship is qualified in two highly significant ways. First, God is not limited by the material he shapes; he is not like a sculptor who might be frustrated by a flaw in the marble he is chiseling. God alone creates without benefit of preexisting media, out of nothing (ex nihilo). All things owe their existence to the Lord; what he has created has a real existence apart from his as a result of his creative acts (they exist per se), but only he exists eternally, out of himself (a se). Further, all of God's creatures are ultimately dependent on him. He sustains and preserves them, he upholds their very existence by his power.

Of the ordered, "mechanistic" course of the heavens Isaiah says,

Lift up your eyes and look to the heavens:
Who created all these?
He who brings our the starry host one by one,
and calls them each by name.
Because of his great power and mighty strength,
not one of them is missing. (40:26)

The psalmist, speaking about all creatures great and small, adds,

How many are your works, O LORD!
In wisdom you made them all;
the earth is full of your creatures. . . .
When you hide your face,
they are terrified;
when you take away their breath,
they die and return to the dust.
When you send your Spirit,
they are created,
and you renew the face of the earth. (104:24, 27-29)

More tersely and comprehensively, Paul concludes, "From him and through him and to him are all things" (Rom 11:36).

So creation is dynamic, finite and dependent. It is an orderly system, to be sure, bearing the marks of the Creator's orderly faithfulness, but it is in continuous dynamic interaction with its Creator, who upholds the universe "by his word of power" (Heb 1:3 RSV).

Creation out of Nothing

That God creates "out of nothing" focuses and undergirds two important truths. It underscores the reality of the unrivaled majesty of the Holy One. If something existed that he did not make, we would be faced with a reality equal to Yahweh in its eternity, limiting him in his purpose and direction of the cosmos. Strictly speaking, the Holy One would be neither infinite nor ultimate. We could not be certain that he is adequate to meet our needs (this other reality might intrude intractably). Nor should we pay him our rivaled attention or devotion (this other reality would demand our significant attention). Seen in this light, creation out of nothing is the necessary corollary to all this book has said about the majestic greatness of Yahweh. Without this conviction it would be impossible to speak of the transcendence or the holiness of the Holy One.

One further clarification of "creation out of nothing" should be made. A long tradition in Western philosophy insists on viewing "nothing" as an existing thing and creation as the realization or actualization of potentialities or possibilities contained within "nothing." So Nicholas Berdayev writes, "Out of the divine nothing, God the Creator was born"; Paul Tillich speculates about "the nihil out of which God creates." Process theology, following A. N. Whitehead, and the existentialism that follows Martin Heidegger's *Das Nichts* continue to elaborate such views.

A number of difficulties arise from these philosophical treatments of "nothing." They lead to bad theology (a finite deity) and bad science (a necessary, noncontingent cosmos). But most basically there is a semantic fallacy here, the fallacy that the existence of a word or concept entails the existence of a thing. While these thinkers' discussions have an air of profundity about them, in the final analysis they are naive and misleading. One is reminded of the dialogue between the King and the Messenger in Lewis Carroll's *Through the Looking Glass:*

"Who did you pass on the road?" the King went on, holding out his hand to the Messenger for some more hay.

"Nobody," said the Messenger.

"That's right," said the King: "this young lady saw him too. So of course Nobody walks slower than you."

"I do my best," said the Messenger in a sullen tone. "I'm sure nobody walks faster than I do."

"He can't do that," said the King, "or he'd have been here first."

"Nothing" turns out to be a remarkably difficult concept to wrap our minds around. Clearly we do not and cannot attribute any positive meaning to this concept. It is a negative, limiting concept; "not anything" and "not something" are its nearest synonyms. But equally clearly, "nothing" is not something alongside the Creator out of which he realizes the world as it must be. All created reality springs into being because the uncreated Creator wills it to do so. Creation might be quite different; its "necessities" arise only from the self-consistency of the Creator and the givenness of his actual work of creation. So it is that creation is a mystery, a reality that surpasses our complete understanding.

Creation out of nothing also helps us understand something of the Holy One's motive for creating. God created not because of some unmet need in himself, nor because he was constrained by some external force. He creates freely and spontaneously for the sheer joy of creating, ultimately because of the satisfaction and glory it brings him. Creation springs into existence as an overflow of his eternal love of life, and it results in the joy of giving, sharing and fellowship between the Creator and his creatures.

Creation by God's Word

To speak of creation ex nihilo, however, does not explain *how* the Lord created; it only says how he did *not* create (by shaping equally eternal matter). So second, we need to note that God created by his word *(per verbum)*.

By the word of the LORD were the heavens made,
their starry host by the breath of his mouth. . . .
Let all the earth fear the LORD;
let all the people of the world revere him.
For he spoke, and it came to be;
he commanded, and it stood firm. (Ps 33:6, 8-9)

The whole creation narrative in Genesis 1 is determined by, and focused on, the word of God. These two dimensions of creation, ex nihilo and *per verbum,* are drawn together in Romans 4:17, where Paul describes God as the one who "calls into existence the things that do not exist" (RSV). Thus the biblical idea of creation is well defined as a free act of the triune God whereby in the beginning, according to his own will and for his own glory, God brought into being the whole visible and invisible universe by his word, without the use of preexisting material, and gave it an existence independent of his own existence but dependent on his will.[3]

In the final analysis, creation (like all truths about God) surpasses our understanding. Even the light of God's spoken revelation takes us only so far. We are no more able to fully comprehend creation than a character in a story is capable of standing outside of the story to describe the motive and plan of the author.

No, he is too quick. We never
catch him at it. He is there
sooner than our thought, our prayer.
Searching
backward, we cannot discover how
or get inside the miracle.

Even if it were here and now
how would we describe the just born trees
swimming into place at their green creation,
flowering upward in the air

with all their thin twigs quivering
in gusts of grace? or the great
white whales fluking
through crystalline seas
like recently inflated balloons? Who would
time the beat of a man's heart
as the woman came close enough to fill
his newly hollow side? Who will
diagram the gynecology
of incarnation, the trigonometry of trinity?
or chemically analyze wine
from a well? or see inside
joints as they loosen, and whole limbs
and lives? Will anyone stand beside
the moving stone? and plot the bright
trajectory of the ascension? and explain
the tongues of fire
telling both heat and light?

Enough. Refrain.
Observe a finished work. Think:
Today—another miracle—the feathered
arrow of my faith may link
God's bow and target.[4]

In particular two points remain a mystery to us: how God created without media (ex nihilo) and how any of his creatures could be both dependent and distinct, possessing truly independent wills. On both counts God's craftsmanship and human craftsmanship are of utterly different kinds.

Interpreting Genesis 1

The Old Testament begins with a strikingly majestic affirmation of the glory of the Creator and his work of creation. While most would agree about its literary merit, there is much less agreement about the exact interpretation of this passage. Alas, it has become something of a battleground, with rival interpreters hurling accusations at one another and even launching heresy trials against their adversaries.

As we approach the passage the question we must struggle with is, What exactly does Genesis 1 teach? A wide variety of answers to this question confront us. Rival views arise because of at least two factors. The Genesis account is an *ancient* text, a fact that easily slips from our consciousness because of its familiarity. The biblical account uses literary conventions foreign and ancient to us, and their exact meaning can easily be ignored or mistaken. What is required of us is to enter into the thought world of the text and its author without imposing anachronistic preconceptions. This is no easy task. As always, our greatest danger is thinking that we already know what Scripture says.

Our work as interpreters is also burdened by scientific theory and theological interpretation. Like it or not, we are the heirs of the controversies surrounding evolutionary theory and modern cosmology. Embarrassment at the folly of some older, more conservative interpretations and recoil from the arrogant unbelief of some scientific interpreters push some one direction and others in the opposite direction, depending on their background and sensibilities. Better we should be consciously aware of these psychological and sociological factors rather than allow them to close our eyes to an uncongenial truth.

Nevertheless, it is a sad commentary on our failure to grasp what is actually going on in this text that the biblical teaching about creation has been allowed to become almost exclusively a battleground with evolutionary science. So much more is involved; indeed, all of life is touched. How could it be otherwise? To be alive in the world means we live as creatures owned and ruled by the Creator, surrounded by God's good creation.

Something of this life-embracing breadth can come home if we identify and reflect on the main theological themes presented by the literary structure of Genesis 1. Four themes stand out most sharply: a celebration of the supremacy of the Creator, a contrasting polemic against the false worldview of paganism, an appreciation of the goodness of the creation, and affirmation and balancing of work and rest. Each of these creation themes contributes to our appreciation of the Holy One and expresses an aspect of his holiness. And each theme grounds and offers perspective for our living as creatures of the Holy One.

The vistas offered us by this creational angle of vision are broad and basic. A whole book on each theme written with the expertise of a specialist could hardly do justice to their profundity. Yet here I hope to suggest some visionary foundations that will allow for more faithful and fruitful living as creatures of the Holy One. Along the way we can see just how breathtakingly broad the idea of creation actually is. All of life can be transformed when we accept the humility and glory of living as creatures within the good creation of our uncreated Creator.

God Supreme

The first aspect of God's holiness we confront is his supremacy as the Creator of all reality. It is impossible not to be struck with the elegant simplicity of Genesis 1. The majesty and beauty of the Holy One are made luminous by this carefully crafted piece of writing. This impression is created in the reader principally by the stately repetitions in the text.

The repetitions are of several sorts. God repeatedly is the active subject of the sentences, and his name appears here some thirty-four times. He speaks the word of command, sees and evaluates on each successive day, effortlessly and powerfully accomplishing his work. The goodness of his work is another repeated refrain, punctuated by the verdict that it all is "very good." The repetition of the day-to-day framework drives the whole story forward to its climax in the Creator's rest. Creation finds its crown and joy outside itself, in the transcendent majesty of the Holy One, its uncreated Creator. The force of these stately repetitions is thus to focus our attention on the supremacy of the Holy One.

The creation story was conceived in praise and designed to lead us to worshipful and dependent communion with our God. This is our highest calling as creatures made in God's likeness. The author says, in effect, "Let me introduce you to the One who made this wonderful world. Because he is the unmade Maker, his greatness must exceed even the greatest wonder of his creatures. Judge his goodness and wisdom from what he has made." Contemplation of the beauty, power and excellence of the creation is the strongest possible stimulus to praise the transcendent Creator.

Praise the LORD.

Praise the LORD from the heavens,
  praise him in the heights above.
Praise him, all his angels,
  praise him, all his heavenly hosts.
Praise him, sun and moon,
  praise him, all you shining stars.
Praise him, you highest heavens
  and you waters above the skies.
Let them praise the name of the LORD,

for he commanded and they were created.
He set them in place for ever and ever;
    he gave a decree that will never pass away. (Ps 148:1-6)

Contemplation of the supremacy of the Holy One reflected in his work of creation encourages us to pray. Consider the case of Jeremiah, living in the days just before the collapse of Jerusalem. The Lord had already led him to prophesy that Jerusalem would fall to the advancing Babylonians. His faithfulness to the Lord had been extremely costly. Then the opportunity arose to purchase a piece of real estate in Anatoth, a city he said was ticketed for destruction. The Lord ordered him to buy the property as a sign of trust in God's continuing faithfulness. Was this not a futile gesture? No. Jeremiah prayed, "Ah, Sovereign LORD, you have made the heavens and the earth by your great power and outstretched arm. Nothing is too hard for you" (32:17).

Here, then, is the key to vital and rich prayer: not great faith in God but faith in a great God. When we contemplate the ordered vastness of the creation, we can never allow ourselves to think that our God lacks either the knowledge or the power to answer our requests. This principle of faith in a great God is well expressed in John Newton's prayer hymn:

Thou art coming to a King,
Large petitions with thee bring;
For his grace and pow'r are such
None could ever ask too much. ("Come, My Soul, Thy Suit Prepare")

A Challenge to Polytheism

Alongside of and contrasting to this note of celebration is a polemical theme, for Genesis 1 criticizes and rejects the gods of the cultures that surround Israel.[5] In the ancient Near East, myths of creation were quite common. They were recited at religious festivals to induce the gods to uphold the order of nature and look favorably on the worshipers. The whole fabric of life was thought to be upheld by incantation and magic. In addition, the future was predicted and guaranteed by various forms of divination and the cataloging of omens.

The vocabulary and literary form of these myths were borrowed by Israel's writers, but not their theology. The similarities in literary form between Genesis and other creation myths actually sharpen and underscore the profound differences between the biblical and pagan views of creation.

Four elements of this critique of polytheism stand out. First, God is one. Notice how the heavenly bodies are treated in Genesis. In other ancient Near

Eastern cultures they were divine, often the most important deities. But Genesis 1 moves in a totally different world of thought. Light is created before the sun or moon, for God is not trapped within natural forces. Indeed, the luminaries are not even named. They are lights, candles or lamps set in the sky, with power to illuminate but not to control. The stars have no potency as they do in astrology. "Hear, O Israel: the LORD our God, the LORD is one" (Deut 6:4).

Second, as the creation of the One God, the cosmos has stability and orderliness. Warring gods do not upset the way of life of men and women through their inscrutable characters and sordid squabbles. There are no gods that need to be placated by magic and incantation. Even the great sea monsters, symbols of chaos and confusion for the ancients, are expressly noted as creatures of God (note the use of *bārā'* in 1:21). The creation is not a chaos of competing principles. It is a cosmos, a wonderfully ordered, inviting setting for human life.

Third, over against magic stands the Word of God. His majestic and powerful will is expressed in intelligible speech. No magical rite keeps the world going. There is no place for mind-deadening superstition. Genesis 1 is a measured and thoughtful expression of praise of the Word of God which made and rules the creation. The creation is, in all sober truth, a universe. It sings one song. The "music of the spheres" is a song of praise to the Holy One (see Ps 19, where this worked out directly in poetry and doxology).

Fourth, humanity's place in God's creation is vastly different in the Genesis story. In the texts from ancient Mesopotamia human beings are a last-minute invention made out of the divine substance. They are not God*like;* they contain a divine spark, a bit of the divine essence. Their purpose is to serve as slaves for the gods. In particular they are to feed the gods with sacrifices. In Genesis human beings are made as the crown of creation and given the world to tend, rule and enjoy as God's stewards. Food is given by God to meet the needs of his creatures. Man and woman are made for relationships of deep intimacy within the family as the basic building block of a wider society. And, wonder of wonders, men and women are made for friendship with the Creator himself.

Genesis 1 and Science

This polemical theme introduces us to the second aspect of God's holiness in the creation story. The supremacy and transcendence of our holy Creator demand that we interact in a thoughtful and critical manner with our own culture. Notice that the author of Genesis 1 is both appreciative of the literary achievements of his culture (using its language and literary art forms) and severely critical of the religion and philosophy of his culture. Embracing the reality of our own creatureliness and the holiness of our Creator mandates and enables a similar posture toward our own cultural world. We too must be thoughtful appreciators and critics of our cultural projects and surroundings.

No project is more influential or central to the culture of the modern West than science. And the scientific quest for the origins of our universe and life has been immensely fascinating and quite challenging to readers of Genesis 1. How should we think about these matters of central importance in our culture, given the holiness of our Creator? What is there to appreciate and what is there to criticize in the name of the Holy One?

To begin, we must pay careful attention to the language of the creation story. The language of Genesis 1 is the language of ordinary speech in everyday conversation. As John Calvin commented, "The Holy Spirit had no intention to teach astronomy. . . . He made use by Moses and the other prophets of the popular language."[6] Consequently, the language of the creation story is nontheoretical. It neither entails nor seeks to communicate any astronomical or cosmological theory.

Perhaps an illustration will clarify the nature of the ordinary speech found in Genesis. We speak of "sunrise" and "sunset." Early one fine morning our son came running into our bedroom to announce, "Mommy, Daddy, the sunset is rising!" In using this language we mean to offer no scientific theory about the solar system. A wooden literalist might accuse us of believing in a geocentric solar system. But in doing so he would miss the intention of our speech. From the perspective of simple, nontheoretical observation, the sun does rise and set. So as Charles Hummel sagely observes, Moses and Einstein, although they doubtless held widely divergent cosmologies, could easily go fishing together if they agreed to meet "at sunrise."[7] The great value of ordinary language is illustrated by this wry observation. It guarantees that the Bible can be understood regardless of a culture's scientific sophistication.

Looking at the creation story from this perspective we may note that it shows remarkably little detailed interest in the mechanics of creation, nor does it offer anything like an attempt at a comprehensive list of the creatures. Sometimes creation occurs by divine fiat (vv. 1, 3, 14, 17, 26), sometimes by direct divine action on existing material (vv. 6, 7, 9), sometimes by divine overruling of the productive capacities of the creation (vv. 11, 20, 24). However, none of these is presented to us as a scientific model. The focus of attention in the creation story is on the ultimate cause, the *who* of creation, rather than the immediate secondary causes, the *how.*

This distinction of ultimate cause and secondary cause is biblically based and a very significant thought construct for us as we seek to understand the relationship of biblical statements to scientific statements. The God of the Old Testament is supremely the God of the exodus, the great divine act of redemption. But Scripture shows no hesitation in attributing the separation of the Red Sea to "a strong east wind" (Ex 14:21). The meteorological and theological explanations are complementary. To set them against one another is a basic error that leads to confusion and misunderstanding.

Typically biblical narrative focuses on the theological level of explanation. But in doing so it does not intend to deny secondary causes. The mark of an act of God is not the absence of secondary causes. We feel no necessity to pit the psalmist's theological assertion "you created my inmost being" (Ps 139:13) against genetics and embryology. Equally, to set the creation account's claim of an ultimate cause ("God created the heavens and the earth") against scientific claims of secondary causes is confusing and mischievous.

Cosmology seeks to study the history of the earth and cosmos as a "going concern," extrapolating backwards to origins. If we are to study the how question at all, we have no other alternative. With this quest for understanding the believer in the Creator has no quarrel. Sadly, a bias has often entered into the discussion of origins—a bias we must resist. By a philosophical conjurer's trick, biological evolution has become "evolutionism," and science has been transmuted into "scientism." Thus "evolution" is expanded into an explanation of origins in an antitheistic worldview, a philosophy of life that is mechanistic, random, relativistic and reductionist. Such views are not science. They could never be derived directly from the data of astronomy, biology, chemistry or physics. They are philosophy, plain and simple. The philosophy here is naturalism, the view that reality is nothing but matter plus time plus chance. Donald McKay has rightly labeled this outlook "nothing-buttery."[8] Indeed, if the creation story were being written today, this philosophy might be the target for its polemic.

Equally confusing and harmful is to reject, in the name of scientific method, any *direct* divine acts of creation. We have no real basis for assuming that the Holy One acts only through secondary causes. If he is the ultimate Maker of material reality out of nothing, his power and creativity are certainly sufficient for him to act directly (without intermediate, created means) in or on the created order.

The question that confronts us, then, is, How shall we best understand this creation that God has made and in which he has placed us? What sources of information should we use? The glory and strength of science are that it tells us to get up out of our armchairs and take a look at the world God made—a world full of contingencies and particularities. Test theories, science says, by what you actually find. But equally clearly we should employ whatever is useful and enlightening, including what we know about God and his relation to the world *and* what we know from God's revelation. Couldn't we sensibly conclude that God created life—or human life—specially and directly if that is what the evidence, the fruit of our careful looking, suggests?

By paying careful attention to the world itself rather than to naturalistic philosophy, physicists have developed a scientific cosmology that is very congenial to the biblical faith in the Creator. Big bang cosmology explains that the universe as we know it was flung into existence by a giant cosmic explosion that occurred "in the beginning." Because of the violence of this creative conflagration, ordinary science has no capacity to extrapolate back to the event itself. The original "fireball" remains a mystery in principle, just as it seems to be an almost incontrovertible fact. Recent science developed the big bang despite the open hostility of many scientists toward the idea of a finite, contingent cosmos that had a discrete beginning beyond our ability to describe or analyze. For example, Einstein failed to solve his own special relativity equation due to a simple algebraic error. It is clear from his comments that he found the correct solution, which would confirm the big bang cosmology, philosophically distasteful. Thankfully, however, the integrity of the scientific community led to the development of several crucial experiments that clearly confirmed big bang cosmology. Describing the history of the development of big bang cosmology for an audience of laypeople, Robert Jastrow concludes in *God and the Astronomers,*

This is an exceedingly strange development, unexpected by all but the theologians. They have always accepted the word of the Bible: "In the beginning God created the heaven and the earth." To which St. Augustine added, "Who can understand this mystery or explain it to others?" The development is unexpected because science has had such extraordinary success in tracing the chain of cause and effect backward in time. . . .

Now we would like to pursue that inquiry farther back in time, but the barrier to further progress seems insurmountable. It is not a matter of another year, another decade of work, another measurement, or another theory; at this moment it seems as though science will never be able to raise the curtain on the mystery of creation. For the scientist who has lived by his faith in the power of reason, the story ends like a bad dream. He has scaled the mountains of ignorance; he is about to conquer the highest peak; as he pulls himself over the final rock, he is greeted by a band of theologians who have been sitting there for centuries.[9]

Those who trust in the Holy Creator have nothing to fear from the careful study of the Creator's handiwork. God's Word, which made the cosmos, and God's world will never finally be in conflict. The efforts of science may present problems from time to time. But all true science thinks the Creator's thoughts after him.

Genesis 1 does speak to science, but not by providing it with ready-made, divinely guaranteed scientific theories. Rather, it sketches out a worldview that is uniquely congenial to the development of science.[10] According to Genesis 1, the cosmos is God's creature, made in an orderly way. We humans too are God's creatures made like God, able to trace his ways in the things he has made. The quest for understanding is not a futile imposition of rationality on a finally random system.

For thus says the LORD,
who created the heavens
  (he is God!),
who formed the earth and made it
  (he established it;
he did not create it a chaos,
  he formed it to be inhabited!):
"I am the LORD, and there is no other.
I did not speak in secret,
  in a land of darkness;
I did not say to the offspring of Jacob,
  'Seek me in chaos.'
I the LORD speak the truth,
  I declare what is right." (Is 45:18-19 RSV)

The fact that mathematics, the formal (logical but contentless) working of the human mind, can repeatedly be applied descriptively to the creation should strike us as a wonder. As we seek to grasp the order in the world around us, we ought to recognize that order and our capacity to recognize it are the work of the Holy One who spoke all things into existence. So it is that true science, no less than true theology, terminates in praise and admiration of our mighty Maker.

A Good Creation

A third aspect of God's holiness is that he is the good Creator of a good creation. Genesis 1 repeats four times that God's creation is good, and concludes with the verdict that it is very good. It is a delightful and beautiful world that our Maker has crafted out of nothing. Simply to be alive in it is a privilege and a joy. True holiness, in God and in us, includes joy, delight and the affirmation of life in the world as good. The fact that our Creator is also our Redeemer makes it doubly joyful, since we are being restored to our proper place as he reclaims what properly belongs to him.

One implication of the basic goodness of creation is that our lives ought to reflect enjoyment and delight in the world. Such is not always the case. Too often we think of holiness as only soberness and a denial of pleasure. Often we have been nervous about taking pleasure in God's good gifts. We live tentatively, withdrawing into a spirituality that rejects the body and the physical world as sinful or as snares to trap us in sin. Certainly sin has come into the creation and affects our enjoyment of the creation. But sin lies not in the things God made but in our willful and selfish use of things. Pleasure is not wrong. Selfish pleasure, or pleasure in a wrong use of the creation, is. Ironically, such "pleasure" never satisfies; it always backfires and never really pleases. In the words of the hymn "Glorious Things of Thee Are Spoken," "solid joys and lasting pleasure none but Zion's children know."

Jesus, by his example, consecrated pleasure and enjoyment. It was our Lord who, as his first miraculous act, turned water into fine wine to keep a wedding party going. No frowning disapproval, no superpious withdrawal from life can be found in the Lord of life. We need to follow this example of our Lord. We need to listen to and act upon the apostle Paul's carefully balanced instruction in 1 Timothy 4:1-5:

> The Spirit clearly says that in later times some will abandon the faith and follow deceiving spirits and things taught by demons. Such teachings come through hypocritical liars, whose consciences have been seared as with a hot iron. They forbid people to marry and order them to abstain from certain foods, which God created to be received with thanksgiving by those who believe and who know the truth. For everything God created is good, and nothing is to be rejected if it is received with thanksgiving, because it is consecrated by the word of God and prayer.

So holiness includes our taking pleasure in the goodness of the Holy One's creation.

Joyful and thankful use of the good creation does not include the misuse of its goodness for selfish or destructive ends. Because the Holy One is the creator of all things, "the earth is the LORD's and everything in it, the world, and all who live in it" (Ps 24:1). The role of men and women as creators and builders of culture is not that of owner and master. The world is not our possession to use as we please. The Holy One is the owner, and the world is to be treated and acted upon in such a way that its latent, created potentialities are exploited for the good of all God's creatures to the glory of God. Human beings manage God's world according to God's directives for God's benefit.

What results when this basic notion of the Holy One's ownership of his good creation is applied to the economic order? Initially one might ask, "What sense can be made of the concept of private property?" In the capitalist West we have been told that it is tyranny to say the state owns everything. And so it is. But what are we to make of the alternative that we, or at least the wealthy among us, individually own everything? Does that not also deny that the earth belongs to God?

In Old Testament law the creational perspective of God's ownership was clearly enshrined in the law of jubilee (Lev 25). According to this law, every fifty years all debts were canceled and possession of the land was returned to those who held original land grants from the time of the conquest of Canaan. This agrarian reform was to take place because the land belonged to the Lord and its human "owners" were merely responsible stewards of God's gracious gift. The Bible knows the rights of responsible stewardship (hence the prohibition of theft) but not a right of private property.

So God's holiness demands in us a life of radical and generous stewardship. One of the tragedies of our day is that almost no one seems to be willing to think and act economically on the basis of faith in the Creator's ownership of all that he has made. Thus a distinctively Christian contribution to economic life is stillborn, and believers in the Holy One simply ape the fashion of unbelieving economic schools of thought.

Or, again, how does the truth that the Holy One owns his good creation apply to our exploitation of natural resources and the creation of a healthy and balanced environment? Certainly it must mean that we are not free to destroy parts of the earth in our desire to create wealth and human comfort. Yet that is exactly what we have done. The good creation of God has been turned all too often into a slag pile, a chemically fouled cesspool, a gas chamber of noxious and deadly fumes. The very earth cries out against our rapacious exploitation. One day we will face the Creator, who will come "destroying those who destroy the earth" (Rev 11:18). So God's holiness demands in us a life of active environmental stewardship and care. Another of the tragedies of our day is the failure of those who profess faith in the Creator to act as if this were their Father's world.

The Creation of Beauty

A further crucial implication of the goodness of God's creation is that beauty and the creation of beauty (arts and craftsmanship) have a central place in God's scheme of things. It is a strikingly beautiful world in which we are blessed to live—beautiful in diverse and wonderful ways. All of this aesthetically delightful profusion is the handiwork of the Creator. His love of beauty cries out to us from all that he has made. God's holiness includes beauty and aesthetic design.

Indeed, the LORD himself is the supremely beautiful One, and beauty in the creation reflects the unsurpassed beauty of his person. Scripture makes a special connection between holiness and beauty. We are summoned to "worship the LORD in the beauty [splendor] of his holiness" (Ps 24:2: 96:9; 1 Chron 16:29). Jonathan Edwards observes,

> For as God is infinitely the greatest Being, so he is allowed to be infinitely the most beautiful and excellent: and all the beauty to be found throughout the whole creation, is but the reflection of the diffused beams of that Being who hath an infinite fulness of brightness and glory; God . . . is the foundation and fountain of all being and all beauty.[11]

We conclude, then, that beauty is crucial to life. Beauty is anchored objectively in God's own character and expressed in all that he has made. Certainly God could have made a merely functional world devoid of aesthetic qualities. He did not have to fill the world with symmetrical and complementary forms. Gray grass and olive-drab flowers could have been the order of the day. He did not have to fill the air with lovely sounds, various pitches and timbres to delight our ears and stimulate our imaginations. All might have been the soul-deadening drone of machine, grinding out its daily quota of goods. Thankfully, it is not so! God has crafted the world not just to function but also to delight. He has made us as his image bearers, able to shape the stuff of creation into aesthetically delightful forms and able to delight in the beauty he and we have made. He has made glorious provision not only for survival but also for joy, not just for life but for a real and satisfying quality of life.

Beauty is not an optional extra to be tacked onto life if we have the time and inclination. We shrivel up and die in our spirits, we fail to realize our true identity as creatures of the Creator, if we surround ourselves with ugliness or a drably functional artificial environment. Remember that the tabernacle, the most holy place in Israel, was provided with the most beautiful and costly artistic decorations. So the Holy One's demand on us is a life of active creativity and enjoyment of beauty. The creation and enjoyment of beauty are central, indispensable parts of our calling as men and women living under the good Creator in a good creation.

Rhythms of Work and Rest

A fourth aspect of God's holiness is in its relationship to work and rest. Because the creation story is based on the extended metaphor of a work week, it affords us much-needed insight into the Holy One's creation of work and rest.

Work plays a central role in our lives. We exist in a love-hate relationship with it. On the one hand we view most of the work we do as boring and beneath our dignity. There are certain kinds of work we would never think of touching (leave those things to the uneducated). And we mostly live for the weekends. We toil with mindless and mind-numbing repetition, partly for the sake of technological efficiency but mostly to slake the insatiable thirst of a consumer economy that demands cheap, disposable "creature comforts."

Yet we are almost compulsive about work. Our jobs define our identity. "What do you do?" we ask a newly met person; and what is the invariable answer? "I work for . . ." Equally often we are ruled by our work and unable to set it aside. Our economic life goes relentlessly on twenty-four hours a day, seven days a week, 365 days a year. We are so busy making, selling and buying that we miss life. We are trapped, not enjoying what we do (we must be better than this, we daydream) and equally unable to stop. Thus we show ourselves alienated from work, as Marxists rightly insist, but for reasons they never take into account in their God-denying philosophy. Our alienation runs deeper, for it is alienation from our Creator and his creation.

In Genesis 1 the Creator is a workman, a craftsman who does not shrink from involvement with the physical stuff of his creation. His is not merely the intellectual or aesthetic work of design, leaving the task of shaping the world to some blue-collar demigod. No, work has an inherent dignity. It is Godlike to work. No work is beneath the dignity of those who bear God's image when it is done to serve the Creator. So God's holiness imparts great dignity to even the most menial work, and it commands us to work six days out of seven!

Yet God's work of creation is not dull, drab, repetitious, driven by greed. It has variety, not mind-numbing repetition; beauty, not soul-deadening ugliness. His work resulted in a product worthy of its Maker, one he could take pride in and pronounce "very good." It has real value for others and for the earth, not greedy acquisitiveness as its driving motive. We are alienated from work not because work itself is bad, but because we have organized our work life thoughtlessly and selfishly. If we could take the biblical view of creation seriously, it would revolutionize our work life and our workplaces.

The view of rest in the creation story would revolutionize our life even more than its view of work. The Holy One ceased from work on the seventh day. He was complete and satisfied in himself. He was not driven to demonstrate his value by numerous accomplishments. He could rest. His work neither defined him nor ruled him.

We can find rest, if only we will, knowing and trusting in the Creator. Living apart from him, we are driven to secure our own rest. But then rest takes the form of sloth (we despise work as much as we need it) or an unreal escapist holiday in the sun. In both cases work still rules and defines us, if only in our temporary withdrawal from it and our need to return to it to pay for our next holiday. Security always lies beyond our grasp, just over the horizon if only we can scramble fast enough to take hold of it.

True rest, by contrast—rest of spirit and body—comes only in knowing that the world and our work are God's.

Unless the LORD builds the house,
    its builders labor in vain.
Unless the LORD watches over the city,
    the watchmen stand guard in vain.
In vain you rise early
    and stay up late,
toiling for food to eat—
    for he grants sleep to those he loves. (Ps 127:1-2)

So God's holiness commands and imparts real rest to faithful workers.

Christian people have been divided through the years over what to do with the Old Testament's sabbath command. Some have seen it as part of the passing levitical order and feel under no obligation to obey it. Others have taken it legalistically and find themselves bogged down in a frightful mess where sabbath-keeping becomes a veto on life in one day out of seven. The Creator's rest, however, is a matter of joyous celebration and affirmation of the goodness of life. It is built into the very fabric of created existence. It is re-creation to our weary spirits and bodies. It is affirmation of our trust in our Creator. It is a necessity to our humanity, which is shaped by and for our Creator. Our hearts are restless until they find their rest in the Holy One.

The Scope of Creation's Meanings

Consider, in conclusion, the range of concerns we touch on when we begin to think through the glorious reality of creation: our possessions, the economic order, environmental concerns, enjoyment of the world, beauty and the arts, work and rest, worship and prayer. This list is amazingly, perhaps even dauntingly, broad. Notice that it includes both concerns that we might call "spiritual" or "religious" and those we normally label "secular." To separate these spheres into airtight compartments can easily cause us to lose our focus on the Creator and his claim over all creation. The breadth of this list (and it could easily be extended) comes as no surprise, however, if we reckon that all reality exists only under the mighty creative hand of the Holy One.

In the creation story the Creator charges men and women with the task of ruling and caring for the newly formed creation and promises to bless them so that this noble task can be accomplished (Gen 1:28-29; 2:15). God has entrusted us with the whole breadth of his marvelous, orderly creation. The challenge to us is to live obediently with a God-honoring breadth. Certainly we will never manage to be experts in most things. But we can identify areas of special concern which the Holy One calls and equips us to master for the sake of his glory. We can determine not to establish a false ranking of callings, viewing some as spiritual and others as merely secular. We can determine to challenge and encourage other believers in the Creator to aim to serve their Maker in their own callings. We can consciously seek to fulfill the Lord's creation commandment to the glory of the Creator.

4

OUR GOD
REIGNS

HOW SHOULD WE CONCEIVE OF THE HOLY ONE'S ONGOING RELATIONSHIP TO HIS creatures? Scripture answers, "The Lord reigns." The incomparable greatness of God, his majestic transcendence, demands that he be viewed as freely controlling all dimensions of his creation, including the immense depths of space and the tortured events of human history.

The Lord Yahweh is neither a passive onlooker nor one finite actor among many in the course of history. He relates to the universe as its ruler, ordering all its vast dimensions to accomplish his purpose according to his plan. This basic biblical conviction is clearly expressed, for example, in Psalm 93:

> The LORD reigns, He is robed in majesty;
> the LORD is robed in majesty
> and is armed with strength.
> The world is firmly established;
> it cannot be moved.
> Your throne was established long ago,
> you are from all eternity.

The seas have lifted up, O LORD,
  the seas have lifted up their voice;
  the seas have lifted up their pounding waves.
Mightier than the thunder of the great waters,
  mightier than the breakers of the sea—
  the LORD on high is mighty.
Your statutes stand firm;
  holiness adorns your house
  for endless days, O LORD.

The sea here is a powerful natural phenomenon, perhaps the most powerful on the face of the earth. Yet the Lord controls it easily, without threat to the stability of his throne. God rules all natural forces, according to the Bible writers, from the raging tempest of the thunderstorm (Ps 29:3) to the penetrating, paralyzing cold of winter (Ps 147:14-18) to the insignificant fall of the sparrow and the numbering of the hairs of our heads (Mt 10:29). Unceasingly and with overflowing generosity (Ps 104; 145:8-9; Mt 5:45-48) the Almighty Creator upholds his creatures, governs all events and guides all things to their appointed ends.

Verses 3 and 4 of Psalm 93 take on added significance when we understand that the Hebrews were landlubbers. The endless tossings of the sea symbolized the power of chaos and disorder. Rising tides of chaos threatened to engulf life, then as now. Indeed, we moderns are also deeply affected by the question "Who's in charge here?" In our day the proud confidence of secular modernity's answer, "We humans aim to be," has given way to the haunting despair of the answer, "No one and nothing." Threatened by the thought of nuclear weapons in the hands of a mad dictator or by a global environmental disaster or by the intractable irrationality and perversity of the human spirit, people lurch from day to day in fear. All seems to be chaos in the final analysis.

This despairing thinking leaves the Holy One out of account. The psalmist frankly admits that tides of rising chaos threaten to engulf life. No rose-colored glasses are demanded by his robust faith. But his vision of life is focused on the Lord, on his transcendent majesty and power and his stable, eternal rule. God's throne is firmly established, unthreatened by the pounding seas of chaos (v. 2). His decrees, the sovereign statements of his purpose, are "sure" (v. 5), true in the sense that they will be accomplished in the Lord's time and way. Here, then, is a stable base for life in a threatening world.

King of Kings

This strong biblical conviction about divine sovereignty seems to come to clearest expression as the people of God are brought into contact with powerful earthly sovereignties. In the exodus the Lord demonstrated not only his power, justice and goodness but also his control over the occult powers of the magicians in Pharaoh's court and finally over the earth's most powerful monarch. Moses' song of praise concludes, "The LORD will reign for ever and ever" (Ex 15:18).

Later, faced by the calamity of national defeat and deportation to Babylon, Isaiah's faith in Yahweh's rule remained unshaken. The sack of Jerusalem was an expression of God's justice, a part of his plan. By the same token, future deliverance would also come as Yahweh shaped the proud ambition of another pagan king to work for his people.

Remember this, fix it in mind,
　take it to heart, you rebels.
Remember the former things, those of long ago;
　I am God, and there is no other;
　I am God, and there is none like me.
I make known the end from the beginning,
　from ancient times, what is still to come.
I say: My purpose will stand,
　and I will do all that I please.
From the east I summon a bird of prey;
　from a far-off land, a man to fulfill my purpose.
What I have said, that will I bring about;
　what I have planned, that will I do. (Is 46:8-11)

Daniel's relationship with Nebuchadnezzar repeats the pattern. The final crisis comes when Nebuchadnezzar dreams about a tree that is cut down to a stump at the command of a watcher from heaven. Daniel bravely interprets the dream as applying to Nebuchadnezzar himself. It is a decree of the Most High that has come against the great king, showing that Nebuchadnezzar will be driven mad and removed from his kingdom and even the human community until he acknowledges that "the Most High is sovereign over the kingdoms of men and gives them to anyone he wishes" (Dan 4:25).

Daniel urges repentance on Nebuchadnezzar to no avail. So God's decree comes to pass. The king Nebuchadnezzar is brought low and comes to repentance. In his own words,

At the end of that time, I, Nebuchadnezzar, raised my eyes toward heaven, and my sanity was restored. Then I praised the Most High; I honored and glorified him who lives forever.

His dominion is an eternal dominion;
 his kingdom endures from generation to generation.
All the peoples of the earth
 are regarded as nothing.
He does as he pleases
 with the powers of heaven
 and the peoples of the earth.
No one can hold back his hand
 or say to him: "What have you done?" (Dan 4:34-35)

Sanity is restored when human pride is deflated by an honest acknowledgment of God's sovereignty.

Initiator and Planner
We should not think of the Holy One as acting merely in response to his creatures, interfering in the affairs of history willy-nilly. His interactions with his creation are not just powerful and continuous; they are also purposeful and planned. He is the great initiator who acts powerfully and constantly in all events to bring all things to their appointed end. The Lord rules over all events in the natural world and overrules the events of human history according to his own plan.

The Old Testament uses a wide variety of terms to speak about God's sovereign plan. One of the central terms is the Hebrew noun *'ēṣâh,* a word often translated "counsel" or "purpose." The basic meaning of *'ēṣâh,* however, can be discerned in 2 Samuel 15:34 and 17:14, where it is used in a nontheological context to speak about the "counsel" of a human being. The *'ēṣâh* of Ahithophel was a plan he had proposed. That plan was opposed by the *'ēṣâh* of Hushai. Interestingly, while both these advisers proposed plans, it was the Lord who ruled, ordaining the overthrow of Ahithophel and the just downfall of Absalom according to his plan (2 Sam 14:14).

If *'ēṣâh* means not only the "advice" of a counselor and "intention" but also "purpose" and even "plan," consider the following statements about God's purpose and plan:

Let all the earth fear the LORD;
 let all the people of the world revere him.
For he spoke, and it came to be;

he commanded, and it stood firm.
The LORD foils the plans of the nations;
   he thwarts the purposes of the peoples.
But the plans of the LORD stand firm forever,
   the purposes of his heart through all generations. (Ps 33:8-11)

Many are the plans in a man's heart,
   but it is the LORD's purpose that prevails. (Prov 19:21)

The LORD Almighty has sworn,
"Surely, as I have planned, so it will be,
   and as I have purposed, so it will stand.
I will crush the Assyrian in my land;
   on my mountains I will trample him down.
His yoke will be taken from my people,
   and his burden removed from their shoulders."
This is the plan determined for the whole world;
   this is the hand stretched out over all nations.
For the LORD Almighty has purposed, and who can thwart him?
   His hand is stretched out, and who can turn it back? (Is 14:24-27)

O great and powerful God, whose name is the LORD Almighty,
great are your purposes ['ēṣâh] and mighty are your deeds. (Jer 32:18-19)

A Hymn to Sovereignty

Perhaps the most important statement of God's sovereign plan, however, is found in Ephesians 1:3-14. In this wonderful expression of high praise to God, the Lord describes himself as the one "who accomplishes all things according to the counsel of his will" (v. 11 RSV). Every creature, all things in space and time, comes under God's rule and works according to his plan. And God's plan is a plan to bless, to rescue his creation despite humankind's bent to destroy and to freely bring benefits to the undeserving. God is the subject of all the verbs here, the great actor, initiator and benefactor.

What makes this great hymn of praise difficult for us moderns is its consistent God-centeredness. Our habitual modes of thought never quite rise to the level of its view of the Holy One's majesty and grace. We instinctively feel there must be some central contribution we human beings make. "Surely," we reason, "God makes a blessing possible and we secure the blessing by our response." Yet without denying the significance and reality of our choices, this passage insists that all is from the Lord. He "has blessed us in the heavenly realms with every spiritual blessing in Christ" (v. 3). He plans, accomplishes and completes for his own good pleasure. This great plan to bless is a plan based truly and throughout in grace alone.

The coming of Jesus provides us with a much fuller disclosure of both the grace and the sovereignty of God's plan. We can see quite clearly that God's plan centers in Jesus (note the repetition of "in him" or "in Christ" in Eph 1:3-14). Now resurrected from the dead, he rules "far above all rule and authority, power and dominion, and every title that can be given, not only in the present age but also in the one to come" (v. 21). One day this invisible rule of Jesus will visibly encompass all reality according to the Father's "plan for the fullness of time, to unite all things in him, things in heaven and things on earth" (v. 10 RSV).

The purpose of God's sovereign and gracious plan is "the praise of his glory" (vv. 12, 14; also v. 6). God plans and works and accomplishes all these things so that we will know his incomparable greatness, be moved to adequately praise him and thus be enabled to enjoy him more thoroughly.

To some this emphasis on the glory of God seems inadequate and even offensive. "Are we not imputing our small, self-centered motives to the Lord?" they ask. But consider, what greater end could the Lord seek to attain? For us to seek our own glory as an ultimate aim inevitably is destructive. Neither our praise nor our self-realization could ever be an adequate purpose for even our own life. We are just not ultimate. But surely the one true and living King *is* ultimate. When his glory is the central and highest aspiration of life, the cosmos is returned to its original created goodness. True reality asserts itself like a ray of sunlight shining through our window as we awaken from a murky and horrible nightmare: amazingly, our highest and most lasting enjoyment is attained as God is all in all. We can rejoice that God plans, works and accomplishes all things to "the praise of his glory," for therein is found our deepest truth, healing and happiness.

Of Cause and Choice

This powerful biblical view of the Lord's relationship to the world (the Lord reigns) stands in sharp contrast to three other pictures frequently in the minds of modern people. Each represents a further step taken away from the fully biblical view under the pressure of modern skepticism.

For more than three centuries the naturalistic leaven in the Renaissance outlook has been working like a cancer in Western thought. Seventeenth century Arminians and Deists, like sixteenth century Socinians, came to deny . . . that God's control of his world was either direct or complete, and theology, philosophy and science have for the most part combined to maintain that denial ever since.[1]

As heirs of this process of decline we find it easy and even natural to fall into images and modes of thought that limit God.

The most common image among American Christians might be called "the Lord interacts" or, more graphically, "the Lord does the tango." It takes two to tango, as we all know. In this picture the Lord is limited (or allows himself to be limited) by the free choices of human agents. Otherwise, so those who adopt this outlook insist, we make God a puppet-master and ourselves puppets. And worse still, we make, and end up making, the Lord the author of evil.

Two important biblical truths are highlighted by views of this sort. The Bible throughout assumes that all human beings have the power of making real choices, choices that arise from within us and are therefore unconstrained and voluntary. These choices are truly our own psychologically and morally, and we are responsible for them. Evil results from human choice. Second, God, according to Scripture, is simply incapable of conceiving or doing evil. He is too pure to even look upon evil (Hab 1:13). "God cannot be tempted with evil, nor does he tempt anyone" (Jas 1:13). A strong and biblical view of God's sovereignty must not lose sight of these verities.

Nevertheless, wrong conclusions are drawn from these truths by those who think in terms of "God does the tango." Free will does not imply that our future choices and actions are utterly unpredictable, open-ended or random.

Imagine two friends who know each other intimately. One faces a major decision and is pondering several possibilities. For the person facing the choice, the future must be indeterminate until he actually decides. But that does not make his choice unpredictable. The friend who knows him well may be quite capable of predicting what the final choice will be, based on his intimate knowledge of his friend's past, character and interests.

Each of us has a particular physical makeup, moral and spiritual character, personal history and set of life circumstances. All of these things together cause us to think and act predictably and with reasonable consistency. Otherwise it is doubtful that any of us would be a person with normal faculties. Yet none of this eliminates the reality of our choices or our responsibility for those choices. Relative to our own physical, moral and psychological constitution, our choices are indeed open and free.

So there is what might be called a complementarity between causal explanations, which arise from external observation, and the free choices of personal agents, which arise from within the person. Both accounts seem to be true simultaneously. To eliminate one for the sake of the other leads to serious distortion. The two must be held in tension if we are to understand what it means to be a human person exercising free will, even if an element of impenetrable mystery remains. Remove the mystery, and something of our humanity is also irretrievably lost.

But if those who know us well can and do predict our free choices, what can be said of the Holy One, who made and sustains us and our whole environment? All who believe in the living God of the Bible would agree that he is able to foresee, in his unlimited wisdom and knowledge, all that comes to pass. Those who hold to the "God does the tango" picture insist that God's rule is limited by this foreknowledge: the Lord's plan and rule takes into account and is conditioned and limited by his foreknowledge of our plans and choices. To justify this understanding, an appeal is made not only to logic (no contradiction between freedom and divine plan results) but also to the New Testament passages that speak of God's foreknowledge as the basis of his plan.

But two objections must be raised to this approach. First and foremost, the biblical passages about divine foreknowledge, our only sure insight into the truth about the Holy One, do not lead to this conclusion. Like our English *foreknowledge,* the Greek word used in the New Testament is a compound word, the prefix *pro* (fore) attached to the verb or noun *gnōsis* (knowledge) or *ginōskō* (to know). So we start with the meaning "to know beforehand or in advance." Our English word *prognosis* is a transliteration of the Greek word.

This word is used with the meaning of factual knowledge in the two New Testament passages where it refers to advance knowledge possessed by human beings (Acts 26:5; 2 Pet 3:17). The picture changes, however, when the words are applied to God (Acts 2:23; Romans 8:29; 11:2; 1 Pet 1:2, 20). In these references the language of foreknowing is deepened and enriched to express something of the wonderful truth of God's gracious and sovereign planning. In the Holy One foreknowledge amounts to foreordination.

> Thus in the few relevant passages both the [verb] and the noun speak chiefly of God's action towards Christ or towards man, and witness to His activity as planned and directed. Any interpretation in terms of an impersonal constraint (such as destiny, fate or doom) or of an autonomy which removes itself from the normal course of world events, would contradict the [New Testament] use of these words.[2]

Three factors lead to this conclusion. In each of these New Testament references to God's "foreknowing," the objects of his knowledge are either Christ or people. In each case these objects are people who have been set apart to accomplish God's active purpose. The thought of God planning and choosing and working actively and sovereignly is present in the context of each reference. Significantly, it is not some bit of information about people, like their choices or their faith, that God foreknows. Nor is it a mass of people whom God foreknows in the abstract. It is the particular people themselves in their totality and their place in his plan and purpose that God foreknows.

Second, since *foreknow* merely adds the thought of "beforehand" to the word *know,* we need to look carefully at the biblical use of *know.* Many times in Scripture it has a pregnant meaning that goes well beyond mere cognition. *Know* is used in a sense practically synonymous with *love:* to set regard upon, to know with peculiar interest, delight, affection and action (a few key examples are Gen 18:19; Ex 2:25; Ps 1:6; 144:3; Jer 1:5; Hos 13:5; Amos 3:2; Mt 7:23; 1 Cor 8:3; Gal 4:9; 2 Tim 2:19; 1 Jn 3:1). So for the Holy One to foreknow means "to know with distinguishing affection and delight" and is virtually equivalent to "forelove."

Third, the *fore* prefix adds a further dimension to our understanding when we compare *proginōskō* to the other *pro-* compound verbs and nouns that have God as their subject. We find that these nouns and verbs are given a *pre* temporal reference (see especially Mt 25:34; Eph 1:4; 1 Tim 1:9). The "beforehand" of God's knowing, planning and ordaining is "before the foundation of the world." Nothing in his creatures drives the Holy One to act in mercy. His foreknowing is synonymous with his sovereign plan to bring men and women into friendship with and enjoyment of their God. Foreknowledge and foreordination are bound up together in the uncreated, eternal reality of the Holy One.

There is a second objection to the understanding of foreknowledge as mere divine precognition. This objection has to do with the use of logic in "God does the tango" thinking. Such thinking is attractive because it seems to resolve the contradiction between human freedom and divine sovereignty. But notice how the contradiction is resolved. The reality of human freedom and ability is taken as basic and allowed to limit biblical assertions of divine freedom and rule. God reigns by getting things to turn out well in the end, but only after having submitted himself to the choices of his creatures.

The tension is relieved, to be sure. But the cost is very great. It involves a virtual denial or ignoring of exactly the sorts of things the Bible teaches about God's foreknowledge. The proper name for this use of logic is *rationalism.* Here the truth about God is dictated by the limits of our conceptual schemes. The glorious reality of the Lord's sovereign freedom is rejected. The

Almighty King is reduced to the role of a very clever reactor, continually developing contingency plans in response to our free initiatives.

Gone too is the necessary reverence for the majestic mystery that attends all true knowledge of the Holy One. Such rationalism distorts the full range of the data of revelation with its attempt to organize that data into a coherent whole. But such distortion isn't just an intellectual error. For the object of that distortion is the living person who made and rules over us. The Lord, if he truly is the Holy One, must be greater that the measure of our minds and our finite understanding. To eliminate the tension between divine sovereignty and human freedom in a rationalistic way is to disrespect the greatness and transcendence of God. As in our understanding of other persons, we must allow for a complementarity between biblical statements about human freedom and those about divine causality. Such complementarity guards the wonderful mystery of our created personhood and the Holy One's uncreated personhood.

Evil represents a special case of this more general situation. True, the Lord is not the author of our evil choices. He allows (or "gives up"—see Ps 81:12; Rom 1:24-28) sinners to practice the evil that they prefer to God's own counsel and commands. But this judicial "giving over" is already part of God's wider plan. According to Scripture, God takes evil up into his plan to accomplish good.

Three cases are worth considering. First, the story of Joseph demonstrates both human responsibility for evil choices and God's overarching sovereignty. Joseph says to his brothers, "You intended to harm me"—you are morally responsible for your act of selling me as a slave to Egypt—"but God intended it for good to accomplish what is now being done, the saving of many lives"—your evil choice only accomplished God's plan to get me to Egypt to do good to you and many others (Gen 50:20). A second illustration of this principle of complementarity is found in what Isaiah says about Cyrus (Is 45:4-6). Though Cyrus acts for his own motives of national and personal pride and conquest, God has chosen him and empowered him as Israel's deliverer to glorify Yahweh:

I form the light and create darkness,
I bring prosperity and create disaster,
I, the LORD, do all these things. (Is 45:7)

The supreme illustration of the interplay of evil human choices and God's dynamic sovereign overruling is found in the birth, ministry and death of the Lord Jesus. The occasion of Jesus' birth in Bethlehem was a decree from the Roman Caesar (Lk 2:1), but can there be doubt that the hand of God was orchestrating all these events? Indeed, as John the Baptist was propelled into his ministry of preparation, the word of God came to him in the wilderness—not to the political and religious dignitaries who, by all human estimate, controlled the flow of events (Lk 3:1-2). But it is in the death of our Lord that the mystery of divine sovereignty is most clearly to be seen. As Peter said, "This man [Jesus] was handed over to you by God's set purpose and foreknowledge; and you, with the help of wicked men, put him to death by nailing him to the cross" (Acts 2:23). The evil, unjust crucifixion of Jesus, an act to be repented of, is the centerpiece of God's whole plan. The Lord allows and overrules evil so that "the wrath of men shall praise thee" (Ps 76:10 RSV).

Of course there is a deeper, darker side to our evil choices, for sin is not, in biblical thinking, merely a cosmetic defect. It reaches deeply into all of life, to the depths of our very being, like some horrible cancer that saps vitality and kills. Evil in us enslaves, binding us in its powerful clutches. Evil blinds, so that we cannot see the truth about ourselves and God; in fact, we resist that truth. Evil destroys, making us hard and insensitive even to God. Spiritual rigor mortis has set in so deep that the human race is frozen into rebellion against God. So deep does the effect go that we, in and of ourselves, are powerless to respond to or seek for God. The good we do is never good without qualification, as selfishness and self-glorification infect all of our motives and deeds. We are incapable of good toward God, even the good of receiving and believing the gospel (see Jn 6:44; Rom 8:5-8; Eph 2:1-10).

What we need is not new resolutions, a change of heart, a social revolution or a new political system. Nor do we need shallow platitudes about human freedom, goodness and ability. We fallen humans need resurrection. We need a sovereign work of God to transform us from enemies and rebels to obedient children. If God were not sovereign over all, including our fallen person, all would be hopelessness and despair.

Our evil choices and deeds (which flow from our evil characters) do not veto God's rule and plan. By his mighty and sovereign grace they are made to work for our good and his glory.

A Clockmaker God?

The second modern picture of God's relations to his creatures can be described as "God stands back" or "God butts out." Involved is the deistic conception of the clockmaker God who constructed the world and left it to run according to its own "laws." Indeed, any intervention of his part would be an act of supreme self-contradiction, since God would be breaking his own laws. So miracles must be banished and God reduced to the status of onlooker in the name of science. This picture was the dominant outlook of America's founding fathers, along with their great optimism about human goodness and ability. The U.S. Constitution is informed by the notion that God stands back to allow a mechanical cosmos to work and give place to proud achievement of "life, liberty and the pursuit of happiness." And something like this notion is not far away when modern Americans say they believe in a god.

But this picture can claim neither Scripture nor science as an ally. As Scripture teaches, the regularity of the natural world depends directly on God's will. So the thought of an occasional miraculous irregularity poses no problem. God does what he wills in the world, and nothing is too hard for him (Gen 18:14).

The view of "scientific law" invoked by deism is sadly dated and unscientific. The laws of science are not "things" to be discovered like subatomic particles or planets. They are descriptive statements of how the creation functions under given conditions. They in no way prescribe what can or cannot happen. In the world of Einsteinian physics and quantum mechanics anything can happen, since the universe must be conceived of as an open system. The God of deism turns out to be an unnecessary appendage, soon to be either discarded for pure naturalism or exchanged for the more robust and intellectually satisfying God of biblical theism.

World out of Control?
The third modern picture is "God struggles for control" or "God fights the wheel"—the wheel of an automobile, that is, careening sickeningly out of control toward disaster. Reflection on the extreme atrocities and calamities of modern history has made this view persuasive to many. "How can we bring a concept of God into relation to the Holocaust?" ask those who think in these terms. And with global environmental and nuclear disasters looming ominously, it certainly is easy to view the world as careening out of control.

But our most striking observations of social disorders and monstrous evils simply do not mandate such radical skepticism about the Lord. The Holocaust is, sadly, not a unique event in human history. In Old Testament times the military and colonial policies of the Assyrians were every bit as horrible and monstrous as those of Nazism. And their policies were carried out on nearly as broad a scale, even in Israel. Yet this moral monstrosity did not destroy Isaiah's robust faith in the sovereignty of Yahweh. Assyria was a tool used by the sovereign Lord to punish evil in Israel and other nations. The tool exalted itself and was rapacious in conquest. So Isaiah warned,

Does the ax raise itself above him who swings it,

> or the saw boast against him who uses it?
> As if a rod were to wield him who lifts it up,
> or a club brandish him who is not wood!
> Therefore, the Lord, the LORD Almighty,
> will send a wasting disease upon his sturdy warriors;
> under his pomp a fire will be kindled
> like a blazing flame.
> The Light of Israel will become a fire,
> their Holy One a flame;
> in a single day it will burn and consume
> his thorns and his briers.
> The splendor of his forests and fertile fields
> it will completely destroy,
> as when a sick man wastes away.
> And the remaining trees of his forests will be so few
> that a child could write them down. (Is 10:15-19)

It is more than passing strange that terrible atrocities lead moderns to lower thoughts of God, but often seem to leave our confidence in humanity untouched. One would think that the Holocaust would have permanently wounded our optimistic faith in human goodness. All of our utopias flounder on the hard rock of human evil. Evil seems more destructive than ever before. Nothing fundamentally new is introduced into the cosmos by modern technology except the scale on which we can wreak havoc on the creation and our fellow human beings. Perversity still springs from our fallen hearts. Final control still lies in the Lord's hands. He sits on the throne still, and his purpose is certain still. Yet we will not open our eyes.

I am reminded of the spiritual blindness of Elisha's servant in 2 Kings 6. The two have been surrounded by "an army with horses and chariots" (v. 15), the heavy artillery of ancient warfare. Quite a show of force by the Syrians this is, against only two men! Interesting, is it not, that the pagan enemy suspects that something powerful is connected to the prophet? But the servant is very impressed with the show of force. Elisha prays, and the Lord opens the servant's eyes to see the host of heaven ringing the enemy forces.

The powers of destructive evil are huge, but not greater than the Lord of hosts. Clear-sighted (and therefore great) thoughts of God turn us from the pathetic picture "the Lord fights the wheel" to "the Lord reigns."

Applying God's Sovereignty

This ebb and flow of discussion, criticism and analysis may suggest to some that Scripture's teaching on divine sovereignty is primarily an intellectual puzzle given to tease us. For many it has been just that, an excuse for speculation, an occasion for reading the mind of the Almighty, an uncomfortable thought to be whittled down, a theological sledgehammer used to assault those with defective theologies. But it is never so in God's Word. So it is worth asking, What should this teaching on God's sovereignty do to us? Four applications stand out as primary.

1. God's sovereignty quenches pride and stimulates humble obedience. In our "let's give God a hand" (applaud, everyone) Christian culture, we have lost a sense of wonder and dependence on our Almighty God. This shows most clearly in our prayerlessness. Too often prayer is for us a matter of a perfunctory invocation and benediction. Otherwise we take over and do quite nicely, thank you. Lost is the sense of our weakness and inability to plan and of God's greatness and his sovereign plan. Indeed, we often find ourselves bristling at the Lord's ways and works, which so infrequently correspond to our own. In hard, bitter pride we fling accusations at the Most High: "Why have you made me thus? Why are you acting this way?" We need to hear the rebuke of Isaiah and Paul: "But who are you, O man, to talk back to God? 'Shall what is formed say to him who formed it, "Why did you make me like this?" ' " (Rom 9:20; see also Is 45:9-13).

Another form of pride afflicts especially those who heed the biblical teaching on divine sovereignty, the pride of second-guessing God's plan. We do know the broadest outline of the Lord's plan. But we do *not* know the details. And Scripture tells us that God works in surprising ways, using the simple and the weak to confound the wise. As Isaiah says in a section of his prophecy that deals with God's sovereignty, "Truly you are a God who hides himself" (Is 45:15). Note, he *hides* himself in providence as he *reveals* himself in his Word (Is 45:18-19).

An inexplicable reversal of fortunes, a sudden death, a disastrous accident, and we quickly lose the ability to trace God's ways. As the Preacher says, "There is a time for everything, and a season for every activity under heaven [the Lord reigns!]. . . . He has made everything beautiful in its time. He has also set eternity in the hearts of men; yet they cannot fathom what God has done from beginning to end [we have an inkling but no comprehensive knowledge]" (Eccles 3:1, 11). Yet in shallow optimism and spiritual pride we pontificate about what the Lord is doing, like Job's false comforters.

Rather than basing our lives on mostly ignorant speculation about God's largely secret plan, we need to take the medicine of humility and submission ("I don't know, especially when it hurts, but God is still in charge here to do me good, even when good is a severe mercy"). Then we can be free to build our lives on the revealed precepts of God's Word and not the quivering bog of our own "insights." Such is the message of the Preacher (see Eccles 12:13), of Isaiah (45:15-19) and of Moses in the covenant (Deut 29:29).

2. God's sovereignty quiets fear and stimulates courage. Often the Lord addresses our fears with reassurance that he has not vacated his throne. Consider the prophet Micaiah, dragged from prison to stand before Ahab and Jehoshaphat to "advise" them on a potential alliance (1 Kings 22:14-28). Already he has had bitter experience with the apostate Ahab ("he never prophesies anything good about me"—22:8) and has been warned to speak approvingly like the other "kept" prophets. What gives such a man the courage to speak only the word of the Lord? I daresay that few if any of us ever face such active and powerful hostility in our work for the Lord. The key to Micaiah's faithfulness is "I saw the LORD sitting on his throne with all the host of heaven standing around him on his right and on his left" (v. 19). Ahab and Jehoshaphat, with all their regal splendor, are as nothing compared to that abiding reality. Human kingship or authority is literally a trifle compared to the heavenly King, whose servant and children we are!

3. God's sovereignty banishes passivity and stimulates prayer, evangelism and service. Some would have it that a robust faith in divine sovereignty leads inevitably to human fatalism and lack of zeal. "Let George do it" becomes "Let God do it." God's initiative is thought to cancel our effort. Not so! In Scripture, confidence in God's strong rule gives our only hope of success in serving the Lord. What we could never do God is doing, and he graciously includes us as his coworkers in accomplishing his plan. So obedience is encouraged, zeal is produced, and faithfulness is maintained.

Two passages of Scripture demonstrate this. In Isaiah 45, a strong passage on the sovereignty of God, the Lord addresses the nations:

Gather together and come;
    assemble, you fugitives from the nations.
Ignorant are those who carry about idols of wood,
    who pray to gods that cannot save.
Declare what it is to be, present it—
    let them take counsel together.
Who foretold this long ago,
    who declared it from the distant past?
Was it not I, the LORD?
    And there is no God apart from me,
a righteous God and a Savior;

there is none but me.
Turn to me and be saved,
all you ends of the earth;
for I am God, and there is no other.
By myself I have sworn,
my mouth has uttered in all integrity
a word that will not be revoked:
Before me every knee will bow;
by me every tongue will swear. (vv. 20-23)

God's sovereignty leads to world evangelism in much the same way as the lordship of Jesus ("all authority in heaven and on earth has been given to me") leads to discipling the nations ("therefore go and make disciples"—Mt 28:18-20). The embattled early church responded to the first tides of opposition by praying, "Sovereign Lord . . . you made the heaven and the earth and the sea, and everything in them. . . . Now, Lord, consider their threats and enable your servants to speak your word with great boldness" (Acts 4:24-30). Clear sight of God's sovereignty leads to confident prayer, bold witness and active care for the poor.

4. God's sovereignty overcomes self-absorption and stimulates worship and praise. Influenced by our narcissistic culture, we habitually turn to ourselves as our ultimate frame of reference. When we are preoccupied with self-fulfillment and self-realization, worship—delighting in the ways and work and person of our Lord—becomes very difficult. To focus on the sovereign Lord is to be transported out of ourselves. "I saw the Lord seated on a throne, high and exalted," says Isaiah (6:1). The only thought of self here is "Woe to me! . . . I am ruined!"—he realizes he is a sinner through and through—and "Here am I. Send me!"—he is a servant by grace.

Were we but more conscious of the depth of our depravity and moral failure, the thought of God's sovereignty would be our deepest spring of overflowing praise. And we would be able to say too that "by the grace of God I am what I am, and his grace to me was not without effect" (1 Cor 15:10). Liberated from proud self-centeredness and achievement, we would be free for God, for service, for others and even for our true selves. Worship would become the ultimate frame of reference of our lives.

Do you long to live a life of humility, obedience and praise? Do you aspire to be a brave and faithful servant of the living God, eager for prayer, service and the spiritual welfare of our world? Then remind yourself that the Lord is sitting on his throne. The Lord reigns. Hallelujah! Amen!

5

The Goodness
of God

THE COMMON ATTITUDE ASSOCIATED WITH *GOOD* IN ALL ITS MANY USES IS APPROVAL or commendation. We call a thing "good" because of the satisfaction it gives or because of its usefulness or because of some value inherent in it. The Bible often uses *good* in this way in describing things (for example, to mean "of high quality" in Gen 2:12, "useful" in Mt 5:13, "productive" in Lk 8:8). But the biblical view of moral and spiritual good stands in stark contrast to the view of goodness in both the ancient and the modern worlds.

According to Scripture, the Holy One, the Lord, is good. *Holiness* and *goodness* become virtually synonymous. This thought is so basic that it seems natural, inescapable and almost trivial. But it was not always so. In fact, the revolutionary quality of this vision of holiness and goodness becomes apparent when we think about what the ancients meant and our contemporaries mean when they use the word *good.*

Definitions of Goodness
For ancient paganism, even of the most noble sort, goodness was thoroughly human-centered. Polytheism invariably led in that direction for two compelling reasons. Because there were many gods, no one of them could be ul-

timate. Many spiritual principles and entities contended for primacy. Any principle that unified and gave overall purpose to life had to lie outside and above the gods. Real transcendence was lacking in ancient religion. So therefore was real moral goodness. The gods themselves were often evil. They treated each other and humans despicably. Exemplars of real nobility in the ancient world inevitably seem to be men and women whose courage and cunning overcame the gods.

Hence the religious heritage of the ancients is more of a problem in understanding "the good" than a help. Some philosophical solutions to this dilemma tended toward monotheism. But it comes as no surprise that by late Greco-Roman times most thoughtful people had ceased to believe in the gods at all, except as a means to return to "the good old days." In practice humankind at its best (note—just a superlative of *good,* and hence no real answer!) became the measure of goodness.

For modern paganism the situation is little different. The gods are dead, God is dead. There is no overall purpose to life, nor is there any transcendent foundation for values. What remains, virtually by default, is humankind as the linchpin of reality. So *good* is, typically, "good to us."

Applied consistently in the moral realm, this leads to the "boo-hurrah" school of ethics. According to this outlook, while ethical statements appear to be about external states of affairs and to invoke objective principles, close inspection shows that they actually refer only to personal taste. One says, "I [or we] do not like stealing," for example, in much the same way as one might say, "I do not like chili." "Honor your father and your mother" means "I [or we] like it when children respect their parents," again with much the same meaning as "I like ice cream." In short, "stealing, chili—boo!" and "honoring parents, ice cream—hurrah!" Morality is reduced to a matter of purely subjective personal preference. Not surprisingly, the characteristic modern way of settling "moral" disputes is to take an opinion survey.

This analysis of ethics, technically known as the emotivist view, is certainly not new. In ancient times Thrasymachus plied ethical wares no less cynical and corrosive than those of modern emotivists. "Justice is but the interest of the strongest," he proclaimed, leering at a dumbfounded Socrates, who never gave him a satisfactory answer. What is new is the fact that in our day the "boo-hurrah" approach has been widely and typically adopted by Western cultures.

As Alasdair MacIntyre suggests, three archetypal characters, or typical figures, mark the landscape of modern culture.[1] At the doorway to our era stands the Aesthete, as envisioned by Friedrich Nietszche and Søren Kierkegaard. He is the seductive prophet who bids us throw off the confining straitjacket of the old repressive morality. Fragmentation and meaninglessness are but harbingers of a new liberation, self-realization and heroism. Finally human beings will come of age and be all in all as they exercise their free and beautiful choices and options.

Sitting by a couch ready to help us after our shattering confrontation with the Aesthete is the second stock character of modernity, the Therapist. He aims to transform neurotic symptoms into directed energy, maladjusted individuals into well-adjusted ones. "Directed to what? Adjusted to what?" we ask. Unfortunately, that is outside his sphere of expertise. The Therapist treats all ends, all ultimate values, as beyond his concern. Under his ministrations modern culture has well-nigh completely replaced truth with psychological effectiveness. So, for example, we extol a play or a lecture as "meaningful" or "absorbing" or "satisfying" or "delightful" or "moving" or "honest." Nothing is or can be said of its *veracity*. The whole of life tends to be measured internally and subjectively. Larger questions of truth and purpose are unanswerably beyond us.

Having adjusted our private inner world with the therapist, we move off to the public world, where we confront the third archetypal character of modernity, the Manager and his spokesperson, Max Weber. He offers the exoskeleton of authoritative bureaucracy to moderns who have lost their moral spines. In place of moral good the Manager moves in the morally "neutral" world of efficiency and instrumental rationality. His concern is with technique, with effectiveness in transforming raw materials into finished product and investment into profit. But ask about the purpose of all this brilliant technology, about the value of the product, about the moral uses of profits, and you are met by a blank stare—and perhaps the suggestion that another session with the Therapist is in order! Like the Therapist, the Manager is unconcerned with ultimate answers, overall purpose or "good" in any ultimate sense. That we should be well-adjusted, happy and productive is the whole moral horizon. These qualities are "good" under emotivism—these and nothing more.

We should also note what happens to "God" when he is brought into this sort of framework. Certainly, we reason, God is good. But *good* is "good to me [or us]," good according to my standards and preferences. So two things result in our theology, both ultimately blasphemous. First, we make ourselves the judges of God, shaping and conforming him to our dictates. When we encounter things in Scripture that puzzle us, that do not seem good to us, we discard or ignore them, hastening to our favorite passages. Second, God becomes just one more justification, perhaps even the ultimate rationale, for our way of life. Thought of God invokes images of the flag or the revolution or material prosperity and motivates us to carry on in the way we have already decided to go. Perhaps we need some minor personal fine-tuning of the way we live. But there can be no transcendent, prophetic critique of our way of life, since, we are convinced, our way is God's way.

Note that even though the outer forms are quite different, the theologies of ancient and modern paganism are amazingly convergent. And the revelation of God in the Bible stands in starkest contrast to both ancient (polytheistic) and modern (secular) paganisms. Unlike ancient polytheism, Scripture teaches that the spiritual, the holy and the good are one. The biblical view of moral and spiritual good is thoroughly theocentric. The Lord alone is supremely good. The writers of Scripture begin with the supreme glory of God's perfection as he reveals himself to us. Contemplating the Lord's perfections, they apply to him the normal word for acknowledging worth. But in doing so they impart a whole new depth of meaning to the word. God is not being judged by some prior concept of goodness. Neither they nor we have a sufficiently noble standard or the cosmic standpoint or the personal perfection necessary to judge God. Rather than defining God in terms of good, they help us to see that we must define good in terms of God.

The Revelation of God's Goodness
The biblical revelation of God as both transcendently great and morally good constituted a unique island of spiritual sanity in the surrounding sea of ancient polytheism. No longer would there be need of a principle of good and unity other than God himself. Human beings are no longer forced to be the measure of all things, a role they were never fit to play.

This thoroughly theocentric view stands out clearly in four of the most important biblical passages about the goodness of God. In Exodus 33:12-34, having severely judged Israel for erecting the golden calf as an aid to worship, the Lord renews his covenant with his people. In doing so he provides them with a revelation of his character (or a declaration of his name). Here is one of the high-water marks in all of Scripture. This divine disclosure becomes foundational for the rest of Scripture. Its very wording is repeated again and again.

Notice that in Exodus 33:19 the Lord promises Moses, "I will cause all my goodness to pass in front of you, and I will proclaim my name, [Yahweh], in your presence." The proclamation of God's name, the declaration of his essential character, announces "all of His goodness." His name is good. Then in 34:6-7, as the Lord passes in front of Moses, he declares, "[Yahweh, Yahweh], the compassionate and gracious God, slow to anger, abounding in love and faithfulness, maintaining love to thousands, and forgiving wickedness, rebellion and sin. Yet he does not leave the guilty unpunished; he punishes the children and their children for the sin of the fathers to the third and fourth generations." Here is the good Lord with whom we have to do. And note carefully that he is the judge, as well as the standard, of all creaturely goodness.

Psalm 100 is an invitation to the whole earth (v. 1) to worship the Lord with glad and joyous singing. The invitation is based on two fundamental affirmations: Yahweh is God, our Creator (v. 3), and Yahweh is good (v. 5). He alone can lay claim on all nations as their maker and owner. And he alone is permanently good, with a goodness that endures without change and without end. The refrain "Give thanks to the LORD, for he is good; his love endures forever" is central to worship in the Old Testament and among God's people in all eras (see 1 Chron 16:34; 2 Chron 5:13; 7:3; Ezra 3:11; Ps 100:5; 106:1; 107:1; 118:1; 136:1; Jer 33:11). It eloquently expresses our gratitude for the solid foundation our God provides for us. Good comes to us first because he is good himself and can do no evil thing. And as the Almighty, the Creator of the whole universe, he will not change in his character or grow weary in doing good or switch to a new "progressive" ethic. Our worship and our deepest hopes are based squarely on the fact that good is theocentric.

The New Testament largely assumes the Old Testament perspective on the character of God, including the theocentric view of God's goodness. But consider how an affirmation of Jesus and three simple statements from John's writings reinforce and deepen the Old Testament teaching. In Mark 10:17-18 (see parallels in Mt 19 and Lk 18), Jesus is approached by a young man who asks him, "Good teacher, . . . what must I do to inherit eternal life?" Jesus responds, "Why do you call me good? . . . No one is good—except God alone." No clearer statement of the theocentricity of goodness is possible. Nothing and no one but the Lord can stand as either the norm or the judge of goodness in his creatures. People and things are good just as far as they conform to the character and revealed will of God.

It was exactly this fact that Jesus wanted to impress on the young man. Without apparent hypocrisy, the man could say he kept the law. But he was also rich and loved his wealth above all things, including God. How then could he be good—how could he ever find eternal life? Both come as a gift from the God whom he excluded from his life by his love of riches. In fact, in addressing Jesus as "good," given his concept of legalistic and human-centered goodness, he was making a serious error. Jesus' intention was not to disclaim goodness or deity, but to shake up the rich young man and make him think more deeply and theocentrically.

This same biblical perspective is summarized in three basic assertions about God in John's writings. Although none of the three uses the word *good*, combined they help us to analyze the goodness of God:

☐ "God is spirit" (Jn 4:24), not a limited deity like the ancient gods who are localized traditionally in shrines.

☐ "God is light" (1 Jn 1:5), morally perfect ("in him there is no darkness at all") and utterly incompatible with the darkness of evil, exposing and judging sin.

☐ "God is love" (1 Jn 4:7, 16), displaying an overflowing generosity to sinners by sending his Son to take away the penalty of sin and thus making sinners his friends.

Affirming these three deceptively simple statements together is the New Testament equivalent of saying, "Give thanks to the LORD, for he is good."

God Is Generous

Three additional basic aspects of the goodness of God can be seen in these biblical passages. They flow from the fact that it is divine goodness we are speaking of, an absolute perfection of God and not some merely human quality. As noted earlier in the discussion of common language about God, the limitations we tend to import into the word *good* must be eliminated as we think of God's goodness. Further, we should anticipate an intensification of even the purest and highest human qualities in God's perfections just because of the incomparable greatness of God.

God is generous to all. First, then, God's goodness is focused in spontaneous generosity to the needy and undeserving. God's goodness involves the whole cluster of moral perfections revealed to Moses in Exodus 34: compassion, grace, slowness to anger, abundance of love, faithfulness, forgiveness and punishment of sin. Within this cluster of moral perfections, Scripture repeatedly stresses, as the focal point of God's goodness, the quality of generosity.

Generosity means an unselfish willingness to give to others what they truly need. This spontaneous giving consistently goes beyond what people deserve so that others may have what they need to make them happy. God speaks of himself as "abounding in love" (Ex 34:6), overflowing with generosity, in scope and quality exceeding even the noblest human act of generosity.

Generosity is expressed to all in natural blessings, the good things of life that we all too frequently take for granted. As Psalm 145 exclaims,

The LORD is good to all;

   he has compassion on all he has made. . . .

You open your hand

   and satisfy the desires of every living thing. (vv. 9, 16)

Similarly, Jesus notes that our heavenly Father "causes his sun to rise on the evil and the good, and sends rain on the righteous and the unrighteous" (Mt 5:45). The point both make is that God is the Creator and Sovereign of all. Every good thing, everything that ennobles and enriches life, every pleasure, every meal, every night's sleep, every moment of health and safety, every satisfying opportunity for work and rest, every friendship and family bond comes from his hand. As James says, "Every good and perfect gift is from above, coming down from the Father of the heavenly lights, who does not change like shifting shadows" (1:17). God's gifts truly are overwhelming. "Count your blessings, name them one by one," says the simple old hymn, "and it will amaze you what the Lord has done."

God is especially generous to his people. If the Lord is good in this way to all, his generosity to his own redeemed people has an even deeper, more comprehensive quality. His goodness goes out to even those who with thankless hearts rebel against him; he rescues them from the consequences of their rebellion, makes them his friends and surrounds them constantly with his protection.

Psalm 107 gives poignant expression to this special saving generosity. First the psalmist announces his theme:

Give thanks to the LORD, for he is good;

   his love endures forever.

Let the redeemed of the LORD say this—

   those he redeemed from the hand of the foe . . .

Then in four stanzas he recounts the troubles God's redeemed have suffered. Some are wandering refugees, homeless and mired in poverty (vv. 4-9). Others are sailing merchants, tossed by violent storms and thereby brought to the end of their own resources (vv. 25-32). These troubles the Lord brings to them in the course of life to impress them with their need of him. Other troubled folk have brought trouble on themselves by rebelling against the Lord. Some are prisoners in a dank, impregnable dungeon (the dungeon of death, according to older versions), brought to these difficulties because "they had rebelled against the words of God and despised the counsel of the Most High" (v. 11). Others are facing sickness because of their folly and sinfulness. In each case people are brought to a position of helpless need. "Then they cried out to the LORD in their trouble, and he delivered them" (vv. 6, 13, 19, 28). God's

THE GOODNESS OF GOD

goodness overflows to each, regardless of what they deserve—indeed, in defiance of what they deserve.

God's goodness comes to the ill-deserving not just to sustain and enrich created life but to rescue and transform it, to make sinners fit to be the children of God. Their extremity is genuinely God's opportunity, designed to cause us all to think deeply and gratefully about our own thankless and thoughtless ill-desert and God's generosity and steadfast love. "Let them give thanks to the LORD for his unfailing love [goodness] and his wonderful deeds for men" (vv. 8, 15, 21, 31) is the psalmist's refrain; and his conclusion is "Whoever is wise, let him heed these things and consider the great love of the Lord" (v. 43).

Beyond the sheer wonder of God's redeeming goodness, the psalmist helps us to see several important ways in which the Lord works out his generosity: the goodness of the Holy One is extended to the needy, is at work not least in situations of adversity and is designed to enable us to do good works.

The Lord is generous to the needy. First, the Lord's generosity is characteristically lavished on those who have no resources and know themselves to be destitute. When the people in Psalm 107 are driven beyond their capacity to help themselves, they turn and cry to the Lord. As the psalmist declares, "He who pours contempt on nobles made them wander in a trackless waste. But he lifted the needy out of their affliction and increased their families like flocks" (vv. 40-41). Surely one point the psalm makes is that we are *always* beyond the capacity to truly help ourselves, even though we characteristically resist and resent the thought of our helplessness.

This is true not just of our capacity to control our physical environment. We are no less destitute morally and spiritually. Only as we come to grips with our poverty do we find the riches of God's generosity.

Nothing could be plainer in the ministry and teaching of Jesus. He came as a friend of the helpless, the sick, the poor, the notorious sinner, folks who knew their helplessness and were ready to seek God's undeserved help. But the rich, the healthy, the conspicuously religious took offense at Jesus, barred themselves from his fellowship and went away, like the rich young man, sorrowing. God's goodness is good news to the poor.

God works through adversity. This being so, we should observe further that God is doing us good even when he withdraws the outward good of prosperity and brings on us the "evil" of sickness or physical danger or ill treatment by others or homelessness. Other calamities could be added to the list in Psalm 107. The psalmist's point is that God himself brings these troubles to us as a "severe mercy" to drive us closer to himself. Perhaps he chooses to get our attention through "godly sorrow [that] brings repentance" (2 Cor 5:10). Perhaps we need the correction and discipline that a loving Father delights to give his own dear children (Heb 12:5-6). Perhaps we need special and even prolonged practice in the exercise of patience, forgiveness or forbearance. The Lord is certain to give us the perfect opportunity to exercise these difficult graces. In any case, Christians' temporary afflictions are preparing them for an eternal weight of glory that far surpasses any momentary pain (2 Cor 5:17).

The Lord has nowhere promised to make life comfortable for sinners. Rather, he seeks to transform them by his grace so that they are fit to be his friends eternally. It is for this reason that Paul can write, "In all things [prosperity and adversity] God works for the good of those who love him, who have been called according to his purpose" (Rom 8:28). God is doing us good when he brings us up against our weakness and helplessness, when he corrects and trains us.

We who know him to be supremely great and unfalteringly good, we who love him for his redeeming generosity, should seek to regard every circumstance of life as among God's good gifts. In painful times we should not deny the pain or mask our hurt and anger (as if we actually could hide anything from him). He knows us through and through. But rather than being overwhelmed by a false self-pity, we can seek out what he has for us to learn, what weaknesses he seeks to heal, what favorite sins he aims to remove. Then we can cooperate with his fatherly regimen of discipline. Under God every adversity becomes a mercy, a good generously pressed on us in God's steadfast love.

God's goodness teaches us goodness. Finally, God's goodness directs, motivates and leads us to a response of obedience to God's commands. In Psalm 107 the importance of obedience is stressed negatively. People find themselves prisoners because "they had rebelled against the words of God and despised the counsel of the Most High" (v. 11). Others are sick because of folly, but their foolishness ("rebellious ways") is parallel in the poetry with "iniquities" (v. 17). In the Old Testament the fool is not so much a stupid or ignorant person as a person who fails to respect the Lord and heed his commands.

Disobedience to the commands of God brings God's displeasure and sets us on the way of disaster. Conversely, obedience to God's commands is good, because it brings God pleasure and sets us on the way of blessing. Such obedience is fully possible only when men and women have been freed from bondage to sin by God's redeeming generosity, but that bondage is broken precisely so that God's people may live according to the good (righteous) standard set in the law of God to the glory of God (Mt 5:14-16; 2 Cor 9:8; Eph 2:10; Col 1:10; Tit 2:14). This necessary obedience is characteristically called "good works" in the New Testament, "the obedience of faith."

God's law is good. Given that we live in an increasingly relativistic society, this notion of "good works" needs further elaboration if it is to be understood and appreciated. Good works are good from two complementary perspectives: they are done according to a good standard and they proceed from a good motive.

The standard is the law (or commands) of God. Again and again Scripture extols the goodness of God's law. For example:

The law of the LORD is perfect,
    reviving the soul.
The statutes of the LORD are trustworthy,
    making wise the simple.
The precepts of the LORD are right,
    giving joy to the heart.
The commands of the LORD are radiant,
    giving light to the eyes.
The fear of the LORD is pure,
    enduring forever.
The ordinances of the LORD are sure
    and altogether righteous.
They are more precious than gold,
    than much pure gold;
they are sweeter than honey,
    than honey from the comb. (Ps 19:7-10)

Or, again, from Paul, "The law is holy, and the commandment is holy, righteous and good. . . . The law is spiritual. . . . The law is good" (Rom 7:12, 14, 16). Indeed, the law and commands of God must be good if they come from the One who is good. In relation to our humanity they are like a designer's operating manual.

The booklet that comes along with a new piece of mechanical equipment, such as a car, tells us the conditions under which the machine can be expected to function well. There are constraints we must heed (autos require gas and water in the proper places) and regular maintenance practices we must perform because of the way our machine has been designed (oil must be changed, tires properly inflated and so on). If we ignore the instructions, our machine will soon cease to function. And the machine cannot be used for just any purpose we might happen to choose, if it is to function at all well. A freight train can't chug down an expressway; a power drill can't be used to drive a nail. If we try to make them do so, they will soon begin to malfunction, even if they do make a go of it for a while.

In the same way, God's law is not superimposed on life arbitrarily. Rather, it is both a disclosure of the moral perfection of our Maker's character and a statement of the boundary conditions for the proper functioning of our full humanity. We are creatures made in the image of God to live to and for God. Violation of his law leads us away from our true identity and destroys us in the process. We are not free to be what we truly are until we live within the boundaries of the designer's constraints and for the designer's purposes. Thus the law of God is good, a delight to every right-thinking child of God.

When we actually look carefully at the law in both Testaments, we discover that it is not a minutely detailed set of precepts to cover every facet of life. Rather, it is a set of broad guiding principles with some sample applications to get us going in the right direction. It marks off the area for profitable investigation and enjoyment in life and leaves great freedom within that wide area. This open-textured quality has the effect of maximizing the imaginative, creative element in our obedience to the Lord. We seek to make our good works the best we can render to God and our fellow men and women (see Phil 1:9-10).

This means that we must take the consequences of our acts (and inaction) into account and weigh them against the standards and values taught in God's Word. And it also means that in some situations choices will be difficult, and Christian people will come to different conclusions. As J. I. Packer notes,

> Proper Christian obedience is thus as far as possible from the treadmill negativism of the conscientious conformist, whose main concern is never to put a wrong foot and who conceives the whole life in terms of shunning doubtful things. . . . Just as one cannot maintain health on a diet of disinfectants only, so one cannot fully or healthily obey God just by trying to avoid defilements, evading risks, and omitting to ask what is the most one can do to glorify God. For that is the question which the Bible forces us to face all the time.[2]

The question of motives. Good works also include right motives—the love of neighbor and, supremely, the love of God. This is how Jesus summarizes the law (quoting the Old Testament), and Paul reinforces the priority of love when he says, "Love is the fulfillment of the law" (see Rom 13:8-10).

The motive of love for neighbor and God clearly does not do away with the standard of law. Love needs the moral compass of God's law to direct it, to keep it from degenerating into sentimentality or selfishness. The commandments of God, then, should be viewed as invariably directing us to loving actions. They cannot be fulfilled (obeyed fully) apart from love as their driving force. Rather than moving us to ignore or dismiss the commands of God, true love for neighbor (a desire to secure the deepest, truest and fullest good for others) and true love for God (an unquenchable zeal for the glory of God to be seen and known) leads us to an informed, creative, even opportunistic obedience to the law of God.

Packer suggests that we think of the role of love in good works as resembling that of a referee in football.[3] A conscientious referee knows the rule book intimately, not least to aid him in decisions in difficult circumstances. He seeks to place himself in the best position to make the right decision. This requires a wide knowledge of the game and the skills the game requires. It also requires the ability to anticipate the flow of the game, so as to be in the right place at the right time. Further, in close calls the referee will invariably seek the advice of his assistants lest he be deceived by his inability to see all the action. And in all this a good referee seeks to serve the players by helping them to enjoy the game as it is set out to be played.

Love for God and neighbor bids us behave like the referee. First, love requires us to have a thorough knowledge of the law of God. Without this knowledge about the basic, God-given framework of life, no good decisions or good works are possible. Second, love directs us to be in the best position by gathering as much relevant knowledge as is possible and anticipating possible consequences. Third, love leads us to seek counsel from others who are better positioned to understand our situation, to gather information from specialists if necessary. This, of course, is not at all like listening to the crowd, whose bias for the home team is evident. Finally, love thus practiced serves and creates joy.

Referees err, even experienced and well-intentioned referees. So too God's people err and miss the best course of action. Hindsight may reveal either that our love has cooled and become thoughtless and apathetic or that it has made us too eager to please, too simple-minded, to be truly wise and informed. Such an acknowledgment (we need to make it frequently) is deeply humbling. But it drives us to remember that we live only by the goodness of God, by his generosity to sinners like us, expressed most deeply in the cross of our Lord. And this reminder bids us return to the game, set on deeper, wiser and more loving enjoyment of our God and our neighbor.

To summarize, then, God's goodness is focused in spontaneous generosity toward the needy and undeserving. Often that goodness takes the form of a severe mercy that helps us to see just how needy and undeserving we actually are, and awakens us to thankfulness for the goodness of our Lord. And the same generosity comes to us to secure goodness in us and to lead us to our life's work of good works. So we joyfully obey God's good law, the charter of our humanity, the designer's manual for creatures made in the image of God, from hearts made alive and ardent toward our God and our neighbor.

God Is Perfect
The second basic aspect of God's goodness is this: God's goodness involves both his glorious generosity and his moral perfection. Here all the emphasis must fall on *both* and *and.* Each passage of Scripture we have considered brings this truth home. In Exodus 33—34 God's goodness includes compassion, kindness, faithfulness and punishment of sin. In Psalm 100 Yahweh is not just good, he is first and foremost God. His eternal faithfulness must include self-consistency, just as his basic character as Yahweh, the great "I AM," demands that he be the truly and only self-determining, self-defining One. Jesus' teaching that God alone is good clearly states his absolute moral perfection. And in John's teaching God is not only love but also spirit, without physical limitations, and (in this context) supremely light, without mixture of any darkness.

God's generosity does not turn him into a weak grandparent, doting indulgently on our foibles, spoiling us with gifts when our lives cry out for discipline. God's goodness fundamentally involves an incompatibility with evil and sin. He never plays the relativist. As light overcomes and destroys darkness, so God's goodness goes out to destroy and overcome sin. God does not wink at sin or tolerate it. In kindness he forbears the folly and deceit of sinners, for he is slow to anger, reluctant to judge. But as sinners persevere in sin, his goodness becomes a threat. He punishes evil and sin in the unrepentant.

God Is One
Invariably we feel a tension in God's goodness between light and love. And preferring to think of God's generosity just because we are so wicked, we often seek to resolve the tension by reducing or ignoring God's moral holiness. Modern people do this by selecting a divine "master attribute" and reducing all else in God to that attribute. So "God is love" becomes our reductionistic credo. Other more challenging biblical assertions are cast aside as "primitive errors" or reinterpreted to be more consistent with our enlightened and advanced insights.

Now this procedure may indeed be more comfortable. A God who distributes warm fuzzies world without end is comforting, but in just the same way as pagan idols were comforting. They are a pale reflection of some of the truth, but mostly they are an exact representation of our inflated but fallen minds. Stronger medicine is required to heal us, and inwardly we know it.

Not only does this approach to God do violence to God's revelation by ignoring and twisting it, it also devalues God himself by reducing the fullness of his perfections. True, it makes God more understandable to our finite intellects, but that should be a warning to us. A God who does not pass our understanding will invariably be an idol, a product of our fallen, if fertile, imagination.

The "both-and" of this second point is rooted in God's simplicity. Because God is an infinite spirit, he is without body (spirit) and without parts (infinite). Note that the opposite of *simple* here is *compound* or *composed,* "made up of many parts" or even "cobbled together out of otherwise incoherent elements." By *simplicity* I mean not that God is a philosophical abstraction, an impersonal, infinite force arrived at by means of subtraction or negation as in Eastern religions. On the contrary, God's simplicity arises from his incomparable greatness. We ascribe to God creaturely perfections in the most complete and divine manner. His perfections, being uncreated, unlimited and undependently real, clearly must exceed those of his human creatures in their glory and wonder. And these exceedingly wonderful perfections exist in his uncreated being without tension or conflict. God is so rich in majesty that to obtain even a vague idea of his glory requires our holding together many attributes.

At this point, however, our limited, creaturely perspective can easily fail us. For we have never met an uncomposed, perfectly coherent person. Not only are we all limited as creatures, composed by a divine act of creation, but our very creaturehood has been deeply marred by direct personal acquaintance with evil. So we are apt to set attributes of our personhood against one another to suit our own convenience or biases. Or we might discuss and appeal to those attributes and capacities in a capricious, self-serving manner. For example, we trot out compassion in response to our own addictions to caffeine, alcohol and sugar. Certainly we must avoid this sort of limited and limiting outlook as we think about and speak of the Holy One.

What we need to bear in mind is that the Holy One is indeed *one,* completely coherent in his uncreated, majestic reality. Every divine attribute designates the one true God from a special angle in accordance with his revelation. All are true of him, together and in an infinite and divine manner. And always we must fight the tendency to impose unintended limits on his infinite greatness because of the limits of the special angle of view we are necessarily adopting.

Remember, there is nothing above or behind or beyond God. God is infinite; hence goodness, generosity, love, holiness—whatever pertains to him—are infinite as well. All are divine attributes. They must not be thought of as added to his divinity, pinned on him like a name tag. Together they are his divinity. All his attributes are identical with him.

God's Saving Righteousness

This view of God's simplicity is not just a matter of philosophical reflection and deduction. Scripture forces this conclusion on us in two ways. First, it uses not only adjectives to describe God but also nouns. It tells us not only that God is faithful, righteous, living, loving and wise, but also that he is truth, righteousness, life, love and wisdom. He *is* whatever he *has.* He is one in every respect.

Second, words used to describe divine attributes come to designate what seem to us contradictory characteristics. The important biblical word *righteousness* affords us a classic example of this phenomenon. The central meaning of *righteousness* is that which is well pleasing to God, which receives approval in the heavenly court.[4] The biblical writers never lose sight of the fixed norms and standards implied in *righteousness,* because nothing or no one evil could ever be pleasing to the Holy One. As a result it belongs, in our characteristic way of thinking, exclusively with the moral perfection and justice of God, as opposed to God's love and grace.

But we need to be careful here, for to think of *righteousness* exclusively in terms of an abstract concept of "distributive justice," which guarantees that each receives exactly what he or she deserves, leads us away from the dominant biblical meaning of *righteousness.* The active goodness of the Holy One involves an undeserved care for the needy that seeks to bring sinners into relationship with himself. So the "right" acts of the Holy One—those works that characteristically please him—are acts of deliverance, liberation and salvation. *Righteousness* is thus "saving righteousness." "The righteous acts of the LORD" (Judg 5:11) are his mighty acts of salvation on behalf of people who do not at all deserve God's mercy.

A characteristic Old Testament use of the word *righteousness* can be seen in Isaiah 46:12-13, where *righteousness* and *salvation* are used in parallel poetic lines:

Listen to me, you stubborn-hearted,
   you who are far from righteousness.

I am bringing my righteousness near,
　it is not far away;
　and my salvation will not be delayed.
I will grant salvation to Zion,
　my splendor to Israel.

So righteousness is that aspect of God's goodness according to which he saves the undeserving. As the New Testament affirms in one of its most wonderful statements, "For in the gospel a righteousness from God is revealed, a righteousness that is by faith from first to last" (Rom 1:17).

Consider the prayer in Psalm 143, where the two senses of *righteous* stand side by side:

O LORD, hear my prayer,
　listen to my cry for mercy;
in your faithfulness and righteousness
　come to my relief.
Do not bring your servant into judgment,
　for no one living is righteous before you. (vv. 1-2)

For the psalmist it is God's righteousness that will cause the Lord to deliver him and not judge him. But no one deserves such generosity, because no one living meets the standard of God's righteousness. God's holy purpose and God's holy standard stand side by side, and the psalmist feels no inconsistency between them.

Still we must acknowledge some unresolved tension. Wonderful as this saving righteousness shown to the unrighteous is, it still can be asked, "Is this 'saving righteousness' righteous by the standard of God's holy righteousness?" How can it be right for the Holy One to accept the unrighteous into his friendship and fellowship? Is not this righteousness an act of moral relativism?

For the moment I will allow these very critical questions to stand unanswered in order to accumulate additional information and perspective. But let's leave them with every expectation that some resolution *is* possible just because the Holy One is one. All of his acts are divine. Love and justice never compete in him. His justice will be merciful and his mercy just, because he is good in a completely coherent and unified fashion.

This unity of being is not true of any creatures, even of creatures made in the image of God. We are made up of (composed of) various parts, and even sin aside, we just don't have it all together. We are not fully in control of our body, our feelings, our thoughts. We act now in love, now in anger, now in justice, now in mercy. Our feelings are a jumble, constantly it seems, and our thoughts, even when logical, are at the mercy of our body, our feelings and our environment. Thankfully, God does have it together, fully, permanently, infinitely. Love and justice, both infinitely true of him, do not compete, nor does one override the other in his uncreated glory. Because his goodness is infinite, because it is divine goodness, it includes both his glorious generosity and his absolute moral perfection.

God's Goodness Surpasses Ours

So the third basic aspect of God's goodness is this: the goodness of God, as a divine perfection, surpasses the highest human goodness in its mind-boggling intensity. "God is love," says John. But consider this love. It is love not to the righteous, the good, the deserving. It is love not called forth by some beauty or goodness in its object. It is love to enemies and rebels that makes them dear children. It is love not as fickle, passing emotion. It is no "grit your teeth and do them good anyhow" stoicism. It is love, high and deep and wide and long, love as the expression of a sovereign purpose, love more tender than that of any mother. It is "love to the loveless shown, that they might lovely be." Hallelujah!—it is God's love, far surpassing our loves in every way.

"God is light," says John. But consider this light. It is the flashing, blazing, thundering light on Sinai, striking fear into the hearts of Israel. It is the glory-fire that led Israel in the wilderness and settled into the tabernacle's most holy place. It is the refiner's fire, burning away all impurity. "Our God is a consuming fire," says Hebrews 12:29. "It is a dreadful thing to fall into the hands of the living God" (Heb 10:31).

The mind boggles at these awesome intensifications. The contours of these truths are angular and daring. Who would imagine a God like this, so beyond us, so threatening and kind? Who would put themselves completely at his justice and mercy? Surely there must be something we can give him, some indispensable service we could render, some godlike role for us to play? But no! As the children in Narnia are frequently reminded of Aslan, "He is not a tame lion."

The Holy One is good; *holiness* and *goodness* have become virtual synonyms. "Virtual" because just as goodness is focused in active, spontaneous generosity without denying moral perfection, so holiness is focused in active, spontaneous moral perfection without denying generosity.

When men and women actually encounter the Holy One, they feel small, but mostly they feel imperfect and unclean. It is this focus of holiness that we must trace out, not least because it is the part we would ignore if we could. To that we now turn in the next chapters, thinking of God, the holy judge of evil, and God, the holy warrior against evil.

6

GOD THE JUDGE

GOD'S PERFECT GOODNESS, HIS MORAL HOLINESS, DEMANDS THAT HE STAND opposed to evil and sin just as light stands opposed to darkness. The two are incompatible. And because this holiness, this light, is divine goodness, his opposition is not the passive resistance of a mere spectator. His holiness rises up in active resistance to all evil, to all that cheapens and distorts and destroys his creatures. The Holy One, in his perfect goodness, is actively and intensely set against evil. He judges it as the only holy Judge of all his creatures.

The Witness of Scripture

Few themes are stressed more strongly throughout the Bible than the reality of God's judgment. God is frequently called "judge." Abraham, interceding for Sodom and his nephew Lot, exclaimed, "Will not the Judge of all the earth do right?" (Gen 18:25). "It is God who judges," says the psalmist in his praise of God (75:7); "rise up, O God, judge the earth" (82:8). The writer to the Hebrews adds, "You have come to God, the judge of all" (12:23).

The title "Judge" is not an honorary one; on page after page of Bible history we meet the solemn reality of God's action in judgment. God judged Adam and Eve, driving them out of the Garden and cursing them and the whole created order (Gen 3). God judged corrupt and proud human culture, first by a catastrophic flood (Gen 6—8) and then by confounding human languages (Gen 11). God judged Sodom and Gomorrah, consuming them in volcanic conflagration (Gen 18—19). God judged the Egyptians for their harsh treatment of Israel and the pride of their king, unleashing ten plagues (Ex 7—12) that became useful symbols for describing his final judgment of the earth (Rev 15—16). Judging his own people for worshiping the golden calf, God used the Levites to unleash a terrible slaughter (Ex 32:26-29). God judged Nadab and Abihu for irregular and rebellious worship practices (strange fire), striking them dead (Lev 10). For Israel's stubborn unbelief and refusal to invade Canaan, God condemned a whole generation to a lifetime of homeless wandering in the wilderness (Num 13—14). God judged Korah, Dathan and Abiram for their rebellion against Moses, swallowing them in an earthquake (Num 16). Again judging Israel for its ingratitude and grumbling in the wilderness ("we detest this miserable food!" they said of God's provision of manna), God sent serpents to assault them (Num 21). God judged Balak, the Moabite king, by turning the curse against Israel he purchased from Balaam into a blessing for Israel and a curse against Moab (Num 22—24). Yet again, judging the Israelite men when they took up with Moabite women and Moabite worship, God destroyed the chiefs of clans, particularly Zimri, the worst offender (Num 25).

This survey of God's acts of judgment only skims the surface of the first five books of the Old Testament. The same pattern continues throughout. People who don't actually have much acquaintance with the Bible assure us that all is different in the New Testament. But accounts of divine judgment are not confined to the Old Testament. God judged the leaders of a decadent Judaism for rejecting Jesus (Mt 21:33-46; 1 Thess 2:14-15). God judged Ananias and Sapphira for their hypocrisy (Acts 5), Herod for his self-satisfied and destructive pride (Acts 12:21-22) and Elymas for his resistance to the gospel (Acts 13:8-9). God judged Christians at Corinth with sickness and even death because of their gross thoughtlessness in partaking of the Lord's Supper (1 Cor 11:29-33). Again, this is just a once-over-lightly survey. The fact of God's work as Judge of all men and women is incontrovertibly attested throughout the Bible.

Current Caveats

"But why," some ask, "should we hold to such primitive and barbaric views? We no longer cling to the ancients' prescientific view of the natural world. Surely some progress has been made in our understanding of God in the two thousand years since the writing of the Bible. It seems frankly incredible that anyone could believe in a God who would order the wholesale slaughter of innocent Egyptian children or Canaanites, or anyone else for that matter. Surely we can improve on that sort of outlook!" So goes the quite standard litany of modern objection to the Bible's teaching.

Along with this objection to divine judgment, a new view of human destiny has arisen known as universalism. This is quite simply the view that in the end all are doomed to be saved. All human beings (and spirits, if such there be), regardless of their belief or unbelief in this life, will come into a life of eternal blessing and fellowship with God. Their eternal estiny is fixed through no accomplishment, choice or even desire of their own (hence they are "doomed"). Even Judas, Hitler, Stalin and Saddam Hussein will be included.

Several motives lead people to this conclusion. First, there is the conviction that God's love would be defeated if any person were finally condemned. Is such a defeat—such a frustration of divine love—even thinkable? Second, there is the feeling that it is arbitrary to fix the eternal destiny of a person at death. Why should we not imagine further chances for repentance beyond death? And wouldn't a God of love offer chances however many times they are needed, until his love meets with a loving response? Third, there is the realization that many millions of people have lived and continue to live in cultures where it is impossible to hear the biblical message. Do 500 million Hindus in India, or 70 million Muslims, have no place in God's love? Could God write off two billion people just because they never heard of Jesus Christ, to say nothing of countless billions now dead? Fourth, there is a pastoral motive. Can it be right or kind to proclaim God's judgment to people who have lost loved ones who did not seem to be Christians?

This hope, those who hold to it would emphasize, rests not in a fantasy about human goodness. Rather, it rests on the greatness of God's power and love. Indeed, they assert, universalism alone does justice to God's love and Christ's victory. Alternative views make God a failure, if not downright devilish. Therefore we must conceive of God's justice as a function of God's love. Adherents of universalism can cite a series of New Testament texts that, for them, clinch the argument (Jn 12:32; Rom 5:12-21; 11:32; 1 Cor 15:22; 2 Cor 5:19; Eph 1:10; Col 1:20; 1 Tim 2:4; Heb 2:9; 2 Pet 3:9; 1 Jn 2:2).

Who could not wish that the universalist was right? We would be strange Christians indeed if, knowing the love of God, we did not want all people to come to know that love. Perhaps this is why universalism has gained wide acceptance among contemporary believers.

Yet the Bible, clear thinking and a desire to let God be God do not allow me to embrace this hope. Let me state my conclusion at the outset: universalism is a false hope because it distorts the truth about God himself. Its apparently fine emphasis on the love of God turns out to be an illusion because it ignores and distorts the fundamental reality of God's holiness. So universalism turns out to be an opiate that lulls us to sleep in our sin and dulls our zeal to tell those who have never heard.

To understand how this is so, we need first to look more closely at what the Bible actually teaches about God's work of judgment, then think through the considerations that commend belief in divine judgment. After that this chapter will tackle the arguments and motives for the universalist hope.

An Old Testament Theology of Judgment

Rather than survey the many Old Testament passages on judgment, let's look more closely at one, Micah 1—2, which is typical of prophetic oracles of judgment. Two observations about the historical background and the literary character of the passage will lead to greater understanding. Micah's teaching is set in the context of the invasion of Palestine in 701 B.C. under Sennacherib, the great Assyrian general and king. Interestingly, this event is well attested in "secular" history from Sennacherib's own annals, though the proud Assyrian general omits mentioning that his siege of Jerusalem failed. The Assyrian horde rolled right up to the gates of Jerusalem, wreaking havoc on the countryside and the small towns mentioned by Micah in 1:10-16. To this invasion setting we also owe the picture of the divine Savior as the siege-breaker in 2:12-13. Second, Micah makes extensive use of assonance, names and words with the same sounds, in 1:10-16. For example in 1:10 the name Gath, the small country town, sounds like the Hebrew word for "tell"; Beth Ophrah, which means "house of dust," obviously sounds like "dust." So Micah is using puns to drive home his message about the awful certainty of the judgment of God.

> The word of the LORD that came to Micah of Moresheth during the reigns of Jotham, Ahaz and Hezekiah, kings of Judah—the vision he saw concerning Samaria and Jerusalem.

> Hear, O peoples, all of you,
>   listen, O earth and all who are in it,
> that the Sovereign LORD may witness against you,
>   the LORD from his holy temple.

Look! The LORD is coming from his dwelling place;
    he comes down and treads the high places of the earth.
The mountains melt beneath him
    and the valleys split apart,
like wax before the fire,
    like water rushing down a slope.
All this is because of Jacob's transgression,
    because of the sins of the house of Israel.
What is Jacob's transgression?
    Is it not Samaria?
What is Judah's high place?
    Is it not Jerusalem?

"Therefore I will make Samaria a heap of rubble,
    a place for planting vineyards.
I will pour her stones into the valley
    and lay bare her foundations.
All her idols will be broken to pieces;
    all her temple gifts will be burned with fire;
    I will destroy all her images.
Since she gathered her gifts from the wages of prostitutes,
    as the wages of prostitutes they will again be used."

Because of this I will weep and wail;
    I will go about barefoot and naked.
I will howl like a jackal
    and moan like an owl.
For her wound is incurable;
    it has come to Judah.
It has reached the very gate of my people,
    even to Jerusalem itself.
Tell it not in Gath;
    weep not at all.
In Beth Ophrah
    roll in the dust.
Pass on in nakedness and shame,
    you who live in Shaphir.
Those who live in Zaanan
    will not come out.

Beth Ezel is in mourning;
  its protection is taken from you.
Those who live in Maroth writhe in pain,
  waiting for relief,
because disaster has come from the LORD,
  even to the gate of Jerusalem.
You who live in Lachish,
  harness the team to the chariot.
You were the beginning of sin
  to the Daughter of Zion,
for the transgressions of Israel
  were found in you.
Therefore you will give parting gifts
  to Moresheth Gath.
The town of Aczib will prove deceptive
  to the kings of Israel.
I will bring a conqueror against you
  who live in Mareshah.
He who is the glory of Israel
  will come to Adullam.
Shave your heads in mourning
  for the children in whom you delight;
make yourselves as bald as the vulture,
  for they will go from you into exile.

Woe to those who plan iniquity,
  to those who plot evil on their beds!
At morning's light they carry it out
  because it is in their power to do it.
They covet fields and seize them,
  and houses, and take them.
They defraud a man of his home,
  a fellowman of his inheritance.

Therefore, the LORD says:

"I am planning disaster against this people,
  from which you cannot save yourselves.
You will no longer walk proudly,

GOD THE JUDGE ————————————————————————— *107*

for it will be a time of calamity.
In that day men will ridicule you;
   they will taunt you with this mournful song:
'We are utterly ruined;
   my people's possession is divided up.
He takes it from me!
   He assigns our fields to traitors.' "

Therefore you will have no one in the assembly of the LORD
   to divide the land by lot.

"Do not prophesy," their prophets say.
   "Do not prophesy about these things;
   disgrace will not overtake us."
Should it be said, O house of Jacob:
   "Is the Spirit of the LORD angry?
   Does he do such things?"

"Do not my words do good
   to him whose ways are upright?
Lately my people have risen up
   like an enemy.
You strip off the rich robe
   from those who pass by without a care,
like men returning from battle.
You drive the women of my people
   from their pleasant homes.
You take away my blessing
   from their children forever.
Get up, go away!
   For this is not your resting place,
because it is defiled,
   it is ruined, beyond all remedy.
If a liar and deceiver comes and says,
   'I will prophesy for you plenty of wine and beer,'
   he would be just the prophet for this people!" (Mic 1—2:11)

Observe five aspects of what Micah says about judgment.
   1. Judgment is a natural expression of the character of God. The devas-

tation, the upsetting of the natural order and the destruction of the towns and cities of Palestine occur because the Sovereign Lord witnesses a judgment word against the people (v. 2) and "the LORD is coming" (v. 3). Yahweh has resolved to judge. His very presence in power explodes sin and evil, for he is holy, he is light that dispels darkness, he is justice that sentences evil.

2. The heart of the justice that expresses God's character is retribution. Retribution is the giving to men and women exactly what they deserve— rewarding good with good and evil with evil. This comes to clearest expression in 2:1, 3, "Woe to those who *plan* iniquity. . . . I am *planning* disaster," and 1:7, "Since she gathered her gifts from the *wages of prostitutes,* as the *wages of prostitutes* they will again be used." God has resolved to reward each person according to his or her deeds.

Retribution is a natural, inevitable expression of God's holiness. In our hearts we all know that this is right. When put in a corner and wronged by a stronger person, even the theoretical relativist blurts out, "It isn't fair!" revealing from his heart what his theory denies.

3. When we fall afoul of the judgment of God, our plight is something we have chosen for ourselves. In Micah God's judgment falls on Israel and Judah for two principal reasons: idolatry (1:6-7) and greedy materialism that oppresses the poor (2:1-2; see this theme also in Mic 3:9-11; 6:9-12). Both of these offenses were well known to be evil violations of God's covenant with Israel. Prohibitions of idolatry abound in the law (see Gen 20:3-4 for the basic covenant stipulations in the first two commandments), and Israel had been repeatedly judged for idolatrous practices (see Ex 32—34 for the golden calf incident). And Israel had been commanded in the law to care for the helpless and to act with strict justice in business dealings (see Lev 19). Israelites were forbidden to amass large estates and give control of the agrarian economy to a wealthy few, because the land belonged to the Lord (Lev 25, especially v. 23). Judgment fell because of willful violations, because of deeds Israel knew to be wrong.

So we see that God's judgment is *according to our knowledge.* This is no less true for the Gentile nations neighboring Israel. Amos pronounces judgment on the nations around Israel and Judah according to their own standards (see Amos 1—2). Every culture has standards of right and wrong, be they ever so far from God's law; every culture also violates those standards when it appears advantageous to do so. But it follows, then, that if we fall afoul of God's judgment, it is not because God has some hidden agenda to spring on us. Judgment falls because we fail to live up to the knowledge we have, and that failure robs us of any excuse. Further, it follows that the more knowledge we possess, the graver our danger. Privilege always carries responsibility. God's chosen people, his vehicle for bringing his truth to the nations, are judged by a stricter standard and subjected to harsher treatment. There are no favorites and no exceptions. Judgment must begin with the family of God (1 Pet 4:17). With God there is justice.

4. God's judgment is universal. Micah forces this conclusion on us in two ways. His teaching begins, "Hear, O peoples, *all of you,* listen, *O earth and all who are in it."* He calls everyone to hear the Lord's verdict. God is "Lord of all the earth" (4:13). This universal perspective allows no sentimental exceptions. Notice that even Micah's hometown, Moresheth (compare 1:1, 14), is included in the devastation of God's judgment. Truth demands that we allow no exceptions, sentimental or otherwise. All the people of the earth must face their God.

5. The judgment of God is at work within the ordinary course of human history. God uses nations, individuals and natural events to bring partial justice, to reward and encourage good, to limit and restrain the growth of evil.

Micah discerns this temporal, historical judgment in Sennacherib's campaign in Palestine. From one perspective there was nothing unusual in the situation at all. Nations and their leaders have always had a lust for power and conquest. Israel and Judah were small states ripe for the plucking by the more powerful Assyrians. But behind this "natural" event is the sovereign hand of God, restraining and punishing evil, rewarding and encouraging good. And the prophet has been given God's interpretation of the events so that we may understand it. While we do not have Micah's pipeline to the Lord and therefore lack his certainty about the meaning of contemporary events, we may be certain that the same God is working for the same ends in similar ways in the events of our time.

Typically the Old Testament moves within the circle of God's temporal judgments. And we must admit that only partial justice is done in the ordinary course of history. The righteous suffer along with the notoriously unrighteous. Sometimes evil people prosper and seem to suffer not at all. But God is not a relativist; he is faithful to himself and his promises. Temporal judgments cry out for some perfect judgment where full justice will be done.

Judgment in the New Testament
If we turn to the New Testament, we find not only agreement with this teaching on God's work of judgment but indeed an intensification of it. For what the Old Testament gropes toward in the way of perfect justice, the New

Testament declares as a certainty—a final, universal judgment with eternal consequences.

It is not a widely recognized fact, but the main New Testament authority on God's final judgment on the lives of all people with abiding, eternal consequences is found on Jesus' lips frequently. The principal passages are Matthew 7:13-27; 10:26-33; 12:30-37; 13:24-49; 22:1-14; 24:36-25,46; Luke 13:23-30; 16:19-31; John 5:22-29. "Hell" is his image for the eternal consequences of falling afoul of God's judgment. "Hell" is Gehenna, the valley of Hinnom outside Jerusalem, a despicable place of infant sacrifice in Old Testament times, which became the city dump. It was an unclean, horrible, forsaken place. This is an image Jesus employs; the eternal punishment to which it points to must be unimaginably worse. This teaching represents not a suspension of the Old Testament view of judgment, as is popularly supposed, but a deepening and intensification of it.

Three additional aspects of our Lord's teaching about divine judgement further deepen and intensify the Old Testament teaching.

1. Jesus himself will be the judge; his word of acceptance or rejection will be decisive. Jesus taught,

> The Father judges no one, but has entrusted all judgment to the Son. . . . [The Father] has given him authority to judge because he is the Son of Man. . . . A time is coming when all who are in their graves will hear his voice and come out—those who have done good will rise to live, and those who have done evil will rise to be condemned. (Jn 5:22, 27-29)

Or again,

> When the Son of Man comes in his glory, . . . he will sit on his throne in heavenly glory. All the nations will be gathered before him, and he will separate the people one from another. . . . Then the King will say to those on his right, "Come, you who are blessed by my Father; take your inheritance." . . . Then he will say to those on his left, "Depart from me, you who are cursed, into the eternal fire prepared for the devil and his angels." (Mt 25:31-32, 34, 41)

By the Father's design, each of us faces a confrontation with Jesus at the end of life's road. His kind but searching gaze will bore its way into our innermost self. We may be certain that Jesus, who is true God and perfect man, acquainted firsthand with our weakness and God's holiness, will be a perfectly just judge. Rightly the Anglican burial service addresses Jesus as "holy and merciful Savior, thou most worthy eternal Judge."

2. Jesus' teaching highlights attitudes and actions that place us in particular danger of his condemnation. He warns against the accumulation of wealth and material possessions, which dull our spiritual vision and crowd God out of our lives. We see this in the rich young ruler, who sorrowfully refused to follow Jesus because of his great wealth (Mk 10:17-31), and in the parable of the rich fool who toiled to store up his treasure but was utterly impoverished toward God (Lk 12:13-21). Jesus teaches the absolute priority of the kingdom of God over any material good.

Do not store up for yourselves treasures on earth, where moth and rust destroy, and where thieves break in and steal. But store up for yourselves treasures in heaven, where moth and rust do not destroy, and where thieves do not break in and steal. For where your treasure is, there your heart will be also. . . .

No one can serve two masters. Either he will hate the one and love the other, or he will be devoted to the one and despise the other. You cannot serve both God and Money. . . . For the pagans run after all these things, and your heavenly Father knows that you need them. But seek first his kingdom and his righteousness, and all these things will be given to you as well. (Mt 6:19-21, 24, 32-33)

In an age profoundly committed to the lie that life does consist in the abundance of possessions (see Lk 12:15), we should tremble at the thought of judgment.

Similarly, lack of concern and care for the poor and helpless is another sure way of coming under God's condemnation. This warning is present in the parable of the rich man and Lazarus (Lk 16:13-31) and in the last judgment scene where the sheep and the goats are separated (Mt 25:31-46). It is striking that although they did not realize it, in caring for or rejecting the poor the sheep and the goats were caring for or rejecting Jesus. Nothing could express more clearly the truth that what people *do* gives us a true picture of their character. Deeds of which God approves flow naturally from a right relationship to the Lord, and deeds that bring God's disapproval reflect our distance from the Lord. Judgment of our deeds, when carried out with perfect wisdom, is actually judgment of our true character.

Again, Jesus warns that unforgiveness puts us beyond the reach of God's forgiveness. He tells a parable about an ungrateful servant who, having been forgiven an immense debt that could never be repaid, refused to write off a small debt for a fellow servant. On hearing of this hardness of heart, his master slapped the servant into prison until he repaid. Jesus concludes, "This is how my heavenly Father will treat each of you unless you forgive your brother from your heart" (see Mt 18:21-35). Notice again that the ground for condemnation, an unforgiving heart, reflects inner spiritual emptiness, an unforgiven heart.

In the same vein, Jesus has stern condemnation for those who cause children or the spiritually young and weak to stumble: "If anyone causes one of these little ones who believe in me to sin, it would be better for him to have a large millstone hung around his neck and to be drowned in the depths of the sea" (Mt 18:6). Those who are teachers, as well as those who shape public opinion through the communications media, will find themselves with a great deal to explain when they face the Lord. All of us will answer for merciless and graceless treatment of those who are weaker than ourselves.

Finally, Jesus warns against the danger of being "religious" and falling into that besetting sin of "religious" folk, self-righteousness. We find it difficult to feel just how shocking the parable of the Pharisee and the tax collector was to Jesus' hearers, because we already know that the Pharisees are bad guys. For Jesus' hearers they were not bad; on the contrary, they were held in highest esteem. There was no question of their sincerity or sanctity. Think of a class of people today whose integrity is generally unquestioned (if such a class of people exists in our morally jaded day). Perhaps a pastor might afford a parallel—a pastor involved in all of the "right" social causes. In any case, in the parable it is not the esteemed and self-esteeming Pharisee who is justified, pronounced "not guilty" before the bar of God's justice. It is the despicable tax collector who can hardly lift his head. He knows he needs mercy, and he cries out for it from the depths of his heart.

Further, Jesus warns that it is possible to be a formal part of God's people and still to reject God's Messiah (Mk 12:1-9). Church membership affords no shelter from Christ's judgment. It is even possible to be active in performing great deeds of religious service and still be a stranger to Jesus: "Many will say to me on that day, 'Lord, Lord, did we not prophesy in your name, and in your name drive out demons and perform many miracles?' Then I will tell them plainly, 'I never knew you. Away from me, you evildoers!' " (Mt 7:22-23). Again, as with each of these grounds for judgment, the reality of our hearts is what the Lord will lay bare. Our deeds come under scrutiny as an index of our true character.

3. God's final judgment involves a present process as well as a future climax in the coming of Jesus. In Jesus, God has acted decisively to deliver men and women from evil. His kingdom has broken into this present evil age like light shining in darkness. Because Jesus' coming is so decisive for the destiny of humanity, so final, it has dragged (so to speak) the last judgment forward into time. As we are confronted with Christ and his gospel, we are forced to respond. This response to Jesus is our response to God. (All is lost when Jesus is rejected.) In this response we bring God's verdict on ourselves, as John declares:

For God did not send his Son into the world to condemn the world, but to save the world through him. Whoever believes in him is not condemned, but whoever does not believe stands condemned already because he has not believed in the name of God's one and only Son. This is the verdict: Light has come into the world, but men loved darkness instead of light because their deeds were evil. Everyone who does evil hates the light, and will not come into the light for fear that his deeds will be exposed. (Jn 3:17-20)

On the other hand, *justification* is God's final verdict of "not guilty" pronounced on us sinners because of the work of Jesus on our behalf. We have received God's last-day verdict of acquittal if we have given our hearts and lives to the Lord Jesus, and we have nothing to fear in God's judgment.

This wonderful, liberating confidence of being shielded from a deserved condemnation by the gracious work of God in the Lord Jesus is expressed in the judgment scene in Revelation 20:11-15. Alongside the books that record each person's works and constitute the ground of our condemnation is "the book of life." Those whose names are found in the book of life are not "thrown into the lake of fire" like the rest of humanity; they enter into the joy of the new heaven and earth. Those who seek the Lord Jesus now, calling on the coming Judge to be their Savior, can sing with truth and great joy:

No condemnation now I dread;
Jesus, and all in Him, is mine!
Alive in Him, my living Head,
And clothed in righteousness divine,
Bold I approach the eternal throne
And claim the crown, through Christ, my own.
(Charles Wesley, "And Can It Be")

The Reality of God's Judgment

Given this clear and pervasive biblical teaching, five reasons can be given for holding firmly and unapologetically to its truth. First, and most basically, judgment is demanded by the character of God. The truth is that God's judgment is an aspect of his moral perfection. Would a God who did not care about the difference between right and wrong be good? Would a God who makes no distinction between a Hitler and a Mother Teresa be worthy of our praise? Wouldn't such a failure to distinguish good and evil be a sign of moral indifference? Or perhaps it would signal some moral inconsistency within God himself. To ask these questions is immediately to recognize their absurdity. God is no relativist; he is not morally indifferent, nor is he spiritually impotent. That God has committed Himself to judge the world is the ultimate expression of his holiness.

Second, full weight must be given to the fact that Jesus is the New Testament theologian of judgment par excellence. The theme of judgement runs throughout his teaching. And as he said, "Heaven and earth will pass away, but my words will never pass away" (Mk 13:31). Certainly we are not at liberty to contradict our Lord, the one who is true God and true man. His position as God's ultimate spokesman and God's last and best Word is overturned if we choose to disagree with him on such a central issue. To reject the thought of God's work of judgment is to reject Jesus.

Third, the reality of divine judgment imparts a moral significance to human life. Final judgment means that in the end all people are accountable to God for all their actions. No person, no situation, is insignificant. Even when actions are too private or too insignificant for others to notice, God sees, and he will bring all things under review. Each unnoticed kindness, each unrewarded act of faithfulness, every thoughtless word and unkind thought will be brought to the light of day by our God. Nothing good will be lost; nothing evil will prevail.

Though we live in an age when people have worked hard to create the feeling that we answer to no one but ourselves, all of life is lived in the light of eternity. Even the humblest action has immense dignity. Even the least significant life by human standards is freighted with cosmic meaning and significance because of the certainty of divine judgment.

Fourth, the reality of divine judgment is an important basis for a prophetic challenge to the status quo in society. Because God is good, he stands against every social evil. The one true and living God is no convenient prop for our preferred way of life. Unlike idols, which are a projection of our own image, he stands over us and against us. Thus the faith of the Bible is profoundly troubling and socially revolutionary. Nowhere is this clearer than in Amos 1— 2, where Yahweh speaks a word of judgment against both the heartless cruelty of Israel's neighbors and the selfish materialism, exploitation, immorality and idolatry of Israel itself. No less has the Sovereign Judge more recently condemned the vicious racism of apartheid, the heartless oppression of the gulag and the greedy, exploitive materialism of the West. All of these will be judged one day, and for that reason God's people are called to faithful and loving resistance against their own society's entrenched evils.

Apart from this holy perspective, apart from the holy light of eternity, we simply collapse into the massive evils around us. But we will not conform if we keep the thought of God's judgment firmly in our minds.

Fifth, the reality of God's judgment assures us of the outcome of the struggle of good and evil. Judgment ensures the triumph of God and of good. The present conflict between good and evil will not last forever. Judgment means that evil will be disposed of decisively, finally, completely. The cynicism and moral indifference so characteristic of our day have no foundation in reality. Even in the thick of battle, even when we seem to face overwhelming odds, the reality of final judgment brings us calmness, assurance and faithfulness.

Another Look at Universalism

What, then, of the case for universalism? In the light of this extensive biblical teaching and the solid reasons for holding fast to the judgment of God, we must reject the universalist perspective. The universalist may raise some real problems for us, and we ought to be humble enough to admit the limitations in our knowledge. But the problems raised simply are not significant enough to overturn the witness of God's Word and the supporting force of arguments for the reality of divine judgment.

Upon inspection, the arguments advanced by universalists prove to have uneven force. The biblical passages they cite cannot plausibly be interpreted to teach universal salvation. If we look at their wider context, their "universalism" disappears. For example, can Paul plausibly be interpreted to teach a universal salvation in Romans 5 and 11 in the light of his explicit teaching about God's wrath and judgment in Romans 1—3? Or consider Colossians 1:20 in the light of Colossians 1:19-23. God's plan "to reconcile to himself all things" includes the Colossians *if they continue in their faith.* Such statements declare the wide scope of God's saving purpose even though some refuse to enter that purpose. *All* in these passages refers to "both Jews and Gentiles" or "the whole created order renewed in the new heaven and earth," not each and every human or spirit.

Universalists make a great deal of the love of God. But I wonder if this is not a too exclusive emphasis. As I noted in the last chapter, God's majestic goodness and uncreated simplicity make it impossible for us to reduce the Holy One to love. Even if we think deeply about God's love, we discover that judgment cannot be eliminated. How can love ignore the whole shape of a person's life as if it had no relevance to eternity? Even if we conceive of God as a superpsychologist (as John Hick seems to do in *Death and Eternal Life*[1]) guiding people to their appointed end, what of the person who refuses to go to the psychiatrist?

Indeed, the universalist's "love" tends to degenerate into pure sentimentality. The love of God is not soothing like a lullaby; it is so unimaginably

great that it demands our all. To turn a deaf ear to its demand, to stand
unmoved by it, is to damn ourselves. As Leon Morris affirms,

Love does not mean that there is no judgement; love guarantees judgement, because it points up the ugliness of sin like nothing else does. Sin
against one's fellowman or against oneself is bad enough, but sin against
the sacrificial love of God is infinitely worse. The man who spurns the love
he sees on Calvary writes a damning judgement against himself.[2]

The love of God that ceaselessly works to save sinners is ruthlessly acting to
root out evil from the world he loves. If we identify ourselves with evil, his
love must become the wrath of God for us and destroy us. Judgment is thus
a true and ardent corollary of God's love. It flashes out suddenly and certainly
to destroy all that would injure and cheapen his beloved creation.

"But what of the millions who have never heard of Calvary?" the universalist
would hasten to ask. In the absence of any direct discussion of this question
in Scripture, two biblically based truths about divine judgment seem relevant.
First, *final judgement will be according to our knowledge as well as according
to our deeds.* So Jesus can speak of the obvious fairness of a man's being
condemned "by [his] own words" (Lk 19:22). No one will be condemned
for not believing in a Jesus of whom they have never heard. But every human
being knows something of God and his truth through the medium of God's
creation. And every person is guilty for falling short of the best they know.
As Jesus instructs us, "From everyone who has been given much, much will
be demanded" (Lk 12:48; compare Rom 2:12).

In addition, *final judgment will be administered according to the perfect
mercy and justice of God.* All our questions about the destiny of any person
must be left with him in the confidence Abraham expressed when he asked,
"Will not the Judge of all the earth do right?" (Gen 18:25). For those living
in cultures where the gospel has never been heard, due to no fault of their
own, the thought of God's justice and mercy is a great comfort.

Questions of Final Destiny

Beyond these biblical principles, anything we might say about the destiny of
any person is a matter of pure conjecture. Consider, for example, what Steven
Travis has to say about such a case: "If a Hindu finds salvation it is not by
virtue of being a good Hindu, any more than a Christian is saved by being
a good Christian. Whatever a person's religious background, 'saving faith'
involves coming to an end of one's own 'religion' and abandoning oneself
to the grace of God."[3]

These wise words express well a God-honoring confidence. But they also cry out for both expansion and qualification. Clearly Travis rightly envisions his hypothetical Hindu as coming to a point of genuine repentance, a repentance that rejects not only his own efforts to be good but also his culture's and even his religion's understanding and standard of goodness. But this depth of repentance and faith generally requires the contrast of an alternative and true view of the good and of God. Very rarely are we able to spontaneously imagine a radically new outlook on these most basic questions. So it is the proclamation of the truth of God that itself awakens faith and repentance: "Faith comes from hearing the message, and the message is heard through the word of Christ" (Rom 10:17; see the context of which this is the summarizing conclusion, vv. 12-17).

Travis wishes to maintain that the salvation of his hypothetical Hindu rests completely on the way to God won by the Lord Jesus on the cross and in his resurrection. There are not many ways to God created by human insight, ingenuity and sanctity. There is only the way of the cross, which will avail for the repentant Hindu who has never heard of Jesus in much the same way as it avails for the repentant Old Testament Israelite who also knew nothing of Jesus as a historical personage.

Still, a qualification needs to be added. The hypothetical character of this whole scenario must be acknowledged. All these observations are quite speculative, seeking to apply what we do know from direct biblical statements to a situation never directly addressed in Scripture. Indeed, this situation of the genuinely repentant person who is ignorant of the gospel through no fault of his or her own is strikingly poignant. But in all sober truth it must also be judged to be very rare indeed, if what Scripture teaches about the fallen human heart and mind is taken into account. Even having the living Word of God directly before them did little to awaken repentance in Jesus' contemporaries.

Certainly we can entrust such persons to the mercy and justice of the Holy One. But equally certainly we must acknowledge the speculative character of this whole discussion and admit our own ignorance. We do not know, nor can we know, the destiny of men and women under these conditions.

There is such a thing as a "reverent agnosticism." Where the Holy One has chosen to remain silent, reverence demands that we too maintain silence. Equally, reverence demands of us that we hold faithfully and tenaciously and obediently to those things that *have* been revealed to us in God's written Word. Says Scripture, "The secret things [God's silences] belong to the LORD our God, but the things revealed belong to us and to our children forever, *that we may follow all the words of this law*" (Deut 29:29). We must avoid the pride that presumes to give definitive answers where God has not given them in his Word *and* the false humility that arbitrarily dismisses or avoids the clear teaching he has provided to direct our living.

The Dangers of Suppressing the Truth

The judgment of God is an essential aspect of his holiness as it confronts sin. It is a sober reality, more certain than any physical law. Do not steer clear of this important truth.

Some suggest that this is a crude and primitive notion to be discarded. But interestingly, what turns out to be crude and primitive is the desire to suppress this truth. Notice that Micah's contemporaries were not thrilled with his message. They react by rebuking him: "Do not prophesy about these things; disgrace will not overtake us" (2:6-7). They propose that his talk of judgment is unworthy of a gracious God whose words do good to the upright. Sounds vaguely familiar, doesn't it? We think our similar reaction to be so very progressive. Actually, no sinner, ancient or modern, likes to hear of God's judgment. But this is the radical medicine we need in order to be healthy. When the truth of God's judgment is suppressed, a number of destructive results follow.

Zeal for the communication of the gospel is quenched. Under the myth of universalism, people are thought of as being OK and are left to live and die apart from a knowledge of their plight and the power of God's love. People in the church ask, "Why should we disturb the religion and the way of life of other people? Why not spend our offerings on new cushions for the sanctuary?" One might as well ask, "Why should we disturb the people asleep in a burning house?" We need the perspective of God's judgment if we are to see the world aright and respond appropriately.

Zeal for personal holiness is quenched. Apart from the sensitivity to sin that comes from knowing that we will one day give account of all our ways to the Lord, we become dull of heart and conscience. We cease to live in the light of eternity and begin to live for the approval of others or for our own selfish ends. Cutting corners is easier because "no one will know and no one cares." Rationalization becomes a way of life. Right and wrong are determined by the latest Gallup poll. Morally, all of life becomes a dull gray fog. We need the blazing light of God's holy judgment to dispel the fog, to reveal the destructive bog that sin is and to illuminate the moral glory of the image of God in which we are made.

Universalism also results in a quenching of zeal for social justice. Apart from a vibrant sense that God will bring all nations, including our own, into judgment, we slip comfortably into the ordinary reality around us. We find it easy to assume that only our enemies are evil—that we ourselves, despite a few minor superficial problems, are basically good. The gospel is emasculated by alien ideas drawn from our favorite ideology, whether of the right (God-and-country chauvinism) or the left (the myth of revolutionary violence). Perhaps this accounts for the lack of truly prophetic preaching in our churches and the tragic lack of resistance to social pressure among Christian people.

Consider the confrontation between Amos, the prophet whose message centered on Yahweh's justice, and Amaziah, a professional prophet attached to Jeroboam's royal court (Amos 7:10-17). Amaziah sought to silence Amos with threats and reports to the king. To be sure, Amos was an unpatriotic nuisance: he prophesied the death of the king and the defeat and exile of Israel. But Scripture and history make it clear who was right. I fear that many of us would side with Amaziah in his conventional nationalism and support for the state religion. Only a lively sense of the judging hand of God in history and at history's end will deliver us from Amaziah's comfortable conformity.

Finally, universalism quenches zeal for the true worship of God. As God is done over in the guise of a gentle, harmless, loving grandfather, worship's central focus is distorted and shifts from God to us. We think of his love in the rather pathetic terms of our own loves. The High and Holy One becomes the dispenser of warm fuzzies, not the lover of justice and judge of the living and the dead. Naturally, God approves of what we approve. Especially he approves of us.

Not only is this dreadfully low view of God a great intellectual error, but this most prevalent modern form of idolatry also cuts us off from true worship of God. As we conform God to our manageable images, we begin to think we can do as we please in worship. Surely he will be glad for whatever we bring him. Our focus shifts from pleasing God to meeting our own needs and desires. As a result, questions of truth or purity rarely arise for modern worshipers. Reverence, even thoughtfulness, in approaching the Lord is strange to us. We do not find it offensive to come to worship unprepared in heart and mind to meet the Lord. We do not worry very much about whether our worship lives up to biblical standards. What we will not tolerate is upsetting truths or encounters in our worship, like Isaiah's encounter with the Holy One. The experience must be tasteful and orderly. As long as worship is soothing, as long as we are made to feel good about ourselves, all is well.

Consider the plight of Nadab and Abihu, the priests who were Aaron's sons. At Sinai the Lord had given quite explicit instructions for leading the worship life of his people, and they had been present at this majestic revelation of

God's will for worship under the old covenant (Ex 24:1). Leviticus 10:1-9, however, tells how both offered unholy fire before the Lord. Exactly what made the fire unholy is not clear. What is clear was that this burning of incense was "contrary to his command" (v. 2). The text hints that perhaps drunkenness was involved (vv. 8-9). In any case God's judgment was immediate and severe. Fire flashed out from the Lord's presence and consumed the two priests.

Perhaps the severity of this judgment arose from their privileged place in history, so close to the pivotal events of the exodus and Sinai. Further, the temptation to ape the worship practices of the surrounding cultures had to be carefully resisted if the purity of God's revelation was to be preserved. Moses, however, interpreted the event to Aaron, their father, in the following terms: "This is what the LORD spoke of when he said: 'Among those who approach me I will show myself holy; in the sight of all the people I will be honored' " (v. 3).

God's response to Nadab and Abihu reflects his true and holy judgment on all disobedient, thoughtless and self-serving worship. If in his long-suffering mercy he does not deal with us so severely, we may also be certain that in the final judgment we will have much to account for, in our laxness and unconcern for purity in worship. But a due regard for that judgment is a key part in moving us to purity and obedience in the worship of our holy Lord.

A thoughtful regard of God's judgment is an important aspect of our whole life as creatures and children by grace of the holy Creator. It is not the whole, to be sure. But the disregard of divine judgment by modern Christian people is a great loss. We suppress this sobering, but wonderful, truth to the impoverishment of our souls. Only in its light will we develop a true, proper concern for the communication of the gospel, for personal godliness, for social justice and for pure, God-pleasing worship. If these fruits mean anything to us, we must get back to their root by embracing the truth of the judgment of the Holy One in our minds and hearts.

7

GOD THE WARRIOR

U NBELIEVERS ASSURE US THAT OUR FAITH IN GOD IS A QUITE UNDERSTANDABLE matter of wish-fulfillment. The spiritual descendants of Freud insist that our belief is a neurotic obsession. Made insecure in our passage to adult life, we "blow up" the image of a loving father to cosmic proportions to protect ourselves from the meaninglessness, ambiguity and loneliness of adult life.

The spiritual descendants of Marx offer a socioeconomic explanation. The thought of reward from God in a coming life is used by the dominant classes to secure their position of advantage. Meanwhile, the oppressed are kept in comforted subjection with promises of future bliss. "God" becomes a sinister tool for oppression in the hands of the privileged and a narcotic that paralyzes any efforts toward change among the oppressed.

At best, faith in God is said to be a comforting illusion. One sick joke goes, "How is God different from Santa Claus? Answer: Santa Claus is real." Naturally, as we mature, as we cease to be children, we will leave this myth behind. At worst, faith in God is psychopathic, a lamentable barrier to personal growth, self-discovery and freedom. Or it is a cause of social aberrations, a lamentable support for prejudice and a barrier to political and economic freedom.

Believers must admit that there is some truth to these accusations. The promise of future reward was used by professing Christians to maintain the institution of slavery in the United States and has more recently been used in support of apartheid in South Africa. Doubtless, some believe in a god neurotically, only because it keeps them from facing either reality or their fears. But as a total explanation of belief in God, the neo-Freudian and neo-Marxist approaches are guilty of both logical fallacy and serious misunderstanding.

Of Projections and Illusions

The logical problem is known as the "genetic fallacy." A moment's thought reveals that the origin of an idea tells you nothing about its truthfulness. Often the profoundest truths and the silliest errors come to us in flashes of intuition, even in dreams. Think of Francis Crick's "discovery" of the structure of DNA. His laboratories were connected by a spiral staircase, which he naturally ran up and down frequently. One day the idea simply dawned on him that DNA was a double helix, a double spiral staircase. Knowledge played a role in the formulation and testing of this discovery, but the origin of the idea was rooted in the accident of the spiral staircase in his laboratory. The psychology of this discovery can be seen to be irrelevant to its truthfulness. We need to examine any idea in terms of its truthfulness, not its origin.

The logical inconclusiveness of Freudian "projection" arguments is further demonstrated by their reversibility. Human fatherhood, for example, could be a finite copy of God's infinite Fatherhood, a reality projected downward, as it were, rather than an illusion projected upward. In fact, Ephesians 3:14-15 seems to say just that.

C. S. Lewis exposes the projection fallacy in his children's story *The Silver Chair*. Prince Rilian has just been freed from the Green Witch's enchantment in her underground world by the children Scrubb and Jill and the froglike Marshwiggle Puddleglum. Immediately they encounter the awful witch, who seeks to enchant them again with burning incense, rhythmic mandolin playing and clever arguments.

The Green Witch seeks to reenslave Rilian and his rescuers by persuading them that their real world, Narnia, is an illusion merely projected in an imaginary way from the only real world, her underground kingdom. The children desperately cling to their memories of things in Narnia, but the witch's enchantment and cleverness keep undercutting them. Puddleglum recalls the sun, and all four rally around this wonderful thought. But the Green Witch responds with condescension, asking them to describe the sun that they remember.

"Please it your Grace," said the Prince, very coldly and politely. "You see that lamp. It is round and yellow and gives light to the whole room; and hangeth moreover from the roof. Now that thing which we call the sun is like the lamp, only far greater and brighter. It giveth light to the whole Overworld and hangeth in the sky."

"Hangeth from what, my lord?" asked the Witch; and then, while they were all still thinking how to answer her, she added, with another of her soft, silver laughs. "You see? When you try to think out clearly what this sun must be, you cannot tell me. You can only tell me it is like the lamp. Your sun is a dream; and there is nothing in that dream that was not copied from the lamp. The lamp is the real thing; the sun is but a tale, a children's story."

Desperately the four remember Aslan, the great lion who is Lord of Narnia (and the Christ-figure in these stories). Again the witch undercuts them with clever, enchanting projection arguments.

"What is a lion?" asked the Witch.

"Oh, hang it all!" said Scrubb. "Don't you know? How can we describe it to her? Have you ever seen a cat?"

"Surely," said the Queen. "I love cats."

"Well a lion is a little bit—only a little bit, mind you—like a huge cat—with a mane. At least, it's not like a horse's mane, you know, it's more like a judge's wig. And it's yellow. And terrifically strong."

The Witch shook her head. "I see," she said, "that we should do no better with your lion, as you call it, than we did with your sun. You have seen lamps, and so you imagined a bigger and better lamp and call it the sun. You've seen cats, and now you want a bigger and better cat, and it's to be called a lion. Well, 'tis a pretty make-believe, though, to say truth, it would suit you all better if you were younger. And look how you can put nothing into your make-believe without copying it from the real world, this world of mine, which is the only world."

Finally the enchantment of the witch is broken by Puddleglum, the melancholic and brave Marshwiggle. He plunges his webbed foot into the fire on which the incense is burning, replacing the sweet smell of incense with the not at all enchanting smell of burnt Marshwiggle. The shock of the pain makes Puddleglum absolutely clear-headed for the first time.

Indeed, clear-headedness is a quite uncommon quality, even here in our reality. But a small bit of it lets us see through the impressive-sounding but logically inconclusive projection arguments.

Not only are projection arguments fallacious and reversible, but they are capable of being stood on their head and used against those who employ them. Perhaps, we would like to suggest, nonbelief in God can best be explained by an unwillingness to be accountable to anyone or anything, by a proud and basically egocentric view of life. God cramps our style, so the myth of his nonexistence is convenient and comforting. Consider this admission by Aldous Huxley:

> I had motives for not wanting the world to have meaning; consequently I assumed that it had none and was able without any difficulty to find satisfying reasons for this assumption. The philosopher who finds no meaning in the world is not concerned exclusively with a problem in pure metaphysics; he is also concerned to prove that there is no valid reason why he personally should not do as he wants to do, or why his friends should not seize political power and govern in the way that they find most advantageous to themselves.... For myself the philosophy of meaninglessness was essentially an instrument of liberation, sexual and political.[1]

Not often do we hear such an honest admission that God was found to be an inconvenience and therefore cast aside.

Those who view God as merely a comfort are also mistaken. Their understanding of what it means to face up to God is hopelessly defective and shallow. God does not just cramp our style. To face the one true and living God is a shattering experience. Amiable agnostics, who speak dismissively of the comforts of believing in God, know nothing of this Holy One from whom heaven and earth flee. Or perhaps they do have some inkling of the terror of facing the living God and neurotically repress the thought with sophisticated rationalizations.

There is such a depth of intensity in God's uncreated holiness, goodness and judgement, that for a fallen human being to face Him is shatteringly traumatic. "Note then," says Paul, "the kindness and the severity of God" (Rom 11:22 RSV). This severity, this traumatizing intensity, comes to focus for us in what the Bible teaches about the wrath of God and particularly in its description of God as a mighty warrior.

God Hates Evil

Scripture praises God not only for his goodness to his people but also for his wrath against evil and those who become his enemies by identifying with evil. Consider:

> The LORD is a jealous and avenging God;
> the LORD takes vengeance and is filled with wrath.

The LORD takes vengeance on his foes
    and maintains his wrath against his enemies.
The LORD is slow to anger and great in power;
    the LORD will not leave the guilty unpunished.
His way is in the whirlwind and the storm,
    and clouds are the dust of his feet.
He rebukes the sea and dries it up;
    he makes all the rivers run dry.
Bashan and Carmel wither
    and the blossoms of Lebanon fade.
The mountains quake before him
    and the hills melt away.
The earth trembles at his presence,
    the world and all who live in it.
Who can withstand his indignation?
    Who can endure his fierce anger?
His wrath is poured out like fire;
    the rocks are shattered before him.

The LORD is good,
    a refuge in times of trouble.
He cares for those who trust in him,
    but with an overwhelming flood
he will make an end of Nineveh;
    he will pursue his foes into darkness. (Nahum 1:2-8)

The wrath of God is being revealed from heaven against all the godlessness and wickedness of men who suppress the truth by their wickedness. (Rom 1:18)

God is just: He will pay back trouble to those who trouble you and give relief to you who are troubled, and to us as well. This will happen when the Lord Jesus is revealed from heaven in blazing fire with his powerful angels. He will punish those who do not know God and do not obey the gospel of our Lord Jesus. They will be punished with everlasting destruction and shut out from the presence of the Lord and from the majesty of his power on the day he comes to be glorified in his holy people and to be marveled at among all those who have believed. (2 Thess 1:6-10)

Although the word *anger* is never used in Revelation 18:21—19:3, the same intensity and praise are present there:

Then a mighty angel picked up a boulder the size of a large millstone and threw it into the sea, and said:

"With such violence
  the great city of Babylon will be thrown down,
  never to be found again.
The music of harpists and musicians, flute players and trumpeters,
  will never be heard in you again.
No workman of any trade
  will ever be found in you again.
The sound of a millstone
  will never be heard in you again.
The light of a lamp
  will never shine in you again.
The voice of bridegroom and bride
  will never be heard in you again.
Your merchants were the world's great men.
  By your magic spell all the nations were led astray.
In her was found the blood of prophets and of the saints,
  and of all who have been killed on the earth."

After this I heard what sounded like the roar of a great multitude in heaven shouting:

"Hallelujah!
Salvation and glory and power belong to our God,
  for true and just are his judgments.
He has condemned the great prostitute
  who corrupted the earth by her adulteries.
He has avenged on her the blood of his servants."

And again they shouted:

"Hallelujah!
The smoke from her goes up for ever and ever."

The Anger of God

To associate anger or indignation with God is jarring to our sensibilities. We have the suspicion that such language is somehow unworthy of God. Typically *our* anger is anything but holy. Most often it explodes without discipline to express a wounded ego, leading us to treat others unkindly. How then can we praise God for what is typically a vice in us?

Scripture knows that human anger is often wrong. As James says, "The anger of man does not work the righteousness of God" (1:20 RSV). Therefore, true thinking about the wrath of God must begin by eliminating all defects we associate with anger that arise because we are sinful creatures. Such a procedure is not impossible. We speak of "righteous indignation," an outrage fully justified and even praiseworthy. We know that there is something wrong with people when they are not outraged at monstrous evil like the Holocaust or racism or rape.

Something of the quality of righteous indignation is expressed in the following dialogue written by Langston Hughes, the black journalist and poet. The dialogue is taken from Hughes's popular humorous newspaper column, which appeared in the Chicago *Defender.* The hero of this column was Jesse B. Simple, a black "everyman" of the 1930s. Simple recalls having tuned in a white church service on the radio by accident when searching for a Duke Ellington recording. The white preacher spoke of Christ's Second Coming. This set Simple to thinking about the hypocrisy of the white religion that promoted racism. Says Simple,

"And Christ knows what these white folks have been doing to old colored me all these years."

"Of course, He knows," I said. "When Christ was here on earth, He fought for the poor and the oppressed. But some people called Him an agitator. They cursed Him and reviled Him and sent soldiers to lock Him up. They killed Him on the cross."

"At Calvary," said Simple, "way back in B.C. I know the Bible, too. My Aunt Lucy read it to me. She read how He drove the money-changers out of the Temple. Also how He changed the loaves and fishes into many and fed the poor, which made the rulers in their high places mad because they didn't want the poor to eat. Well, when Christ comes back this time, I hope He comes back mad His own self. I hope He drives the Jim Crowers out of their high places, every last one of them from Washington to Texas! I hope He smites white folks down!"

"You don't mean all white folks, do you?"

"No," said Simple. "I hope He lets Mrs. Roosevelt alone "[2]

Even our fallen human anger, when controlled and disciplined by God's grace, has a place; "Be angry but do not sin; do not let the sun go down on your anger, and give no opportunity to the devil" (Eph 4:26-27 RSV).

Anger in the Lord must be this sort of righteous indignation against the sin and evil that maim and destroy his creatures. "The wrath of God" is God's personal active, intense hostility in the punishing of evil and sin.

Three characteristics of God's wrath follow from this basic insight. First, *God's wrath is an expression of his justice.* It is the normal, settled hostility of a just Judge to criminal behavior. We are apt to think of a judge as an impartial figure and picture Justice as a blindfolded woman holding a pan-balance. There is a truth in this picture, for true justice is not influenced by the human standing of the criminal, whether president or pauper. As Scripture says, "Do not pervert justice; do not show partiality to the poor or favoritism to the great, but judge your neighbor fairly. . . . I am the LORD" (Lev 19:15-16). Or again, "God does not show favoritism" (Rom 2:11). But this image errs in the direction of indifference. While a judge must be impartial toward people, he or she must not be indifferent toward issues of justice and injustice. Above all, an adequate judge must be positively and passionately committed to justice.

What is only imperfectly present in the best of human judges is perfectly present in the Lord. He loves justice and hates injustice, and there is a perfect depth, intensity, and consistency to this love and hate. What characterizes us only fitfully when we are at our best is a foundational element of his holy goodness. "Wrath" is the deep and consistent hostility of the Holy One to all injustice. It is a perfection in his character that we should admire and praise.

Second, *in Scripture God's wrath is something men and women choose for themselves.* Before wrath is inflicted by God, it is a state we opt for by turning from God's truth, light and love. Unbelievers prefer to live without God, in defiance of God, and they shall have their wish. The Holy One gives us what we choose in all its implications, nothing more and nothing less. Indeed, talk of God's love for the world would seem to demand this sort of respect for those who bear God's image. There is nothing of cruelty or the thoughtless inflicting of pain in this. The simple justice of it is quite clear.

Third, *Scripture repeatedly stresses that "the Lord is slow to anger."* Now, "slow to anger" does not mean "never angry." Rather, it helps us to see God is not irascible; the Holy One is not a cosmic grouch or killjoy, nor does he "fly off the handle." He is patient. He takes no delight in the destruction of the wicked. When from our perspective his anger erupts into history, it is always after a long-suffering period of patience when issues of great magnitude with eternal consequences are at stake and people have chosen to set themselves against his ways.

A Case of God's Wrath

Consider the famous (some would say "infamous") story of Elisha and the bears (2 Kings 2:23-25). Elisha is sometimes assumed to have been a heartless, savage old man who couldn't take a joke about his baldness. He lashed out against a bunch of mere children, so this representation goes, and worst of all, God responded immediately by sending a savage pair of bears that devoured no fewer than forty-two of the children. We recoil in horror. How could Elisha, God's prophet, do such a thing? And more important still, how could God do such a thing?

On almost every count that interpretation is a misrepresentation. Elisha was in fact a very young man, just being launched into a prophetic ministry that would last for nearly sixty years. He certainly was not ruthless or savage, as his appeal to the king to spare the Syrian army demonstrates (2 Kings 6:1-23). The jeers and insults hurled at him were far more than a personal insult. "Go up" was presumably a sneering mockery of the ascension of Elisha's predecessor Elijah, a request for a repeat performance that would rid Israel of God's prophet and God's word. "Baldhead" was almost certainly not a reference to physical baldness, since men in the Near East usually covered their heads. Most likely it was a reference to a prophetic tonsure, in which case the ridicule is directed not personally at Elisha but at the prophetic office and at the God whose mouthpiece the prophets claimed to be.

"Small boys" (RSV) or "little children" is highly misleading. The Hebrew words used to designate the mob (note that forty-two were injured by the bears and many others must have escaped) applies to older teenagers and young men, even sometimes professional soldiers. We should envision, then, a pack of young toughs more like a contemporary street gang than a grade-school class. The text does not report that any of them were killed. "Mauled" implies severe wounds. If there were fatalities, we do not know it.

But more than getting the facts straight, we need to set the whole scene in context. Ahab and Jezebel are still very much in command of Israel, and the tide of Baal worship and its associated immorality has continued to rise. Elijah was gone, and Elisha is left to attempt to fill his immense shoes. Now he must put his prophetic call to the test.

So he sets out, doubtless with great fear in his heart, from the safety of the Jordan Valley for the northern kingdom where Ahab holds sway. His old master Elijah had been overwhelmed with discouragement when facing this same spiritual battle (1 Kings 19:3-5). Surely this young and more gentle man must likewise quake. His starting point is Bethel, the notorious center of false worship established by Jeroboam when he broke with Judah and erected a Canaanite bull statue for use in worship. For more than seventy years the Lord has been warning against this rebellion and idolatrous act and roundly condemning the worship taking place in Bethel. These warnings have been rejected with hostility. Elisha's approach to Bethel involves a three-thousand-foot ascent out of Rift Valley up to the mountain ridge. He must arrive weary in body and spirit.

Having heard of his approach, the hostile folk of Bethel prepare a hot reception for him. A mob of young ruffians turns out (doubtless with the encouragement and approval of their elders) to show the young prophet a thing or two. Life is cheap in these days, and quite possibly Elisha is in grave danger. But there is also a larger issue, the cause of the truth of God.

It is no exaggeration to call this incident a critical turning point in human history. Because Elisha was called to lead the school of the prophets, if he had been killed the cause of true faith would have been threatened with extinction. But even if Elisha's life was not at risk, his ministry and the proclamation of God's truth would have faced severe limitation if this crowd of young toughs had been able to intimidate him and run him out of town.

From this perspective, Elisha's prayer is fully understandable. Just as Jesus instructed the disciples to solemnly shake the dust from their feet when people refused the message of the kingdom, and himself added, "I tell you the truth, it will be more bearable for Sodom and Gomorrah on the day of judgment than for that town" (Mt 10:15), so Elisha calls on God to judge the mob of youths. He does not ask for the bears. But God answers and sends them to protect his spokesman and his truth.

As an epilogue to this story, I should note that never again was Elisha molested in his long years of itinerant ministry. News of this event must have traveled far and wide and served to give Elisha great liberty to proclaim God's word.

This is no story of an ill-tempered old prophet and his savage, capricious God. The justice and patience of the Lord are quite clear. The folk of Bethel had settled into a hard and vicious resistance to the truth, despite repeated warning. Now they even dared to exterminate the truth. But they left respect for Yahweh out of their schemes, and for that omission they paid. In this case, God clearly is slow to anger and just in his ways.

The Process and Climax of Wrath

We do well to be alert to the way the wrath of God works. God's wrath is expressed in God's handing us over to the consequences of our rebellion and sin. He abandons us as he did the hard, violent idolaters of Bethel, ratifying our rebellious choices and leaving us with their unforeseen consequences. Romans 1 makes this quite clear. Having declared that "the wrath of God is being revealed from heaven against all the godlessness and wickedness of men who suppress the truth" (v. 18), Paul traces out the working of divine wrath in the threefold repetition of the phrase "God gave them over . . ." (vv. 24, 26, 28). There is a downward spiral in these verses. People sink deeper and deeper as God withdraws his goodness and protection and lets sin bear its own destructive fruit.

The wrath of God is a process visible in the world around us, a process within history, which reaches a climax in God's final judgment. In Romans 1 Paul notes the marks of divine wrath on his own culture, and if we but open our eyes we can see them all around us in the greed, lust, violence, rootlessness and meaninglessness of our culture. But Paul also speaks of a climax to this process, a "day of wrath": "But because of your stubbornness and your unrepentant heart, you are storing up wrath against yourself for the day of God's wrath, when his righteous judgment will be revealed. . . . For those who are self-seeking and who reject the truth and follow evil, there will be wrath and anger" (Rom 2:5, 8).

From this perspective we can understand the Lord Jesus' teaching about hell. Hell is the ultimate state under God's wrath of those who persist in rejecting God and his truth. Jesus described it as losing one's life or as forfeiting one's soul (Mk 8:35-36). The metaphors he used are even more horrible: "fire" for the agonizing awareness of God's displeasure, "outer darkness" for the consciousness of the loss of God and therefore of all good, "gnashing of teeth" for intense condemnation and self-loathing, "wailing" for a deep, abiding sense of abandonment. Jesus showed great restraint in the use of this imagery compared to his Jewish contemporaries. But the reality he points out by these phrases is unimaginably dreadful.

It is helpful to realize that this fate is not at all what God intends or desires for us. "Do I take any pleasure in the death of the wicked? declares the Sovereign LORD. Rather, am I not pleased when they turn from their ways and live?" (Ezek 18:23). "God our Savior . . . wants all men to be saved and to come to a knowledge of the truth" (1 Tim 2:3-4). Hell is not designed for human beings but for "the devil and his angels" (Mt 25:41). It is not so much a place as a nothing realm, a kind of terrible negative, a state of God-forsakenness. And when we are truly and fully shut off from God, all good disappears.

Hell is God's underlining affirmation of the relationship toward himself that we have chosen in this life. It is not inflicted on us arbitrarily by a hateful and savage God; it is a state into which we grow as the sum of our selfish and God-denying choices. It is an awful reality, the destiny of those who turn a deaf ear to God's plea to trust in his mercy. Hell brings no joy to God or to his people. Certainly it brings us no comfort; it is the ultimate trauma we confront in facing the Holy One. If honesty allowed us, we would eliminate it from our beliefs. But it does not. If we are to approach the true and living God and not some safe projection of our imagination, we must confront this shattering truth.

But in the end, we must also rejoice that evil will not exercise a continuing veto on good. Our holy Lord is set personally, vigorously and triumphantly against all that distorts and destroys his beloved creatures, and against all those who give themselves to evil. The words of praise in Revelation 16:5-7 ring true:

You are just in these judgments,

you who are and who were, the Holy One,

because you have so judged;

for they have shed the blood of your saints and prophets,

and you have given them blood to drink as they deserve. . . .

Yes, Lord God Almighty,

true and just are your judgments.

The Lord of Hosts

God's holy hostility to evil and sin is also at the root of the Bible's picture of the Lord as a warrior. In Moses' song of triumph the victorious Lord of the exodus is praised:

The LORD is my strength and my song;

he has become my salvation.

He is my God, and I will praise him,

my father's God, and I will exalt him.

The LORD is a warrior;

the LORD is his name.

Pharaoh's chariots and army

he has hurled into the sea. (Ex 15:2-4)

Isaiah, in responding to the redeeming work of the Servant of the Lord, says:

The LORD will march out like a mighty man,

like a warrior he will stir up his zeal;
with a shout he will raise the battle cry
and will triumph over his enemies. (Is 42:13)

Frequently in the Old Testament God is called "the LORD of hosts." He is the
God of armies, either the armies of Israel or, more typically, the armies of
heaven. He leads the angelic host to do battle against his enemies and to
protect his own people. Several psalms speak from this same perspective,
though they do not call the Lord a warrior. Consider Psalm 68:1-3 (RSV).

Let God arise, let his enemies be scattered;
let those who hate him flee before him!
As smoke is driven away, so drive them away;
as wax melts before fire,
let the wicked perish before God!
But let the righteous be joyful;
let them exult before God;
let them be jubilant with joy!

Jesus himself was conscious of participating in a great spiritual battle in his
ministry. He spoke of binding "the strong man" in order to rob his house in
the context of his ministry of casting out demons and his conflict with the
leaders of the decadent Jerusalem establishment (Mk 3:22-27). In the visions
of the last judgment in Revelation, Jesus is described in the following terms:

I saw heaven standing open and there before me was a white horse, whose
rider is called Faithful and True. With justice he judges and makes war. His
eyes are like blazing fire, and on his head are many crowns. He has a name
written on him that no one knows but he himself. He is dressed in a robe
dipped in blood, and his name is the Word of God. The armies of heaven
were following him, riding on white horses and dressed in fine linen,
white and clean. Out of his mouth comes a sharp sword with which to
strike down the nations. "He will rule them with an iron scepter." He treads
the winepress of the fury of the wrath of God Almighty. (Rev 19:11-15)

If these statements about the Lord are taken at all seriously, they are anything
but comforting. Perhaps that is why we steer clear of them. They are another
aspect of the trauma that grips us when we actually face the Holy One.

The enemies of God in these passages fall into two classes. They include
(1) human beings and whole cultures that have so set themselves against God
that they cannot repent and (2) the invisible spiritual forces and beings set
completely in resistance to the Lord. The classic example of this unholy
alliance was the Egyptian Pharaoh, himself a demigod, and his court magicians and wise men, who trafficked in the supernatural. The same configu-

ration of opponents confronted Israel as it entered Canaan. Powerful walled cities and mighty armies were the military foes, but these armies were in the service of a degraded, occult religion. In Jesus' day, he was met with a tremendous upsurge of demonic activity and by a cultural and religious establishment that soon came to thoroughly hate him. In this case, the enemy resisted the Son of God. And in Revelation the focus is the same. Outwardly, the great whore Babylon, the fallen world commercial and political order, persecutes and hounds the people of God. But behind the scenes is the dragon, Satan himself, and all his allies.

The strength and pervasiveness of these twin enemies make us conscious that creation is engulfed in a huge cosmic struggle. Powerful visible and invisible agents are engaged in an unjust and destructive revolt against their Creator. Their rage against him is as implacable as it is destructive. God's enemies are the destroyers of the earth. Great damage has been done and is being done to the creation.

Under these circumstances, neutrality is impossible. God must act if there is to be any hope. And we must not hesitate or waver in our commitment to him and his battle. If we do not or cannot pray for God to arise to vindicate himself, to destroy "those who destroy the earth" (Rev 11:18), we show ourselves to be ignorant of what is going on in the world around us or, worse, to be a part of the enemy forces. Indeed, what makes this biblical picture of God as a warrior against sin and evil so devastating to us is that we know the enemy is not just around us. "We have met the enemy, and he is us."

In the light shed by these hard but important truths of the wrath and warfare of the Lord, let's turn to consider three difficulties that often arise for modern Bible readers. We are frequently at a loss to understand the passages in Scripture that curse God's enemies, particularly in Psalms. The Lord's command to Israel to exterminate the Canaanites is also offensive to us. And many are troubled with the fear that biblical teaching about the severity of God will be used as a mandate for repressive social and political measures in our day, as it has been used in the past.

The Imprecatory Psalms

Consider first the cursing or "imprecatory" psalms. These poems express a desire for God to act against the enemies of his people in ways that are very graphic and sometimes gruesome. A typical example of this sort of prayer is Psalm 58:

Do you rulers indeed speak justly?

Do you judge uprightly among men?
No, in your heart you devise injustice,
and your hands mete out violence on the earth.
Even from birth the wicked go astray;
from the womb they are wayward and speak lies.
Their venom is like the venom of a snake,
like that of a cobra that has stopped its ears,
that will not heed the tune of the charmer,
however skillful the enchanter may be.

Break the teeth in their mouths, O God;
tear out, O LORD, the fangs of the lions!
Let them vanish like water that flows away;
when they draw the bow, let their arrows be blunted.
Like a slug melting away as it moves along,
like a stillborn child, may they not see the sun.

Before your pots can feel the heat of the thorns—
whether they be green or dry—the wicked will be swept away.
The righteous will be glad when they are avenged,
when they bathe their feet in the blood of the wicked.
Then men will say,
"Surely the righteous still are rewarded;
surely there is a God who judges the earth."

Some have simply declared these psalms valueless for Christian use, seeing them as an outpouring of vindictiveness and self-righteousness. Others see them as being transcended in the progress of revelation by the purer New Testament ethic of love for enemies. But a more careful investigation of their Old Testament ethical context, of parallels in the New Testament and of the consistent biblical teaching about God's holiness and justice leads to a different conclusion.

We are helped to appreciate these psalms when we realize that Old Testament ethical teaching does not encourage vindictiveness toward personal enemies. As examples of proper conduct toward enemies, the following commandments and proverbs are worth pondering:

If you come across your enemy's ox or donkey wandering off, be sure to take it back to him. If you see the donkey of someone who hates you fallen

down under its load, do not leave it there; be sure you help him with it.
(Ex 23:4-5)

Do not hate your brother in your heart. Rebuke your neighbor frankly
so you will not share in his guilt. Do not seek revenge or bear a grudge
against one of your people, but love your neighbor as yourself. I am the
LORD. (Lev 19:17-18)

Do not gloat when your enemy falls;
  when he stumbles, do not let your heart rejoice,
or the LORD will see and disapprove
  and turn his wrath away from him. (Prov 24:17-18)

If your enemy is hungry, give him food to eat;
  if he is thirsty, give him water to drink.
In doing this, you will heap burning coals on his head,
  and the LORD will reward you. (Prov 25:21-22)

If these statements set the standard for the ordinary attitude toward enemies,
what should we make of the cursing of enemies in Psalms? The solution to
this dilemma seems to lie in the particular identity of the enemies brought
under these curses. These enemies are not primarily the personal opponents
of the psalmist. They are the enemies of Israel and of Israel's king. Those who
seek to subvert and destroy Israel, however, are first and foremost setting
themselves against God and seeking to overturn the Lord's work of salvation
for the whole world. The enemies cursed are those who openly declare
themselves to be the enemies of God. This is clearly expressed in Psalm
139:19-22:
  If only you would slay the wicked, O God!
    Away from me, you bloodthirsty men!
  They speak of you with evil intent;
    your adversaries misuse your name.
  Do I not hate those who hate you, O LORD,
    and abhor those who rise up against you?
  I have nothing but hatred for them;
    I count them my enemies.
Indeed, in Psalm 58 the enemies are "you gods" (v. 1 RSV). Perhaps this
phrase should be translated "you rulers" (NIV), designating the powerful
human leaders of nations that schemed against Israel and its king. But more

likely the reference is to the demonic deities of surrounding cultures, "the principalities, . . . the powers, . . . the world rulers of this present darkness, . . . the spiritual hosts of wickedness in the heavenly places" (Eph 6:12 RSV). Here are the ultimate enemies of God.

The cursing psalms contain some vividly gory turns of phrase. Think of bathing your feet "in the blood of the wicked" (Ps 58:10). Perhaps the most appalling statement is found in Psalm 137:8-9, where the psalmist prays,

O Daughter of Babylon, doomed to destruction,
   happy is he who repays you
   for what you have done to us—
he who seizes your infants
   and dashes them against the rocks.

Again, what are we to make of this bloodthirsty rhetoric? Certainly it is horrible. But again, the Old Testament, while it treats evil with severity, does not normally advocate or encourage violence. Indeed, it condemns wanton violence in the strongest terms. For example Psalm 58 condemns the demonic gods as those whose "hands mete out violence on the earth" (v. 2).[3] But the Old Testament does not shrink from the realization that full justice demands retribution, a punishment that precisely fits the crime. In Psalm 137 the cry is primarily for this justice: "Happy is he who *repays* you for what you have done to us." The arrogant Babylonian oppressor mocks Zion and its God, having torn down Jerusalem's walls and slaughtered its children. Dashing infants against the rocks is a precise fulfillment of justice against the infant-bashing Babylonians.

Further, the Old Testament does not couch its statements about temporal judgment in bloodless abstractions. There is a concrete realism in its thought and language. Prayer for the victory of God's people and the vindication of God's truth working through the instrumentality of a nation-state, or among nations as he does in the normal course of providence, means battles and sieges and pain and death. So without the destruction there is no justice for either the proud, stubborn enemies of God or their powerless victims.

Turning to the New Testament, we discover some changes in perspective and emphasis. The people of the kingdom of God are no longer a particular nation-state but an international, intercultural community. So human enemies are brought near to God, and God's enemies are more difficult to identify. The messianic King comes to bring a kingdom that does not use the techniques, oppression and violence of the kingdoms of this world. Jesus ushers in the kingdom by a life of gentle, gracious service and, supremely, by a horrible death in the place of his enemies. So love for neighbor and enemy takes on a greater depth and poignancy.

But these changes do not eliminate zeal for or rejoicing in God's work of judgment. New Testament saints in heaven rejoice in God's judgment on his and their enemies in Revelation, as I have already noted. Teaching about prayer, Jesus speaks of God's speedy vindication of his people "who cry out to him day and night" (Lk 18:7). And with a brutal realism reminiscent of Psalm 137 and its dashing of children's heads, Jesus predicts the downfall of unrepentant Jerusalem:

> As he approached Jerusalem and saw the city, he wept over it and said, "If you, even you, had only known on this day what would bring you peace— but now it is hidden from your eyes. The days will come upon you when your enemies will build an embankment against you and encircle you and hem you in on every side. They will dash you to the ground, you and the children within your walls. They will not leave one stone on another, because you did not recognize the time of God's coming to you. (Lk 19:41-44)

Indeed, some of our own prayers are inevitably involved in the carrying out of this awful reality. J. A. Motyer writes:

> Do we stop to consider what we are asking when we pray for the Return of the Lord Jesus? Probably we do not couch our prayer in the following terms: In flaming fire take vengeance on those who know not God and obey not the gospel; give them their due punishment, even eternal destruction from Thy face. But, according to 2 Thessalonians 1:8, these things are inseparable from the coming, and therefore by implication, if not explicitly, we are asking for them.
>
> Or again, do we pray for the deliverance of God's persecuted children in China or elsewhere? How do we imagine that the Lord of history will in the long run rescue them? Will it not be either by the Return, or by some other act of justice and vengeance?
>
> It seems to be exactly the element of realism, which is absent from our prayers, and which gives us such offence in the prayers of the psalms. We are prepared for the prayer (143:11): "In thy righteousness bring my soul out of trouble." We are upset by the biblical realism of 142:12: "And in thy lovingkindness cut off my enemies, and destroy all them that afflict me."[4]

This basic consistency between the New Testament and the cursing psalms arises because the psalms are based on three abiding truths about the Holy One and our relationship to him.

1. The cursing psalms express a passionate longing for God to vindicate his own name. Enemies have arisen, mere creatures who seek to obscure the glory of their Creator. This is plainly intolerable. The Lord must triumph and be all in all. So the psalms give voice to a deep and holy zeal for the glory of God and express a desire for that glory to be seen by all people.

2. *The cursing psalms express a hunger for justice.* The Lord is not some high-level bureaucrat who never dirties his hands. He is the active defender of the weak and poor. Powerful forces have arisen which seek to overthrow truth and violently oppress the weak and poor. But the Holy One is just; he must act justly by bringing speedy judgment on powerful evildoers. To pray for him to act in this just way shows a clear-sighted understanding of both the needs of our society and the character of God.

3. *The cursing psalms express a godly anger.* The Holy One himself is angry in a righteous way, as we have seen. But is righteous anger appropriate in sinners? In Ephesians 4:26 Paul does not forbid Christians to be angry. He calls for an even harder thing: sinless anger. This is an emotion that we only rarely feel. Perhaps we come closest to it when we consider the horror of the Holocaust or the grisly enormities of the slave trade. These massively destructive injustices make our blood boil. Or at least they ought to. But because we so rarely feel a truly righteous indignation, we fail to understand it when we meet it in the psalms.

The Genocidal Commands
A similar set of problems arise for us when we consider the Lord's command to Israel to utterly destroy the Canaanite peoples upon their entrance to the Promised Land (Ex 23:23-24; Deut 7:1-5; 20:16-18).

> When the LORD your God brings you into the land you are entering to possess and drives out before you many nations—the Hittites, Girgashites, Amorites, Canaanites, Perizzites, Hivites and Jebusites, seven nations larger and stronger than you—and when the LORD your God has delivered them over to you and you have defeated them, then you must destroy them totally. Make no treaty with them, and show them no mercy. Do not intermarry with them. Do not give your daughters to their sons or take their daughters for your sons, for they will turn your sons away from following me to serve other gods, and the LORD's anger will burn against you and will quickly destroy you. This is what you are to do to them: Break down their altars, smash their sacred stones, cut down their Asherah poles and burn their idols in the fire. (Deut 7:1-5)

Many people find this highly offensive. Even for some who profess to hold to the truth and authority of Scripture, this is just too much. So they speak of "innocent Canaanites," allow that this command is simply a man-made error that intruded its way into the Bible, and breathe a sigh of relief because the New Testament corrects this ethical monstrosity in its command to love enemies.

But we need not follow this destructive escape route. Again, if we consider the whole situation and the ways of the Holy One, we can make some sense, at least, of these commands.

Canaanite civilization was overripe for judgment. The wickedness of the Canaanites was extreme. Particularly their religion, which provided the foundation for their whole way of life, was degraded and degrading. G. E. Wright evaluates it as follows:

> The amazing thing about the gods, as they were conceived in Canaan, is that they had no moral character whatsoever. In fact their conduct was on a much lower level than that of society as a whole, if we can judge from the ancient codes of law. Certainly the brutality of the mythology is far worse than anything else in the Near East at that time. Worship of these gods carried with it some of the most demoralizing practices then in existence. Among them were child sacrifice, a practice long since discarded in Egypt and Babylonia, sacred prostitution, and snake worship on a scale unknown among other people.[5]

This extreme wickedness God had borne patiently over nearly five centuries (see Gen 15:16). Simple justice required that he visit the Canaanites with judgment. As Moses said to Israel on the plains of Moab, "It is not because of your righteousness or your integrity that you are going in to take possession of their land, but on account of the wickedness of these nations, the LORD your God will drive them out before you, to accomplish what he swore to your fathers, to Abraham, Isaac and Jacob" (Deut 9:5).

Mention of the debased quality of Canaanite religion is of central importance because the basic concern in God's command to Israel was the removal of the influence of false religion. Involved here was both the weakness of Israel (the Old Testament contains a very unflattering account of Israel's persistent unfaithfulness) and the seductiveness of the dominant surrounding culture. Intermarriage was to be impossible because it would lead Israel to serve false gods. Every trace of the Canaanite culture was to be obliterated lest it work its way in like a cancer and waste and destroy the knowledge of the Lord in Israel.

A great battle had begun. And we must be reminded of the enormous consequences of this battle. At risk was nothing less than the bringing of God's saving truth to a lost world. If Israel had been swallowed by a tidal wave of paganism, we would all (humanly speaking) be lost in our sins, without hope and without God.

It is crucial to stress that these commands did not proceed from a narrow ethnic or national prejudice. Individual Canaanites were included among God's people. Think of the mixed multitude that left Egypt (Ex 12:38; Num 11:4), of Rahab (Josh 2:4-6), Hobab (Num 10:29-33) and Ruth. Further, the law made generous and humane provision for the sojourner among God's people (Ex 20:10; 23:9; Lev 24:16, 22; 19:34; Deut 10:18-19). The laws covering warfare distinguished ordinary war, in which the destructiveness of Israel's armies was clearly restrained, from the invasion and occupation of Canaan, where destruction was to be total. The commands to destroy Canaanite culture were clearly not ordinary military practice. They covered a special, limited situation, not to be repeated (see Deut 2:5, 9, 19; 7:26; 20:10-11). Canaanite culture, based as it was on Canaanite religion, had to be judged and obliterated utterly in the name of God's justice and for the sake of God's revealed truth. There could be no peaceful coexistence, no synthesis, no accommodation.

To complete the picture, observe that the same divine severity expressed toward the Canaanites was promised to Israel and ultimately became Israel's experience. The Lord's covenant with his people contained not only a promise of blessing but also the threat of judgment if they were unfaithful (Lev 26; Deut 28—29). Within the covenant community the most severe penalties were reserved for unfaithfulness to God's covenant, unfaithfulness that aped the practices of the Canaanites (see Lev 24:10-13; Num 15:36; Deut 13; Judg 2:13-15). Even in his gracious work of redemption the Lord is the Holy One, just in all his ways, sovereignly bringing his truth and grace to his fallen creatures. To be a part of his people entails acceptance of greater responsibility.

The Social Implications of God's Severity

A further potential problem should be considered. Could not this teaching about the severity of God's dealings with evil be used today to justify harsh government practices and ruthlessness in warmaking? Sadly, it *has* all too often been used this way. But such an approach is a misuse.

Within the Old Testament itself, military and judicial severity is clearly limited, and love for neighbor and mercy toward the weak are commanded. The Old Testament also bears witness to Israel's failure to live up to these lofty standards, of course. But characteristically this failure was a byproduct of the rejection of the Holy One and the adoption of the ways of pagan cultures.

This ameliorating influence comes to full flower in the New Testament. Consider, for example, Romans 12:14-21:

Bless those who persecute you; bless and do not curse. Rejoice with those who rejoice; mourn with those who mourn. Live in harmony with one another. Do not be proud, but be willing to associate with people of low position. Do not be conceited.

Do not repay anyone evil for evil. Be careful to do what is right in the eyes of everybody. . . . Do not take revenge, my friends, but leave room for God's wrath, for it is written: "It is mine to avenge; I will repay," says the LORD. On the contrary:

"If your enemy is hungry, feed him;

if he is thirsty, give him something to drink.

In doing this, you will heap burning coals on his head."

Do not be overcome by evil, but overcome evil with good.

No clearer prohibition of human severity can be found in our supposedly more enlightened day. But notice the rationale for forgiveness and gentleness here. We love our enemies not because God has abdicated his role as judge, nor because the Old Testament is irrelevant. In fact, Paul quotes Proverbs 25:21-22 to guide us into costly service of enemies *because* the final righting of wrongs lies with the Lord and not with us.

When we appoint ourselves the agents of God's wrath, disaster is inevitable. But when we actively embrace the reality, certainty and finality of God's judgment, we are freed from protecting our own rights, freed for kindness and service to all people.

The Heart of Our Struggle

Considering these particular difficulties may be helpful, but it does not take us to the heart of our dilemma. For all this talk of divine judgment, wrath and "holy war" rings strangely in the ears of those who have been nurtured in an age of sentimental, unbiblical Christianity. We do not at all care for teaching so uncompromising and so painful. Gentle and kindly persuasion is all right. But to think that God is angry against our evil deeds, that God punishes sinners, that God works out his purposes through pain, that God wills the destruction of sinners—no!

But this is exactly where we must think clearly and make up our minds. To whom do we owe our first allegiance? If to God, then we must move beyond comforting half-truths to see and love the Holy One as he is. Do we believe that God rules the world? If so, we must accept the fact that pain, destruction and judgment are part of his infinitely wise and loving order. Do we believe the teaching of Jesus? If we do, we must observe that he taught that punishment, pain and destruction are a part of his Father's wise and loving work. It is sheer hypocrisy to limp along in two minds. When by the grace of God we have made up our minds, it is our wisdom and duty (and it should become our joy) to embrace these truths with every particle of our being.

Once we embrace the truths of God's awesome holiness, his wrath against sin and his unflagging opposition to evil, we are confronted with the trauma of facing the living God. For we are sinners left naked before his unblemished purity. No longer can we seek refuge in comforting illusions. Accounts of God's severe judgments against sin can no longer be viewed as products of human error and therefore uncharacteristic of the Lord. These judgments are eruptions into time of eternity's verdict of sin.

What does the Holy One think of our idolatrous, lustful, violent, greedy society? To answer, do not look at his long-suffering treatment of the modern West, but to the fate of Sodom and Gomorrah, the city-states of Canaan, and Jerusalem. Fear for your neighbor, but fear even more for your own complicity in the godlessness of our time.

Or again, what does the Lord think of hypocrisy? Do not look at his long-suffering treatment of us, but at the fate of Ananias and Sapphira (Acts 5). Fear for every time you sought dishonestly to look better than you actually were.

The most urgent question of our lives thus arises: "How can I, a sinner, live before the Holy One?"

PART II

LIFE BEFORE
THE HOLY ONE

8

THE DEVASTATION
OF SIN

ONE OF THE BANES OF MUCH THEOLOGICAL WRITING AND TEACHING IS THAT IT
is so often divorced from real, everyday life. *Theology* suggests to many an
idle, speculative theory. Theology might be of interest to a certain odd sort
of believer, but most can do without its detached, irrelevant mind trips.

Nothing could be further from the way Scripture actually presents its great
teachings about the Holy One. Insistently it presses on us not just a true and
divinely revealed account of God's person, but also an invitation and instruction in how to turn the truth into life.

Given the towering majesty, sovereignty and goodness of the Holy One, we
must investigate the claims his central reality makes on our lives. How can
we sinners live before the consuming blaze of his holiness? What qualities
and practices of living flow from a right relationship to his holiness? What
does life before the Holy One look like?

God's Covenant Initiative

The four aspects of life before the Holy One we will consider in this book
have not been chosen arbitrarily. They flow from the Bible's description of
the people of God. Consider what the Lord says to Moses as he inaugurates

the Sinai covenant (Ex 19:4-6):

"You yourselves have seen what I did to Egypt, and how I carried you on eagles' wings and brought you to myself. Now if you obey me fully and keep my covenant, then out of all nations you will be my treasured possession. Although the whole earth is mine, you will be for me a kingdom of priests and a holy nation." These are the words you are to speak to the Israelites.

The emphasis here is God's initiative and God's intention. The covenant is based on God's gracious deliverance of his people from slavery. The Sinai covenant presupposes and is an expression of God's grace. And that deliverance from slavery was to result in a personal relationship with the Deliverer. "I brought you to myself," says the Holy One.

These redemptive and covenantal realities are reemphasized when Peter describes the New Testament people of God in a way that echoes and quotes Exodus 19:

But you are a chosen people, a royal priesthood, a holy nation, a people belonging to God, that you may declare the praises of him who called you out of darkness into his wonderful light. Once you were not a people, but now you are the people of God; once you had not received mercy, but now you have received mercy. (1 Pet 2:9-10)

In these marvelous descriptions of the people of God we can clearly see four aspects of life before the Holy One:

☐ God's people are to be a priestly people. So sacrifice must be considered as a central aspect of our fellowship with the Lord.

☐ God's people are to be holy people. So we must consider the fear of God and the life of obedience to God as a second central element.

☐ God's people are to be God's own treasure or possession. So we must reckon with the glory of God, his personal majestic presence among and ownership of his people.

☐ God's people are brought to him so that they might declare his praises. So we must seek to understand the sort of worship that does maximum justice to who he is and therefore pleases him.

The Sin Barrier

Before we consider these topics, however, we need to understand clearly the sort of barrier that keeps us from living freely and joyfully before the Holy One. Our creatureliness, our finitude and smallness, is not our basic problem. We humans are made in God's image—that is, with a likeness to and natural kinship with our Maker. We do not possess thoroughgoing knowledge of

God, but that ignorance no more keeps us from relationship with the Holy One than a child's ignorance of the adult world keeps her from relationship with her parents. The barrier lies elsewhere: not in our created human constitution but in the grave distortion of our true humanity introduced by sin.

The Old Testament uses three dominant words for "sin." They appear together in Leviticus 16:21 (RSV), the description of the high priest's confession on the Day of Atonement: "Aaron shall lay both his hands upon the head of the live goat, and confess over him all the iniquities of the people of Israel, and all their transgressions, all their sins." (These three terms appear together thirteen other times; Ex 34:7; Num 14:18; Ps 32:1, 5; Is 59:12; Ezek 21:29). While the three words are synonyms, each also has a distinctive meaning. When we take these meanings together, we can begin to catch something of the character, calamity and destructiveness of sin.

Iniquity (*'āwôn*) in its nontheological usage refers to crookedness. At root, iniquity is deviation from the straight way, from the norm. The word is applied to personal relationships. It refers to deceit and perversity, the opposite of honesty and straightforwardness. It is sometimes translated "guilt" and used to designate that which cries out for severe reprisal. *Iniquity* reminds us of the twisted, deceitful ugliness of evil, the distortion of good that results from sin.

The second term, *transgression* (*peša'*), refers to rebellion and a breakdown in trust. In the political sphere, it refers to armed insurrection. When applied to the moral and spiritual sphere, *transgression* indicates a rejection and violation of God's authority and commands. *Transgression* has an interpersonal dimension as well. Exodus 22:9 (RSV) speaks of "every breach of trust *[peša']*, whether it is for ox, for ass . . ." referring to the failure of a steward to deal honestly and faithfully with his master or employer. So transgressions not only overturn God's commands but also constitute a breach of trust with God's person. They seek to violate the Lord himself.

The third word, *sin* (*ḥēṭ'*), means "missing the mark" and, more broadly, "failure." The term is used in reference to military target practice; for example, Judges 20:16 describes the seven hundred stone-hurling warriors of Israel as being able to aim at a hair and not "miss" (*ḥᵃṭi'*). Its application to moral life is straightforward; "It is not good . . . to be hasty and miss the way" (Prov 19:2). This is the most frequently used word for wrongdoing.

Sin, like our other two words, refers to a failure to keep the law of God. But it also refers—more deeply still—to a failure of person-to-person relationship (see 1 Sam 2:23; 1 Kings 8:46; Jer 16:10-12). Moses says to two of the tribes that have conquered land on the east side of the Jordan and have promised to join the other ten tribes in the conquest of Canaan, "But if you fail to do this, you will be sinning against the LORD; and you may be sure that your sin will find you out" (Num 32:23). David cries, "Against you, you only, have I sinned and done what is evil in your sight" (Ps 51:4). In both cases the moral failure involved other people *and* disobedience of God's law. But the ultimate failure was directed toward the Lord himself.

The Characteristics of Sin

Now, when we take these three terms for sin together and consider them in the overall light of biblical instruction about sin, five basic principles stand out clearly.

First, and most basically, *sin is ultimately against God himself.* The act of sin flies in God's face and rejects God himself. Sin flees from his holy presence. Normally we focus on the destructive effects of sin on individuals and the wider community. But this focus can obscure the most basic character and effect of sin, its Godward dimension.

Scripture does not promote this confusion. David can cry to the Lord, "I know my transgressions, and my sin is always before me. Against you, you only, have I sinned and done what is evil in your sight" (Ps 51:3-4). Paul the apostle defines the root of sin in the following terms: "Although they knew God, they neither glorified him as God nor gave thanks to him" (Rom 1:21).

This is not to deny the disastrous and malicious effect of sin on God's creatures. David's sin, for example, violated both the law of God and other human beings. But the stress must lie on the fact that it is *God's* law and *God's* creatures that are violated. Sin in its most basic character flies in the face of the Holy One, rejects him, rebels against him, flees from him.

Second, *the liability sin produces is that it brings us under the wrath of God—under God's holy, settled hostility.* Sin's liability is consistent with sin's basic character as the rejection of God himself. As the three key words for sin stress, sin is a violation and destruction of our relationship to the Holy One.

We move in the orbit, most fundamentally, of personal relationships. To reduce this liability to basically impersonal categories suggests that somehow God relates to us on less than interpersonal terms. Scripture does use some more impersonal metaphors in assessing our liability as sinners. We are debtors, or criminals before God's justice, or slaves needing liberation. But behind all these pictures is the Holy One himself. The debt we owe is not to some impersonal corporation but to our gloriously benevolent Maker, whose personal generosity we have maliciously, selfishly and destructively exploited. The law and justice we have violated are not just an external legal code. The law is a description of the way of life that pleases the Holy One. It expresses his moral character. When we break it, we violate not just a code but the person of the Lord. In our sin we reject, violate and trample underfoot the Holy One.

Our slavery is self-imposed, the slavery of the treasonous criminal. We have ensnared ourselves in webs of deceit and rebellion of our own making. The cost to be paid for our liberation is not mere money, not even a king's ransom. By rebelling against the good pleasure of our Maker and Owner, we have forfeited our very life. To fly in the face of the Holy One is to become his enemy and thus to fall justly under his mighty disapproval and anger.

Third, *sin is universal among human beings.* The breadth of this universality encompasses us all: "All have sinned and fall short of the glory of God" (Rom 3:23). And its depth is powerfully and clearly expressed in Genesis 6:5-6: "The LORD saw how great man's wickedness on the earth had become, and that every inclination of the thoughts of his heart was only evil all the time. The LORD was grieved that he had made man on the earth, and his heart was filled with pain." We must be clear about what this saying does and does not mean. It does not mean that sinful human beings and the projection of their imaginations in culture are as bad as they possibly could be. Even after the Fall, human beings retain the vestiges of the image of God in which they were created (see, for example, Gen 9:6). That image is horribly defaced and sometimes nearly indiscernible. But its reality means that even fallen human conscience reflects the law of God and serves to restrain the extremes of sin (see Rom 2:14-15). God limits the effects of sin by a variety of created structures, such as the family and government. By the goodness that sends rain on both the just and the unjust, the Holy One restrains the worst and most disastrous reaches of evil.

While the utter evilness of evil is restrained, it is also true that evil touches and maims each and every aspect of human life. Every imagination of the heart of humankind is only evil always. Evil touches the heart, the center and core of our humanity. When the source of a stream is polluted, the whole stream is polluted. Parts of the stream will be unevenly affected, depending on currents and how quickly and thoroughly the toxin is carried, but every part will be spoiled in some measure. So it is with the life of every human being. This is the point Jesus pressed home to the Pharisees when he insisted,

Don't you see that nothing that enters a man from the outside can make him "unclean"? For it doesn't go into his heart but into his stomach, and then out of his body. . . . What comes out of a man is what makes him "unclean." For from within, out of men's hearts, come evil thoughts, sexual immorality, theft, murder, adultery, greed, malice, deceit, lewdness, envy, slander, arrogance and folly. All these evils come from inside and make a man "unclean." (Mk 7:18, 20-23)

Evil specifically corrupts our thought processes. Our thinking is not preserved from the destructive effects of sin. Rather, we fall prey to rationalization, self-justification and the passing fads of culture. Freudian psychology has taught us how our apparently objective arguments are so often controlled by sub-conscious—and often very base—needs and desires. Marxists remind us that our apparently objective views and values are often rationalizations designed to ensure our comfortable position in society. Both the Freudian and the Marxist accounts of life are fundamentally flawed, but at this point they have something to teach us. These modern masters of suspicion alert us to ways in which our thoughts are distorted by our own needs and prejudices and the dictates of our social environment.

Fourth, this depth perspective on the universality of sin leads us to the conclusion that *sin makes women and men unable to please God.* Too often we view sin in a superficial way, as a surface-level blemish that can easily be washed away to reveal a basically good person beneath it all. All we need is a sort of spiritual and moral shower or bath. So we flatter ourselves. But sin corrupts not just in a cosmetic, external way. It reaches to the very core of our being. Indeed, Scripture tells us that we commit particular sins because we *are sinners,* because our basic human constitution has been corrupted. Evil deeds and thoughts arise not from the impact of external influences and conditioning but from our fallen hearts (again, see Mk 7:14-23). Sinners do not and cannot do good toward God, for they are in bondage "under sin" (Rom 3:9-18; 7:7-25). In terms of Jesus' powerful metaphor, the evil tree (the person fallen into sin) must be made good before its fruit can be good (Mt 12:33-35).

Again, it is important to recognize exactly what we mean when we speak about human inability. I am not claiming that fallen men and women never act in formal external conformity to the directives of God's law. Nor am I claiming that fallen humanity is as bad as it possibly could be. By God's continuing created and creative goodness, evil is restrained and fallen men and women often treat one another in conformity with the law of God that has been written on their hearts (Rom 2:14-15).

Rather, our moral and spiritual inability shows itself in two ways. We are not free to be consistently good. By the standard of God's justice, many of our actions must be accounted failures. Occasionally we summon the humility to drop our normal rationalizing and admit that this is so. Characteristically we seek a new beginning. We want to eradicate our weaknesses and failures. We make resolutions and turn over a new leaf. But what becomes of this? Very little, if anything. If you haven't tried this experiment in self-help, try it. You will prove the continuing downward drag of fallen human nature. Sin is a power that overwhelms all our good intentions. All our "new leaves" and New Year's resolutions quickly are aborted. Sin enslaves and destroys. When Jesus says, "Everyone who sins is a slave to sin" (Jn 8:34), those with an even minimally sensitive conscience know him to be speaking the truth.

But consider even our "good" deeds, those actions that are in formal conformity with God's law. Are these good works truly good? Good works are measured from three standpoints. They must be done in accordance with a right standard, in accordance with God's law (2 Tim 3:16-17), from a right motive, from love and gratitude to our fellow creatures and, supremely, to our Creator (1 Thess 1:3; Heb 6:10), and with a right aim, with a view to the glory of God (Mt 5:16; 1 Cor 6:20; 10:31; 1 Pet 2:12). At root, "goodness" in us— in those who are creatures wholly dependent on our Holy Creator—must be God-centered in a thoroughgoing way. But when we reflect on our "good deeds," their formal compliance with God's law is consistently vitiated by a self-serving, self-glorifying bias. Again, we know that God is perfectly right and just when he says of us, "All of us have become like one who is unclean, and all our righteous acts are like filthy rags" (Is 64:6).

Fifth, I conclude this grim portrait of sin by observing that *sin produces abnormality.* Sin has radically destructive consequences for all of God's good creation. At the Fall of humankind God pronounced a solemn curse on the creation. This curse aimed to both judge and restrain the evil that had entered the good creation. It extended not just to Adam and Eve and their children but also to the animal world (Gen 3:14) and even to the ground itself (3:17). The whole created ecosystem is distorted because of Adam's rebellion. It is subject to a frustrating abnormality that will remain until God's work of rescue through "the seed of the woman" is completed (Gen 3:15; Rom 8:22; see also Eccles 1—2 with its catchphrase, "vanity of vanities"—KJV).

Clean and Unclean

Awareness of the fallen abnormality of God's creation helps us to better grasp what Leviticus means when it speaks about "holiness," "cleanness" and "uncleanness." Much of Leviticus is taken up with clarifying the physical perfection that was required of the things and people associated with the tabernacle and the worship of God. Sacrificial animals had to be unblemished; lepers had to be separated and ritually cleansed once cured; women had to be purified after childbirth; all bodily discharges were defiling and disqualified people from approach to God's presence. Contact with death invariably defiled. Priests might come into contact with death only when close kin die, and the high priest was never to have contact with death. Leviticus 21:17-21 lists imperfections that barred a person from the priesthood. One student of these regulations summarizes them thus: "In other words he must be perfect as a man if he is to be a priest."[1]

Expressed in what appears to us as a bewildering array of petty regulations is the important concept that holiness and cleanness involve wholeness, or normality, integrity, soundness and order. Cleanness is the normal state of most things, because they are God's good creatures. They become holy when dedicated to the service of God. In fact, to become unclean the creation must be perverted. Because of the ravages of sin, some things are or become abnormal and substandard. Release from uncleanness could be attained by washing and sacrifice and avoidance of things and situations that were inherently unclean. We could diagram the relationships involved like this:

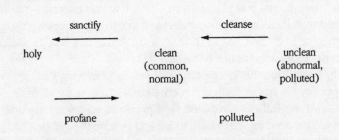

Figure 1. Relationships between the holy, the clean and the unclean[2]

The ultimate state of abnormality and disorder is death. In the sin-ravaged creation there are clearly gradations of abnormality. Again, this gradation between life, wholeness and normality and death, imperfection and abnormality can be represented by a chart listing many of the people and things used in Israel's sacrificial worship.

The exact criteria used by the ancient Hebrews for distinguishing between wholeness and imperfection are often difficult to identify. The categories that can be identified sometimes strike modern ears as rather arbitrary. But a valuable reminder is enshrined in these ancient laws about cleanness and uncleanness. What seem to us meaningless, arbitrary taboos were charged with a depth of significance. We are reminded that in God's created universe

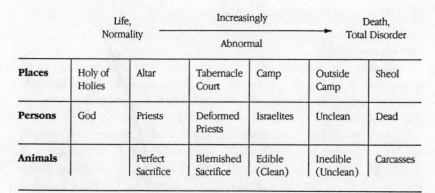

	Life, Normality		Increasingly Abnormal			Death, Total Disorder
Places	Holy of Holies	Altar	Tabernacle Court	Camp	Outside Camp	Sheol
Persons	God	Priests	Deformed Priests	Israelites	Unclean	Dead
Animals		Perfect Sacrifice	Blemished Sacrifice	Edible (Clean)	Inedible (Unclean)	Carcasses

Table 1. Life and death, wholeness and abnormality in Israel's ritual worship[3]

there is a moral order that touches all of life. These rules were symbols of that moral order; they were like

> signs which at every turn inspired meditation on the oneness, purity and completeness of God. By rules of avoidance, holiness was given a physical expression in every encounter with the animal kingdom and at every meal. Observance of the dietary rules would then have been a meaningful part of the great liturgical act of recognition and worship which culminated in the sacrifices of the temple.[4]

Consider how this symbolism might have worked with the dietary laws. Only the normal members of each sphere of creation were counted as clean or pure. So aquatic animals without fins and legless land animals that squirmed along the ground were unclean and to be avoided. This identification of normalcy with perfection was a reminder of God's absolute purity and of the purity he demands in his people. Carrion-eating birds and carnivores were also unclean. They pointed to the sinful, malicious, rapacious instincts of fallen humanity, qualities that make us unsuited for fellowship with the Lord. Exodus 22:31 summarizes the thrust of the laws of uncleanness: "You shall be people consecrated [literally, holy] to me; therefore you shall not eat any meat that is mangled by beasts in the field; you shall throw it to the dogs" (NRSV).

The New Testament teaches that these Old Testament laws are no longer binding. Practiced legalistically, they became a badge of exclusiveness and pride. Viewed externally as an end in themselves, they became an easy way to avoid the larger principles of justice and morality to which they properly point. Jesus dismissed them, but in doing so he also pointed to their deeper significance when he taught that the uncleanness that truly defiles comes out of us, from our defiled hearts (Mk 7:18-23).

The Human Plight
No less than the men and women of the Old Testament, we need to be reminded that we live in a moral universe. Holiness touches all of life, from the most important affairs to apparent trivialities. Everything and everyone stands under the watchful eye of our holy Creator.

Further, we need to be reminded that God's created universe is ravaged by sin. We do not live in a fully normal, fully healthy world. The carnage is all around us. Two symbols of this destruction point to the devastating effects of evil. The air we breathe and need for continuing life has been fouled as a byproduct of human greed and thoughtlessness. Scientists tell us that air pollution is detectable even in the "pristine" Arctic wilderness. Water, another staple of life, is also polluted. Water samples taken from the middle of the Pacific Ocean contain bits of nondegradable plastic. What other animal is so foolish as to foul its own nest? Greed, thoughtlessness and evil have made us destroyers of the earth.

In death we confront the ultimate abnormality. None of the propaganda about the naturalness of death, about its being a normal part of life, quite manages to persuade us. In the face of death we weep for loss, for the sheer irreverence of this enemy of humanity. We know we are made to live for our Creator forever. But we face the verdict that evil, our sin, frustrates what God intended for his image-bearers when he created us. Death is fearful to us not primarily because it forces us to face the unknown. We fear because we know, sometimes deep beneath our rationalizations and professed convictions, that we will face the Holy One without excuse. We know that in our present condition we cannot stand in his presence. Indeed, "the sting of death is sin" (1 Cor 15:56).

Finally, we need to be reminded of the absoluteness of God's holiness. Fellowship with the Holy One is absolutely incompatible with sin and all of its products. We can never approach the one true and living God in our current state of uncleanness. We sinners are both hopeless and helpless: hopeless because our sin has utterly fractured our relationship with the Holy One and helpless because sin enslaves and destroys, making us unable to respond to or obey or enjoy the Holy One.

Sin has left us locked in a debtors' prison. The debt we owe, our very lives, is more than we can afford to pay. A ransom of immeasurable value must be paid, but we are bankrupt morally and spiritually. Sin has left us dirty and infected with a sickness unto death. We need a cleansing beyond our knowledge and our power to provide.

Most profoundly, sin has brought us under God's personal, holy displeasure and wrath. We have no power to avert that wrath. True justice and love demand that we be consumed. Only now, when we are fully aware of the desperate plight created by our sin, can we begin to understand the place of sacrifice.

9

The Necessity of Sacrifice

*S*ACRIFICE IS A TERM WE USE QUITE FREQUENTLY. WE SPEAK OF THE SACRIFICES parents make to give their children a good education. Or we talk about the sacrifices an athlete makes in training to win a championship. For us, sacrifice means cost.

The idea of cost played a part in the way the people of the Bible thought about sacrifice. But they normally had a more specific, less metaphorical and more theological idea in mind. They thought primarily of the animal sacrifices offered up in the tabernacle (and later in the temple) which are described in detail in Leviticus. For the men and women of the Old Testament, these ritual acts were central to their ongoing relationship with God. Sacrifice was "the appointed means whereby peaceful coexistence between a holy God and a sinful man becomes a possibility."[1] In making his covenant with Israel, the Holy One had provided a means to overcome the barrier that sin constituted to the enjoyment of life in his presence. The importance of sacrifice is therefore difficult to overestimate.

The Value of Ritual
That does not mean, however, that the biblical concept of sacrifice is easy for

a modern audience to appreciate or understand. At the outset we are confronted with a complicated ritual that is dull to read about, hard to understand and seemingly irrelevant to our situation. Moderns have a built-in aversion to ritual and symbolic gestures. For us freedom and spontaneity are good, organization and ritual are bad. Indeed, the noun *ritual* is most often associated in our minds with adjectives like *meaningless* and *boring.*

This bias against ritual is evident in most modern study of the Old Testament. The founding father of modern critical study of the Old Testament, Julius Wellhausen, displays this prejudice. Two basic value judgments run throughout his greatest work, *Prolegomena to the History of Israel* (1878). The first is that ritual is bad, while freedom and spontaneity are good. The second is that the earlier eras of Israel's religion were marked by spontaneity, but this spontaneity gradually degenerated into organization and tradition-bound ritualism. So while certain parts of the extant Old Testament appear at first reading to belong to the formative period of biblical history (most of Leviticus, for example), they must actually have developed quite late in Israel's history. While many of Wellhausen's successors have rejected various detailed aspects of his views, the acceptance of these basic value judgments goes a long way to explaining the attraction of his overall reconstruction of the Old Testament.

We must not simply assimilate these value judgments uncritically from our culture. The sheer bulk of ritual law in the Pentateuch indicates its importance to the men and women of the Old Testament. At this point Scripture would seem to be raising a serious objection to our assumptions. Perhaps we need to think more deeply about ritual.

What is the essence of ritual as we find it in the Old Testament? Biblical rituals express basic truth visually as opposed to verbally. They are a drama acted out onstage and watched by human beings and God himself. On the one hand, as dramatized prayers, rituals express the deepest hopes and fears of humankind. On the other hand, ritual dramatizes God's promises and warnings, declaring his attitudes toward humanity.

So ritual may be likened to television in being a vivid, visual medium. But television does not permit the participation that is at the heart of Old Testament rituals. Everyone had his own role to play under the eye of God and other persons. As Gordon Wenham notes,

> It is easy to sing, "Just as I am, without one plea, But that thy blood was shed for me;" but to bring a whole bull, kill it, skin it, chop it up and then watch the whole lot burn on the altar would be quite another matter. Yet this is precisely what someone who offered a burnt offering (Lv. 1) was

expected to do. Without doubt, these Old Testament rituals were a pro-
digiously powerful teaching medium; the most eloquent modern preacher
is dumb by comparison.[2]

Not only is ritual powerful; it is also important and inevitable. Modern anthro-
pological study suggests that rituals express the most basic and central values
of a group of people. If we do not understand the ritual system of a people,
we do not understand what makes them tick.[3] If this is so, it is not at all
surprising that over half of the Pentateuch, the foundational revelation of
Israel, consists of ritual regulations and instructions about the tabernacle,
sacrifices, festivals and the priesthood. Unless we understand these arrangements, we will be in danger of missing the heart of ancient Israel's religion
and values.

Further, ritual seems inevitable. Indeed, ritual and organization reemerge
in our culture despite strenuous attempts to eliminate or minimize them.
Students freed from the shackles of expensive clothing in the radical 1960s
immediately adopted the compulsory uniform of faded jeans and army-sur-
plus backpacks. House churches that dispense with formal liturgy and professional ministers soon develop their own regular, often idiosyncratic way
of conducting worship and a recognized, sometimes authoritarian leadership.
The issue we must face is not whether to observe rituals. We humans seem
invariably to do so. Rather, the question must be, "How satisfactory are these
forms for expressing our most deeply held values?"

With these thoughts in mind, let's try to set aside the prejudices of our time
to consider the sacrificial ritual of the Old Testament.

The Old Testament Ritual Pattern

Despite what may appear to be a bewildering variety of sacrifices regulated
by a multiplicity of rules, it is helpful to note a basic ritual pattern. In all of
the great animal sacrifices, we may discern six steps in the ritual process.

1. The worshiper "brought near" his offering. This may seem no more than
a necessary preliminary. How else could the sacrifice be offered? But to the
Hebrews it was clearly of great significance, so much so that the causal form
of the verb *to draw near* became the technical term meaning *to sacrifice.* The
worshiper came obediently into the presence of God himself. It was an awesome moment. What was "brought near" further reinforces the gravity of the
occasion. The principle of "the best for God" was observed throughout.
Clean, domestic animals without defect were the normal offering. Even when
provision was made for the poor by allowing them to bring a less costly dove
or a cereal offering (Lev 5:11), the Lord was still offered the best, since these

offerings were such as the poor Israelite was able to get (Lev 14:21).

The normal place of sacrifice was the tabernacle, the portable tent-shrine whose plan was given to Moses by revelation from the Lord. It was constructed with exacting, thoughtful and artistically excellent obedience (Ex 36:1; 39:43). The design of the tabernacle itself emphasized the holiness of God. In its central, most holy place God's presence was manifested. This inner sanctum was nearly unapproachable, entered only once a year by only the high priest, when he offered the sacrifices of cleansing on the Day of Atonement. For the ordinary worshiper, to enter the sanctuary with an offering was to draw conspicuously near to the Holy One himself. It was an awesome thing indeed.

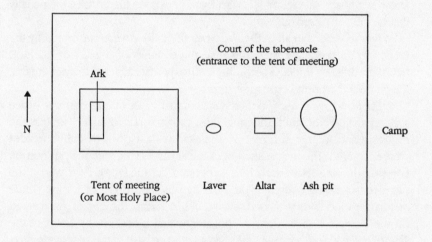

Figure 2. Plan of the tabernacle[4]

2. The worshiper laid his hands on the head of the animal. The Hebrew verb means something like "press down" or "lean on." It was no casual touch. Leviticus mentions only the act, but it is very unlikely that it was done in silence. Most probably the worshiper explained at this point why he was bringing the sacrifice and confessed his sins to the Lord. He may even have recited or sung a psalm. Psalm 40, 51 or 66 could well have been used by the worshiper, while 20 or 50 would have been appropriate as a priestly reply.

Some hold that this act meant only that the worshiper was identifying the offering as his own sacrifice. But "bringing near" the animal would seem to suffice for this purpose. Rather, the laying on of hands effected a symbolic transfer of the sins of the offerer to his offering. Thus when the animal died, it was receiving the punishment due to the worshiper for his sins. It was being treated as the sins it bore deserved.

3. *The animal was slaughtered by the worshiper.* The only exception to this rule was in the sacrifice of a bird. In this case the priest killed the sacrifice. Since the next stage in the ritual of sacrifice required the priest to collect the victim's blood, this exception was probably required by the need to quickly collect the small amount of blood available from a bird. Otherwise little blood might have been left in the bird when the time came for the priest to collect it. But in the more normal sacrifice the symbolism could not be more striking. The worshiper's sin deserved the severest punishment. The worshiper acknowledged and proclaimed this fact by imposing on his sacrifice the penalty that he himself deserved.

So far the actions in all of the five types of sacrifice were performed by the worshiper in the same way. The final three stages of the act of sacrifice, however, differed in detail according to the type of sacrifice. It was here that the work of the priest began.

4. *The blood of the sacrifice was manipulated by the priest.* For burnt, peace and reparation (or guilt) offerings, the priest splashed blood against the northeast and southwest corners of the altar in such a way that all four sides were splattered. The major differences in the ritual came with the purification (or sin) offering. Here variations depended on the person for whom the sacrifice was being offered. If the offering was for a priest or for the whole nation, the blood was sprinkled seven times in front of the curtain that marked off the Holy of Holies. Then the priest smeared blood on the horns of the altar of incense and poured out the rest of it at the base of the altar of sacrifice. When the sacrifice was offered for a ruler or for a wayward member of the community, there was no sprinkling of the curtain, but blood was smeared on the horns of the incense altar and poured out at the base of the altar of sacrifice.

The solemnity of the blood ritual, particularly the elaborate blood ritual of the purification offering, must have made it plain that sin and its polluting effect could not be taken lightly. Sin defiles individual men and women, the whole community in which they live and even the tabernacle where God promised to dwell. This pollution endangers God's people. God's wrath will be aroused where sin is not atoned for and its defilement removed.

The blood ritual symbolically addressed this danger. When a sacrifice was offered, the animal was killed in the place of the worshiper. The manipulation of the blood represented the ritual presentation to God of the evidence that death had taken place to atone for sin. Because atonement had been made, that same blood acted symbolically as a cleansing agent, removing pollution and restoring cleanness.

5. *The sacrifice (at least in part) was burned on the altar.* In the case of the burnt offering, the whole animal was consumed, so that this stage marked the end of the sacrifice. For the other animal offerings, certain prescribed parts were burned on the altar, mostly the internal fat. The smoke rising from the altar fire was described as "an aroma pleasing to the LORD" (Lev 1:9, 13, 17).

The idea expressed by this phrase is seen in its clearest and starkest in the flood story. Before the flood "the LORD saw . . . that every inclination of the thoughts of [the human] heart was only evil all the time" (Gen 6:5). So he destroyed humankind. After the flood Noah offered a sacrifice. "The LORD smelled the pleasing aroma and said in his heart: 'Never again will I curse the ground because of man, even though every inclination of his heart is evil from childhood' " (Gen 8:21). Note that nothing had changed in humankind, but God's attitude toward humankind was altered. Similarly, the rising aroma of sacrifice did not change the offerer. But it did remove God's curse, God's holy hostility against sin. Sacrifice thus made possible fellowship between sinful persons and a holy God.

6. *Finally, any remaining parts of the offering were disposed of in a variety of ways, depending on the type of sacrifice.* Typically, the priest received these offerings and was thus provided food and animal hides. With the peace offering, part was burned, part was set aside for the priests, and the remainder was eaten by the worshipers. This made the peace offering a festive and joyful occasion, a celebration of the manifold blessings of God's shalom.

This review of the sacrificial ritual makes it clear that various types of sacrifice were mandated by God to be used on various occasions. These can best be reviewed and compared in the chart below.

The sacrificial system presents three different models to describe the disastrous effects of sin and the way of overcoming them. The oldest and most frequently used offering, the burnt offering, gives the most basic picture: personal relationship. The human being is a guilty sinner whose sin calls forth the implacable hostility of God's holiness. The sinner deserves to die, but the animal dies in his place, under the wrath of God. God accepts the animal as a ransom for the person, and thus reconciliation is achieved.

The sin offering uses a medical model. Sin pollutes the people of God and his sanctuary, so that God in his awesome purity becomes a threat. He no longer dwells among his creatures. But the blood of the sacrifices disinfects God's dwelling place, the sanctuary, and God's mediators, the priests and

Name	Ref.	Occasion	Offering	Disposition
Burnt offering (*'ōlâ*)	1:1-17	Gaining divine favour	Unblemished male. Individual means governed kind of offering	All burned
Cereal offering (*minḥâ*)	2:1-16	Thanksgiving and securing divine goodwill	Salted unleavened cakes or cereals	Part burned for God; remainder assigned to priests
Peace offerings (*zebaḥ šᵉlāmîm*)	3:1-17 22:18-30	Gratitude to God; fellowship with Him; public rejoicing; deliverance from vows	Unblemished male or female animal according to individual means	Fat burned; remainder eaten by priest and worshipper in fellowship meal
Sin offering (*ḥaṭṭāṭ*)	4:1—5:13	Need for purification from sin or defilement	Bull (priest or congregation); male goat (ruler); female goat, lamb, pair of doves or pigeons; meal offering (individual)	Fat burned for God; remainder eaten by priests
Guilt offering (*'āšām*)	5:14-19	Guilt about misappropriations of holy things or some loss to sanctuary	Unblemished ram	Fat burned; remainder eaten by priests

Table 2. The sacrifices of Leviticus[5]

God's people. In this way God may continue to be present with his people and fill the tabernacle with his glory, the visible token of his presence.

The reparation offering employs a commercial picture. Sin makes people debtors to one another and to God. As we make restitution for our sins against other people, our debt to God is paid through the offering of sacrifice.

Running through the entire Old Testament sacrificial system are five common theological themes. These truths are of such basic significance that failure to grasp them leads us to utterly misunderstand the meaning and place of the sacrifices and also the character of the God to whom sacrifice was offered. So the remainder of this chapter will address these five themes.

Sacrifice Comes at God's Initiative

First, and most basically, sacrifice was an institution established by God at his own initiative. This was not the case in the religions of the cultures that surrounded Israel. In most ways the external forms used by Israel and its neighbors were identical. But among Israel's neighbors, religious sacrifice was offered at the initiative of the worshiper in order to supply something lacking in the deity. In their crudest form, sacrifices provided the gods with food to sustain or entertain them. This view of sacrifice the Old Testament finds ridiculous:

I have no need of a bull from your stall
   or of goats from your pens,
for every animal of the forest is mine,
   and the cattle on a thousand hills.
I know every bird in the mountains,
   and the creatures of the field are mine.
If I were hungry I would not tell you,
   for the world is mine, and all that is in it.
Do I eat the flesh of bulls
   or drink the blood of goats? (Ps 50:9-13)

More typically sacrifices in ancient Near Eastern religions were like bribes designed to secure blessings and favor from an unwilling, irascible, unpredictable deity. The ultimate horror of this mentality was to be found in child sacrifice. One thinks of Agamemnon offering the life of his daughter Iphigenia to the gods in order to influence these unpredictable deities to make the winds blow toward Troy so he could launch his ill-fated invasion fleet. That this horrible practice should have been adopted by Ahaz and Manasseh, two later kings of Judah, shows the extent of their defection from God's laws and ways (see 2 Kings 16:3; 21:6, for example). Needless to say, child sacrifice was strictly forbidden by the Old Testament law (Lev 20:4) and prophets (Jer 7:31).

Lest we moderns become too smug in reviewing the deficiencies of ancient paganism, we ought to be reminded of our own repeated attempts to bribe and buy off God. When my family lived in Pittsburgh, we discovered that one of that city's largest and most impressive church buildings was widely and derisively known as the "fire escape" for one of the wealthy commercial barons of the city. This folly outdoes our lesser follies only in its grand scale. We persist in feeling that somehow we can ingratiate ourselves with God. Somehow we can impress him with our gifts and sacrifices; somehow we can make him beholden to us so that he will be favorable toward us. In our own way we slip back into a mindset just like Agamemnon's, Ahaz's or Manasseh's.

Again, the Old Testament sweeps aside this whole way of approaching God. Sacrifice was his institution established by his grace so that sinners might be his friends. The sacrifices were instituted in the context of God's gracious covenant with his people. They did not establish that relationship at Israel's initiative. They maintained it by God's provision. Sacrifices were covenant ordinances. The sacrifices made atonement for sin not because of any efficacy in the sacrifice itself or any magic in the sacrificial ritual, but because of God himself. God said, "I have given [sacrificial blood] to you to make atonement for yourselves on the altar" (Lev 17:11). P. T. Forsyth comments, "Given! Did you ever see the force of it? 'I have given you the blood to make atonement. This is an institution which I set up for you to comply with, set it up for purposes of My own, on principles of My own, but it is My gift.' The Lord Himself provided the lamb for the burnt offering."[6]

Pardon and blessing are not wrung from an unwilling or unpredictable deity. They are the gracious gift of the Holy One, who is eager to forgive. So the psalmist rejoices,

> Their hearts were not loyal to him,
>> they were not faithful to his covenant.
> Yet he was merciful;
>> he forgave their iniquities
>> and did not destroy them.
> Time after time he restrained his anger
>> and did not stir up his full wrath. (Ps 78:37-38)

The Mediation of a Priest

Second, sacrifice highlights the important principles of priestly mediation. God appointed a class of people and their head, the high priest, to an office of representation. As God's representatives to his people, they were charged with the task of maintaining the purity of the sacrifices in strict obedience to the Lord's commands. Further, they were to instruct the people in these laws and their meanings so that sacrifice would not be a mindless bit of magic, but a spiritual and holy event in the ongoing relationship between the Holy One and his covenant people.

As the representative of the people, the priests were charged with approaching the High and Holy One. I have noted their role in the offering of every regular sacrifice. This representative function reaches its culmination on the Day of Atonement (yôm kippurîm), the solemn national ceremony of cleansing and forgiveness of sin that occurred on the tenth day of the seventh month. This was the one day in all of the year when the high priest was allowed to enter the most holy place.

The special rites used only on this day brought home the seriousness of sin and the importance of dealing with it. The Day of Atonement was a day of fasting. The Jewish liturgical calendar had several feasts but just this one fast. On this most solemn of days the people remembered the holiness of God and the terrible plight brought about by their sin.

The high priest began the day by bathing himself. On normal days he was required to wash only his hands and feet (Ex 30:19-21). But this was a very special day, a day wholeheartedly concerned with cleansing. Then the high priest put on plain white linen clothing rather than his magnificent robes of office. The animals used in the sacrifices of the day were collected. For himself and his household he took a young bull for a sin offering and a ram for a burnt offering; for the people of Israel he took two male goats for a sin offering and a ram for a burnt offering.

The high priest began with the bull, which he offered to make atonement for himself. Having gathered the blood of this offering, a censer full of burning coals and two handfuls of incense, he entered into the most holy place, the little dark room at the heart of the tabernacle. Upon entering, he promptly put the incense on the coals, creating a thick cloud of smoke to cover the mercy seat "so that he will not die" (Lev 16:13). God in his transcendent glory was present above the mercy seat. The cloud of incense apparently hid the mercy seat and the glory from the priest's eyes, thus protecting him. The high priest then splashed the sacrificial blood once against the face of the mercy seat and seven times in front of it.

Next the high priest took the two goats and cast lots over them. One goat was "for the Lord" and the other "for the scapegoat." The one "for the Lord" was offered as a sin offering for the people. The blood of this goat was taken into the Most Holy Place and used in the same way as the blood of the priest's own sacrifice. "In this way he will make atonement for the Most Holy Place because of the uncleanness and rebellion of the Israelites, whatever their sins have been. He is to do the same for the Tent of Meeting, which is among them in the midst of their uncleanness" (Lev 16:16). Now the high priest and the place of worship itself were both ceremonially clean.

Attention then focused on the sins of the people. The high priest laid both his hands on the head of the other goat and confessed "all the wickedness and rebellion of the Israelites—all their sins—and put them on the goat's head" (Lev 16:21). After this general confession he sent the goat away in the care of an appointed man, to be released in the wilderness. Thus the nation's sins were solemnly confessed and borne away in response to God's provision and command. They were no longer laid to the charge of the people.

Now that sin and uncleanness had been dealt with, the high priest took off his simple linen garments, put on his glorious robes and offered the two remaining rams as burnt offerings for himself and the people. At the same time the fat of the other offerings was also burned up to the Lord, while their carcasses were removed from the camp and burned up. These final offerings expressed the joy and devotion of the people of God and their representative.

Such were the events of this special and solemn day according to Leviticus 16. Worshipers must have been deeply impressed with the awful seriousness of sin in the light of God's holiness. Something had to be done if sin was not to separate people from God and bring them under his certain judgment. Further, it must have been clear that the normal sacrifices did not deal with all sin. The very existence of the Day of Atonement suggests that the Holy One had appointed a means in addition to and beyond the sacrifices of individual Israelites to fully deal with the threat of sin. In this way the central representative role of the high priest was underscored.

Two especially noteworthy aspects of the observance stand out. Both placed the high priest at center stage. The first was the placing of the sins of the people on the scapegoat. There is dispute about the meaning of the Hebrew phrase translated "scapegoat." Literally it means "for Azazel." Some hold that this was the name of a demon, perhaps even Satan himself, so that the sins were being sent back to where they belong. Others think that it meant "rocky precipice," because in later times at least the goat was finally pushed off a precipice to its destruction. Still others hold that it meant "complete destruction," so that the sins were no more. With the information available to us at present, it is impossible to be exactly certain what "Azazel" meant. But there is no doubt about the total meaning of the ceremony. The people saw their sins completely removed. The sins were laid on the goat's head by the high priest, and they were taken into the wilderness to trouble them no more. The Holy One had made provision for their cleansing and the exterminating of their sins through his appointed representative.

The second noteworthy aspect is that on this day, and this day alone, after taking the most stringent precautions, the high priest was granted admission to the Most Holy Place. The limitations are obvious: freedom of access to the Holy One for all of God's people was only a dream. Still, true access to God's glorious presence by a God-appointed representative was possible. This held out hope to all of God's people. In these ways the Day of Atonement underscored the importance of priestly mediation.

Atonement for Sin

Third, sacrifice made atonement with the Holy One for the sins of the people. Repeatedly Leviticus describes the effect of the sacrifices on the Lord himself. They were "an aroma pleasing [or soothing] to the LORD" (see, for instance, 1:9, 13, 17). Further, the sacrifice would be "accepted on [the worshiper's] behalf to make atonement for him" (1:4).

The derivation and meaning of the Hebrew verb *to make atonement (kipper)* is a matter of some dispute, despite its rather frequent occurrence. One possible derivation of the term is the Akkadian verb *kapāru,* "to cleanse" or "to wipe." If this is the meaning of *make atonement,* then sacrifices wipe away or cleanse sin. This fits those contexts where the altar or the sanctuary is the direct object of the verb and the action involved smearing or sprinkling the altar with blood (Lev 4:25; 16:14).

Some would see this as the only meaning of *atone.* The Bible, so they assert, consistently leads us away from the false pagan notion that God is bribed or changed by our offerings. We must steer clear of this pagan mode of thought ourselves. By our sacrifices we do not change or affect God. The object of sacrifice is human sin and uncleanness. Sacrifice cleanses or covers over sin so that it no longer constitutes a barrier to fellowship with God. On this view of atonement, sacrifice provides an *expiation* for sin.

Despite the attractiveness of this view, however, it is difficult to escape the conclusion that it does justice to only part of the biblical data. We may be grateful for its advocates' desire to defend our view of God and his holiness from pagan influences. But it seems something of an overreaction, an overdefensiveness. Certainly atonement in Old Testament sacrifices was not a bribe. Nothing a human being does could alter God's justice or his holy, active displeasure against sin. But Old Testament sacrifice was not a human achievement; it was instituted by God. He himself provided the means for dealing with his justice and wrath. Such a view is not pagan. It is Old Testament covenant faith in the justice, mercy and faithfulness of the Holy One.

An alternative view notes that *kipper,* "to make atonement," may be derived most naturally from the Hebrew noun *kōper,* meaning "ransom price." A *kōper* was the money a man condemned to death could pay under certain circumstances to escape the death penalty (Ex 21:30; Prov 6:35). *Kipper* then could be literally translated "to pay a ransom (for one's life)." This meaning is compatible with the passages that speak of sacrifice as "making atonement" for a person as opposed to an object.

In modern parlance, a ransom usually is a large sum of money paid to terrorists or criminals to free innocent hostages. It involves helpless participation in an outrageous and illegal act. But in the Old Testament the payment of a ransom must be seen as a gracious and humane act. It allowed a guilty person to be punished with a lesser penalty than he or she deserved. For example, in a case of adultery the wronged husband would legally exact the death penalty. But as an act of mercy he could spare his guilty wife and her lover if a ransom was paid (Lev 20:10; Prov 6:35). This permission to substitute a ransom for the maximum penalty was common in ancient Near Eastern law, though the Old Testament clearly excluded it in the case of murder (Num 35:31, 33). So the emphasis in a ransom payment fell on showing mercy while still doing justice.

In the Old Testament texts that do not deal with sacrifice, *kipper* means to pay a ransom so that a person does not suffer the death penalty demanded by law. The ransom itself could be money, or the suffering of another person, or even animals that took the place of the guilty person (Num 8:10-12). The overwhelming probability is that the same meaning should be understood in texts dealing with sacrifice, unless such a meaning leads to nonsense or contradiction. Consider Leviticus 17:11 again: "I have given [blood] to you to make atonement for [to ransom] yourselves on the altar; it is the blood that makes atonement [ransoms] for one's life." God in mercy allowed a sinner to escape the death penalty his or her sins deserved by offering as a ransom payment the life of a sacrificial animal.

This view of sacrifice as a ransom payment that made for peace with the Holy One clearly involves the principle of *vicarious substitution*. What was required by God's justice was the death of the sinner. What was offered up at God's initiative in covenant grace to satisfy God's justice was the life of the sacrificial victim. Life was substituted for life. The animal was the worshiper's substitute, dying the death he or she deserved. This substitutionary aspect was further underscored by the worshiper's act of laying hands on the head of the animal and confessing his or her sins. Thus the animal bore the person's sins and their just punishment.

Most basically, this view of sacrifice as a substitutionary ransom payment indicates that sacrifice *had* an effect on God, an effect that God himself designed it to have. Over and over again Leviticus repeats that the burning sacrifice has a "pleasing" or "soothing" aroma to the Lord. The completed sacrificial action touched God himself. Sacrifice did not eliminate sin or change a person's sinful nature. But it made possible fellowship between a holy God and sinful humankind, because sacrifice turned away God's anger against sin

Thus sacrifice provided a *propitiation* for God's holy wrath against sin. Indeed, the Greek verb used to translate *kipper* in the Greek Old Testament (Septuagint) means "propitiate" or "turn away anger."[7] Understood in this way, *make atonement* means everything conveyed by *expiate*—that is, to cover and cleanse sin. But in addition it explains *how* this cleansing and forgiving is accomplished: by turning aside God's holy wrath against our rebellion and iniquity. God in his mercy provides sinners with a means to overcome his holy hostility against their sins by the payment of a ransom, substituting the death of a sacrificial victim for the death they justly deserve. In this way justice is done, but mercy triumphs. In the Old Testament, sacrifice was the expression and execution of God's holy anger on the one hand and the expression and putting into action of God's grace on the other.

To many people, to speak of atonement in terms of propitiation seems hopelessly primitive and quite unnecessary. To judge by current Bible translation practices, *expiate* says all that needs to be said. But this reducing of atonement to covering and cleansing sin is no gain. Such a view ignores the reality of God's holy and just wrath against evil and sin. As we saw earlier, while the idea of God's wrath may make us uncomfortable, it is neither an idea unworthy of God nor a concept to be discarded. When the holiness of God confronts sin, there is inevitably God's wrath to be faced. To ignore this reality is spiritual blindness and self-deception.

There are three reasons that *propitiation* is to be preferred to mere *expiation* if we are to understand the atonement made by Old Testament sacrifice.

1. The Old Testament concept of propitiation avoids the abuses of the pagan conception of sacrifice. The gifts of the worshiper do not bribe God into dropping his just and holy anger against sin. He is not only the object of the propitiation effected by sacrifice but also its subject. On the level of the Old Testament grammar, *God* is characteristically the subject of the verb *make atonement [propitiate]* and almost never its object. God propitiates his own wrath, so great is his love for his people, by the establishment of the covenant and its sacrificial ordinances. Initiative in averting wrath against those who deserve it lies with God, not with sinning men and women. This Old Testament view of propitiation thus magnifies the grace and love of the Holy One without denying his holy justice and wrath.

2. Expiation—that is, covering or cleansing—normally has things as its object. It makes good sense in the context of impersonal relations. At times this does full justice to the assertions of the Old Testament. When sacrificial blood is applied to the horns of the altar (Lev 4:25), as in the sin or purification offering, or to the mercy seat on the Day of Atonement (Lev 16:14), it seems best to understand the atonement being made as a "wiping clean." In this way the place of sacrifice and the priestly agents were cleansed and sanctified to perform their tasks.

But even in these cases a more personal relationship to the Holy One stands in the background. After all is said and done, sin and guilt are not things, but relational concepts. They exist properly in the context of personal agents and personal relationships. Sinful men and women stand before their Holy Maker. Yahweh's righteous anger is aroused by sin. Sacrifice deals with this situation of hostility in strained and broken personal relationships. The concept that describes what happens as a result of sacrifice must be appropriate to this context of personal relations. Specifically, it must relate to the averting of God's personal displeasure with human rebellion and waywardness. *Propitiation,* with the proper biblical safeguards against pagan misunderstanding, seems the most adequate idea and term.

3. To reduce the concept of propitiation to expiation raises more questions than it answers. Why should sin be expiated by the sacrificial action? What is there in the sacrifice that covers and cleanses sin? What would happen if there were no expiation? Would not the hand of God be in those consequences? In Scripture, if sin is not dealt with, men and women face the reality of God's displeasure. But isn't this just another way of saying that the wrath of God abides on them? And isn't this simply to say that "expiation" is necessary to avert the wrath of God? But then what would we gain by abandoning the concept of propitiation? As a matter of fact, no convincing account can be given of expiation of sin before the Holy One that does not also involve the averting of his holy wrath against sin.

So sacrifice made atonement with the Holy One by the payment of a ransom. The life of the sacrificial victim was offered or paid in substitution for the life of the guilty worshiper, under the ax of God's justice. This offering of life for life was instituted by God himself in order to satisfy his own justice and to avert his own holy wrath against sin. In this way sacrifice powerfully witnessed to the awesome reality of God's justice and wrath and the wonder of his overflowing goodness and generosity. Solemnity, awesomeness, wonder and joy were mingled in this covenant ordinance.

Consecration and Communion

Fourth, sacrifice expressed worshipers' consecration to the Holy One and their desire for communion with the Lord. The element of cost enters at this point. Ransoms are apt to be costly, and the sacrifices were a high price to pay. Perfect rams or bulls were even more valuable in Old Testament times than they are today. To select a prize animal, bring it to the tabernacle, slaughter it, skin it, chop it up and then watch it go up in smoke (or be carted off by the priests) was a costly and powerful expression of gratitude to the Lord. When you reckon that sacrifice was a regularly repeated ceremony for all of God's people, both the cost and the real commitment expressed are heightened. Our passing of an offering plate in a worship service seems pale by comparison.

The reality of communion with the Lord and celebration of his good gifts was also expressed. This dimension was especially emphasized in the peace offerings, sacrifices that were offered to accompany special petitions or vows to the Lord or simply as spontaneous acts of generosity and thanksgiving. Peace offerings were often associated with occasions when the reality of God's covenant was emphasized. Even this essentially joyous sacrifice contained a blood rite, reminding the people of their constant need for forgiveness of sin. But most distinctive in the peace offering was the meal that concluded it. People and priests enjoyed a meal together in which God's presence was recognized as especially near. Eating meat—a luxury in ancient Israel—made it a particularly joyful occasion when the goodness of the Holy One and all of his generous blessings were recalled and enjoyed. So sacrifice was an occasion for consecration to and communion with the Holy One.

The Limitations of the Sacrificial System
Fifth, sacrifice in the Old Testament contained intentionally built-in inadequacies. The whole priestly and sacrificial institution was an acted-out promise that God would ultimately deal mercifully with sin and its consequences. But the means employed never fully met the promise, and sensitive men and women in the Old Testament era were left to look for a real and final fulfillment of God's promises.

Consider the limitations that were part and parcel of the sacrificial institution. The Old Testament recognizes kinds of sin for which no sacrifice availed. Rejection of the covenant was the clearest instance of this sort of sin. When Israel rejected the Lord in the wilderness and built the golden calf to worship in his place, Moses sought to make atonement for the people's sin. In his intercession he offered to have his name blotted out of God's book as a sacrifice to secure forgiveness for the people. The Lord refused. He replied to Moses, "Whoever has sinned against me I will blot out of my book" (Ex 32:33). But if a human sacrifice could not secure atonement, how could the sacrifice of animals be expected to atone for sin?

Similarly, Numbers 15:27-31 makes it clear that sacrifice was effective for unintentional sins, but sins committed "defiantly" cut the sinner off from the people of God and made sacrificial atonement impossible. Defiant sin here is undoubtedly more than just intentional sin. It is sin that expresses a rejection of God himself and his covenant mercy. All sin, however, has the basic character of flying in the face of God. All sin breaches God's covenant. It was not obvious when the line drawn by this text was crossed so that sinners would find themselves beyond the effectiveness of the sacrifices of the Old Testament.

The very nature of the Day of Atonement also raises questions about the effectiveness of sacrifices. Why should this day have been necessary if the ordinary sacrifices of the people were truly effective? What are we to make of the high priest's own need to offer a sacrifice for himself? Could he truly and fully function in the mediatorial role set out for him by the law if he himself was a sinner like the rest of the people? What happened if the high priest and other priests themselves became rebels against God's covenant?

Is any real effectiveness or finality in dealing with sin to be found in the Old Testament institution of sacrifice? Sacrifices were offered again and again. Doesn't the repetitive character of these sacrifices suggest that they provided no fully effective or final answer for the problem of sinful men and women who stood before the Holy One?

It is in this light that the prophetic attack on sacrifice is to be understood. For example, consider Isaiah's hard words to the Israelite religious establishment:

Hear the word of the LORD,
    you rulers of Sodom;
listen to the law of our God,
    you people of Gomorrah!
"The multitude of your sacrifices—
    what are they to me?" says the LORD.
"I have more than enough of burnt offerings,
    of rams and the fat of fattened animals;
I have no pleasure
    in the blood of bulls and lambs and goats.
When you come to appear before me,
    who has asked this of you,
    this trampling of my courts?

Stop bringing meaningless offerings!
    Your incense is detestable to me.
New Moons, Sabbaths and convocations—
    I cannot bear your evil assemblies.
Your New Moon festivals and your appointed feasts
    my soul hates.
They have become a burden to me;
    I am weary of bearing them.
When you spread out your hands in prayer,
    I will hide my eyes from you;
even if you offer many prayers,
    I will not listen.
Your hands are full of blood;
    wash and make yourselves clean.
Take your evil deeds
    out of my sight!
Stop doing wrong,
    learn to do right!
Seek justice,
    encourage the oppressed.
Defend the cause of the fatherless,
    plead the case of the widow.

"Come now, let us reason together,"
    says the LORD.
"Though your sins are like scarlet,
    they shall be as white as snow;
though they are red as crimson,
    they shall be like wool.
If you are willing and obedient,
    you will eat the best from the land;
but if you resist and rebel,
    you will be devoured by the sword."
    For the mouth of the LORD has spoken. (Is 1:10-20)

For the sacrifices to be spiritually effective required that a connection be maintained between an inward and personal faith in the worshiper, obedient performance of the outward forms of worship, and the personal nearness of the Lord who receives worship. When this vital connection was broken, sacrifice was particularly liable to abuse. The prophets rose up to emphasize the priority of personal relationship with the Lord. The mere performance of external rites, even rites commanded by the Lord, was of no real avail. Indeed, the rites became a spiritually destructive and deceptive force in the absence of commitment to God and his ways. The whole priestly class could sin defiantly in their offering of sacrifices, when they were not personally committed to living in relationship to the Holy One. Then there was no sacrifice for sin!

The Fulfillment of Sacrifice

Thanks be to God, this sorry record of failure is not the Old Testament's final word on sacrifice and atonement. It is no accident that when priestly and prophetic religion are brought together in the figure of the Servant of the Lord in Isaiah 53, all that is valuable in the institution of sacrifice is realized. Remember these words, as glorious as they are familiar:

> Surely he took up our infirmities
>   and carried our sorrows,
> yet we considered him stricken by God,
>   smitten by him, and afflicted.
> But he was pierced for our transgressions,
>   he was crushed for our iniquities;
> the punishment that brought us peace was upon him,
>   and by his wounds we are healed.
> We all, like sheep, have gone astray,
>   each of us has turned to his own way;
> and the LORD has laid on him
>   the iniquity of us all.
>
> He was oppressed and afflicted,
>   yet he did not open his mouth;
> he was led like a lamb to the slaughter,
>   and as a sheep before her shearers is silent,
>   so he did not open his mouth. . . .
>
> Yet it was the LORD's will to crush him and cause him to suffer,
>   and though the LORD makes his life a guilt offering,
> he will see his offspring and prolong his days,
>   and the will of the LORD will prosper in his hand. (Is 53:4-7, 10)

Here is the person who makes an effective and final sacrificial atonement and calls forth the love and personal commitment of the fallen human heart.

The Old Testament, then, knows the necessity of sacrifice for sinners to live before the Holy One. God's perfect justice must be meted out. His holy wrath against sin must be turned aside. Mere formal compliance with ritual, even a God-given ritual, is insufficient to make atonement effective. But the Old Testament knows no truly effective and finally sufficient sacrifice for sin. Its whole institution of sacrificial worship functioned as an elaborate, dramatic promise by the Holy One that he himself would deal with sin. And the prophets looked forward to a fulfillment of that promise. The Holy One, who is utterly self-consistent and cannot deny himself, would surely make a way for sinners to stand in his presence.

10

THE MAJESTY
OF THE CROSS

THE NEW TESTAMENT BEGINS WITH EVERYONE ON TIPTOE. MOMENTOUS EVENTS are about to unfold. John the Baptist, that strange prophet from the wilderness, commences his ministry, calling for a new level of moral and spiritual reality. He describes himself in the words of Isaiah as "the voice of one calling in the desert, 'Make straight the way for the Lord' " (Jn 1:23). His work is to prepare the way for a mighty one who will fulfill God's promises to inaugurate the kingdom of God and bring in a revolution of grace and peace. Seeing Jesus, John cries out, "Look, the Lamb of God, who takes away the sin of the world!" (Jn 1:29). John's exclamation summarizes the New Testament outlook on sacrifice.

Jesus not only fulfills Old Testament expectations of a coming prophet and king. The promise of the Old Testament sacrifices also is fulfilled in him. He is the Suffering Servant of the Lord. He is God's perfect priest, the one mediator between God and humankind. In his death he accomplishes what the repeated animal sacrifices of the Old Testament could only promise, an effective and final atonement. Sinners who look to him and his cross can stand confidently before the Holy One.

The Meaning of Jesus' Death

The teaching of Jesus and the events surrounding his death are the basis for this New Testament teaching about the cross. Consider Jesus' two most explicit sayings about the meaning of his death. In Mark 10:32-45, Jesus is en route to Jerusalem with his astonished disciples and a fearful group of followers. Sensing that great events are about to unfold, but obviously not understanding their character or true significance, James and John approach Jesus with a request. They want to be given the positions of greatest authority at the Lord's side when he comes into his glory. The other disciples are indignant, but not because of the insensitivity of the two toward Jesus' approaching passion. Rather, they resent having been excluded from this brash request. They also want to be great. A squabble breaks out among them, and Jesus is forced to intervene. He proceeds to instruct them all on the nature of true greatness in his kingdom: greatness demands not the self-assertion and lordliness of the Gentile authorities, but sacrificial service. This sort of service corresponds to Jesus' way. "For even the Son of Man did not come to be served, but to serve, and to give his life as a ransom for many" (Mk 10:45).

Here is Jesus' own synopsis of his mission. Notice that his work finds its end and its crown not in his teaching or his working of miracles or his example, though each of these has an important place in his life as a servant. He has come ultimately to pour out his life as a ransom in the place of many. This saying clearly echoes the description of the Servant of the Lord in Isaiah 53. Jesus comes as the Servant of the Lord to pour out his life as a substitute for the many whose lives were forfeit because of sin. They are liberated from the terrible penalty and bondage of their sin to live before the Holy One by Jesus' sacrificial ransoming death.

Jesus' saying over the cup at the Last Supper also echoes both the language of Old Testament sacrifices and Isaiah 53. He asserts, "This is my blood of the covenant, which is poured out for many for the forgiveness of sins" (Mt 26:28; Mk 14:24; Lk 22:20). In addition to his sacrificial, atoning death, Jesus speaks of another prophetic expectation, a "new covenant." Jeremiah had predicted the coming of the new covenant (Jer 31:31-34). It was to be a day when God overcame all the limitations of the old covenant with Israel and fulfilled all of his purposes. Sin would be fully and finally forgiven, and God's law would be internalized in the hearts and in the minds of God's people. All of God's people would know God intimately and personally. Jesus claimed that all of these wonderful, hoped-for spiritual realities would be inaugurated in the pouring out of his life.

The events surrounding his death also point to the solemnity, wonder and immense significance of Jesus' sacrifice for us. See him in the garden, sweating great drops, as it were, of blood, as he petitions the Father to let "this cup" pass from him. What is it that he shrinks from? Perhaps the "cup" here refers merely to Jesus' divinely appointed agony of death of the cross. But a deeper meaning is more likely. The prophets often speak of a cup filled with the wrath of God (see Is 51:17, 22). What faced Jesus in the cross was not just the agony of a painful physical death. Certainly that would have been enough to face. But more centrally, Jesus dreaded having to face his Father's wrath against our sin. The horror of the cross is the awfulness of the Son of God falling undeservedly under the wrath that was justly due the sin of the world.

This view of the cup that the Lord dreaded is further deepened by his cry from the cross: "My God, my God, why have you forsaken me?" Recall that the wrath of God is at work when God withdraws and leaves sinners to the devastation wrought by their sin. Here is Jesus forsaken by the Father, experiencing the spiritual agony of the wrath of God against sin. Can we ever fully understand what is happening here as God the Father turns his back on God the Son? The One who from eternity had been the object of God's eternal, unfailing love now stands condemned and forsaken. Creation itself reacts with an unnatural darkness. God's holy justice and wrath against sin are revealed. And God, the Holy One, absorbs the full force of that wrath, revealing his goodness and grace. "Note then the kindness and the severity of God" (Rom 11:22 RSV). This is the most awesome event in human history.

One final happening places a wonderful divine exclamation point after Jesus' death. The first three Gospels record that "with a loud cry, Jesus breathed his last" (Mk 15:37 and parallels). John's Gospel adds that Jesus cried, "It is finished" (Jn 19:30). This is a cry of victory. The work of propitiating the wrath of God has been done fully and finally. Redemption was accomplished. At this point the "curtain of the temple," the barrier that marked off the Most Holy Place, was torn in two from top to bottom (Mk 15:38). Remember that this was the place where only the high priest could enter, and then only once a year. God accepted the sacrifice of Jesus as the fulfillment of the Old Testament sacrifices and priesthood, and therefore threw down the barrier to his holy presence. Direct access for sinners to the presence of the Holy One had been won.

These truths of Jesus' redeeming, substitutionary, propitiatory death bring us to the very heart of the New Testament gospel. Human beings face no more foundational problem than their estrangement from the Holy One because of sin. To be sure, the New Testament knows all about our human weaknesses and problems, our fear, physical frailty, loneliness, cruelty, exploitation of the weak, despair, moral cowardice, hypocrisy. But all of these problems are rooted in sin, which brings us under the wrath of the Holy One. They are symptoms of our deepest disease, our justly deserved God-forsakenness. Sin and its judgment are the self-inflicted tyrannies from which we most need deliverance. And it is exactly this deliverance that Jesus achieved in his death on the cross.

The Final Sacrifice

Because of the centrality of these concerns to the gospel, they are treated in great depth in the New Testament epistles. The letter to the Hebrews contains the most thorough discussion of Old Testament priesthood and sacrifice and its fulfillment in Christ. Perhaps the key word in this careful exposition is *better*. The Old Testament contained a real revelation of God's plan for dealing with sin. But it was partial and provisional. It was good; but with the appearing of the eternal Son of God something "better," something complete and final, has come (Heb 1—2, 7—10).

In Jesus we have a better priesthood. He is the perfect High Priest, the one true mediator between God and humankind (Heb 8:6). He needs to offer no sacrifice for his own sin, because he is without sin (Heb 7:26-28). He is truly God and therefore has full and free access to the Father. He is God's last and best Word (Heb 1:1-4). Yet he is fully human, having shared in all our weaknesses and temptations (Heb 4:14-15). Jesus alone is fully able to represent both God and humankind with righteousness, sympathy and compassion.

In Jesus we share in a better covenant (Heb 8:6—9:28), the new covenant predicted by Jeremiah and now inaugurated by his death. Hebrews makes clear that this new covenant completes all that the Old Testament sacrifices pointed to but were unable to obtain. Christ entered not an earthly tabernacle, like the high priest, but into the Holy One's very presence (Heb 9:11). He entered not repeatedly but "once for all" (Heb 9:12, 26; 10:10, 12), to obtain an eternal redemption. He entered not with the blood of bulls and goats, which would never atone for sin (Heb 10:1-4), but with his own blood. All that the Day of Atonement, the high point of the Old Testament priestly work of atonement, expressed and promised Jesus has accomplished in inaugurating a new covenant.

In Jesus we have a better, once-for-all sacrifice. Jesus' sacrificial death was final because it secured what the repeated sacrifices of the Old Testament had promised. Hebrews underscores this glorious note of finality by speaking of Jesus, his priestly work finished, sitting down at the right hand of God:

After he had provided purification for sins, he sat down at the right hand of the Majesty in heaven. (Heb 1:3)

Day after day every priest stands and performs his religious duties; again and again he offers the same sacrifices, which can never take away sins. But when this priest had offered for all time one sacrifice for sins, he sat down at the right hand of God. Since that time he waits for his enemies to be made his footstool, because by one sacrifice he has made perfect forever those who are being made holy. (Heb 10:11-13)

Finally our author exhorts us—on the basis of Jesus' better high priesthood, our better covenant with its better promises, and Jesus' better, final sacrifice for sin—to approach the Holy One directly with "boldness" or "confidence" (another key word in Hebrews). Jesus' completed work on the cross gives us a tremendous liberty of access to the throne of heaven, the very place where the Holy One dwells in glory. No more need we hold back in craven fear. No more must we sinners approach only through the punctilious performance of rituals of sacrifice and the mediation of human priests. We all are invited to regularly do the very thing only the high priest was allowed only once a year under the old covenant. The curtain of the temple has been torn in two. All may enter freely and with great confidence that the Holy One welcomes them in the name of Jesus.

Perhaps this rich teaching of the epistle to the Hebrews is best summarized by its author when he writes about Jesus,

For this reason he had to be made like his brothers in every way, in order that he might become a merciful and faithful high priest in service to God, and that he might make atonement for the sins of the people. Because he himself suffered when he was tempted, he is able to help those who are being tempted. (Heb 2:17-18)

A Great Redemption

The remainder of the New Testament contains no similar thoroughgoing discussion of the Old Testament system of sacrifice. Like Hebrews, however, it sees the death of Jesus as God's means of accomplishing all that the Old Testament sacrifices and priesthood promised. The death of the Lord Jesus is the costly sacrifice that secures our ransom from the penalty and power of sin. He died as our substitute, bearing what was in all justice ours—the wrath of God that consumes and destroys sinners and sin—so that we might enjoy what was in all justice his—the status and enjoyment of being children of the Father.

The New Testament texts that affirm and allude to this gracious achievement of the Father and Son are too numerous to mention. But consider these central affirmations:

Christ redeemed us from the curse of the law by becoming a curse for us, for it is written: "Cursed is everyone who is hung on a tree." He redeemed us in order that the blessing given to Abraham might come to the Gentiles through Christ Jesus, so that by faith we might receive the promise of the Spirit. (Gal 3:13-14)

God made him who had no sin to be sin for us, so that in him we might become the righteousness of God. (2 Cor 5:21)

For all have sinned and fall short of the glory of God, and are justified freely by his grace through the redemption that came by Christ Jesus. God presented him as the one who would turn aside his wrath, taking away sin through faith in his blood. He did this to demonstrate his justice, because in his forbearance he had left the sins committed beforehand unpunished—he did it to demonstrate his justice at the present time, so as to be just and the one who justifies those who have faith in Jesus. (Rom 3:23-26 mg)

My dear children, I write this to you so that you will not sin. But if anybody does sin, we have one who speaks to the Father in our defense—Jesus Christ, the Righteous One. He is the one who turns aside God's wrath, taking away our sins, and not only ours but also the sins of the whole world. (1 Jn 2:1-2 mg)

. . . Because God is love. This is how God showed his love among us: He sent his one and only Son into the world that we might live through him. This is love: not that we loved God, but that he loved us and sent his Son as the one who would turn aside his wrath, taking away our sins. (1 Jn 4:8-10 mg)

The Revelation of God's Grace
Typically when we discuss these passages we focus on what was accomplished for us. And in all sober truth, the great realities of pardon from the just penalty due sin, release from the slavery caused by sin, and the turning aside of the wrath and curse due to sin are wonderful beyond our best and noblest thoughts. But these and similar passages place an even stronger emphasis on what the cross reveals about *God.* Indeed, the cross accomplishes what it accomplishes just because of the character of God that it reveals. At no point in creation or history is the reality of God's character, his holiness, more fully revealed than in the cross of our Lord Jesus Christ.

In the cross God supremely reveals the majesty and wonder of his grace, his overflowing, undeserved goodness to those who deserve only his severity. Notice that God is almost invariably the subject of the verbs in the New Testament's wonderful declarations about the cross: God made him to be sin for us; God presented him as the one who would turn aside his wrath; he did this to demonstrate his justice; he loved us and sent his Son as the one who would turn aside his wrath. He is the great author of pardon and redemption through propitiation. Like the Old Testament sacrifices that prepared for it, the cross of Jesus is a work of undeserved goodness focused on the Holy One's turning aside of his wrath against sin.

Three aspects of this awesome work of propitiation underscore its utter graciousness. First, the cross is God's *costly* propitiation. The costliness of this redemption magnifies the marvel of grace. Release from the penalty of our sins comes with a terribly high price tag. This costly price Jesus paid by pouring out his life in our place. The price was paid when he came under the curse of God that the law of God demands. It was paid when Jesus drank the cup of the wrath of God to its bitter dregs as he hung on the cross. This terrible cost was paid in full so that free grace might flow for the salvation of sinners.

Second, the cross is God's *self*-propitiation. It is all too easy for our thinking to go awry as we ponder Jesus' achievement for us. Unless we are careful, we slip into thinking of a gracious Jesus who intervenes on our behalf with a justly angry Father. But such thinking fails to observe the Father's initiative of love and the unity of Father and Son in the cross. It is the Holy One who presented Jesus to satisfy his own holy demand for full justice. It is the Holy One who loved us and sent his Son to turn aside his wrath. And the Son freely obeyed the Father, expressing his unity with the justice and mercy of the Father in the costly undertaking of our sin and God-forsakenness. This wonderful divine unity reminds us that it was not on some alien third party that the ax of God's justice fell. The turning aside of the wrath of God on the cross was brought about by God himself. It was a self-propitiation, the Holy One absorbing the force of his own wrath so that blessing might flow to those who deserve that wrath.

Third, the cross is a *full* propitiation. The biblical affirmations we are pondering make plain that the Holy One fully and effectively accomplished his gracious purpose in the death of his Son. The cross was not an isolated event but the central act in God's plan to save. It guaranteed the full completion of God's gracious purpose.

Unfortunately, modern Christians are apt to speak of salvation as something that God makes *possible*. But not Scripture. "Christ redeemed us from the curse of the law by becoming a curse for us," declares Paul (Gal 3:13). Or again, "When the kindness and love of God our Savior appeared, he saved us, not because of righteous things we had done, but because of his mercy" (Tit 3:4-5). Notably absent is any suggestion of making redemption or salvation merely "possible." Pardon and redemption are *realities* begun and completed by the Holy One in his amazing grace. We are saved from wrath and restored to fellowship with the Holy One not by some transaction with the Lord that he makes possible and we complete. We are saved only by the cross of Jesus in its majestic finality. And this is so not least because the wrath of the Holy One was fully quenched at the cross. No wrath is left for those whose place Jesus took on the cross.

> O Christ what burdens bow'd thy head:
> Our load was laid on Thee;
> Thou stoodest in the sinner's stead
> Didst bear all ill for me.
> A victim led, Thy blood was shed!
> Now there's no load for me.
>
> Death and the curse were in our cup:
> O Christ 'twas full for Thee!
> But Thou hast drained the last dark drop,
> 'Tis empty now for me.
> That bitter cup, love drank it up,
> Now blessing's draught for me.
>
> The Holy One did hide His face:
> O Christ 'twas hid from Thee.
> Dumb darkness wrapped Thy soul a space,
> The darkness due to me.
> But now that face of radiant grace
> Shines forth in light on me. (Anne R. Cousin, "O Christ, What Burdens")

"It is finished!" Jesus cried out in triumph from the cross. Nothing is left for us to add.

The Revelation of Wrath and Love
In the cross God reveals both the reality of his wrath against sin and the reality of his love for sinners. A full and gracious provision for sinners requires that both of these realities be taken into account. Normally we feel God's justice and love to be in tension with each other. But for sinners to live before the

Holy One, they must somehow be brought together harmoniously. Notice how Psalm 85 expresses this truth:

> You showed favor to your land, O LORD;
>   you restored the fortunes of Jacob.
> You forgave the iniquity of your people
>   and covered all their sins.
> You set aside all your wrath
>   and turned form your fierce anger.
>
> Restore us again, O God our Savior,
>   and put away your displeasure toward us.
> Will you be angry with us forever?
>   Will you prolong your anger through all generations?
> Will you not revive us again,
>   that your people may rejoice in you?
> Show us your unfailing love, O LORD,
>   and grant us your salvation.
>
> I will listen to what God the LORD will say;
>   he promises peace to his people, his saints—
>   but let them not return to folly.
> Surely his salvation is near to those who fear him,
>   that his glory may dwell in our land.
>
> Love and faithfulness meet together;
>   righteousness and peace kiss each other. (vv. 1-10)

It is supremely in the mighty sacrifice of Jesus on the cross that we see God's love and justice "kiss each other." And it takes us to the very heart of this majestic and gracious embrace when we see Christ's cross as God's appointed means for the turning aside of his own wrath against our sin.

In the New Testament's use of this concept of propitiation, witness is clearly borne to two great realities. One is the certainty and the seriousness of the Holy One's personal reaction against sin. The other is the greatness and faithfulness of the Holy One's personal love, which provided the sacrifice that would avert his wrath from men and women. Only this understanding can do justice to the cross as the central and richest revelation of the Holy One.

Consider what happens to our understanding of God when we allow propitiation to disappear from our understanding of the cross. The cross then no longer reveals the wrath and justice of God, only his love. In the minds of some this might be an advantage, but consider the consequences. On one hand we are forced to explain how forgiveness of our sins is not an act of injustice on God's part. How can God be holy and still pass over wrong? Does he not, on this view, wink at our sin? Does not God become a relativist, denying his perfect goodness and violating not only his law but also his character?

When the wrath and justice of God are eliminated from our understanding of the cross, the sacrifice of Christ becomes an act unworthy of the Holy One. But in Romans 3:25-26 it is clear that God's purpose in the atoning death of Christ is to vindicate his own just character and at the same time to declare the believing sinner guiltless before the bar of his justice. No miscarriage of justice is involved, no setting aside of the high demands of God's holiness, no winking at sin. "What then shall we say? Is God unjust? Not at all!" (Rom 9:14).

The just demands of God's holiness must be met when sinners are liberated from the penalty of sin. They are met in Christ's death. He became sin for us by bearing in his person the entire penalty due to us. On the basis of his substitutionary death he extends acquittal and imparts righteousness to sinful men and women. The mighty sacrifice of Jesus Christ reveals the seriousness, intensity and justice of God's reaction to sin.

On the other hand, when we lose sight of the justice and wrath of God in the cross, our understanding of the love of God is also distorted. Notice that John includes the concept of propitiation in his concept of the love of God: "This is love: not that we loved God, but that he loved us and sent his Son as the one who would turn aside his wrath, taking away our sins" (1 Jn 4:10 mg). When our understanding of the love of God is detached from the idea of propitiation, God's love begins to be regarded as an infinite expansion of human affection. Judgment is viewed as a temporary device of the "loving" Father instead of an expression of his holy Fatherhood. Little wonder that "love" goes thin and loses power. It has ceased to be understood as *holy* love. God becomes not only a relativist but also a sentimentalist.

This descent into sentimentality is one of the most striking aspects of our present religious pathology. What we are left with is a shallow, cute greeting-card theology, with trite slogans and poetic doggerel. God is only the god-of-happy-endings and warm, gushy feelings.

Listen to the repetitive lyrics of contemporary Christian music or the thousand and one bestseller testimonials of how my personal god (do we indeed own him who made us?) made me healthy, wealthy or wise. No longer the holy Father, God becomes a doting grandfather, pathetically waiting for us to give him the time of day, only one step short of senility. Or the Holy One is reduced to a cosmic bromide: "Take god three times a day and you will feel no pain." Or worse still, god is identified with our better self and our deepest childlike desires, yearning to break free from the smothering weight of adult repression and pathological guilt.

Such sentimentalized, greeting-card theology could not be more destructive of real faith. Notice how unreal it seems, how unrelated to the actual lives that we live. "We often seem to revere a god who is just too touchy-feely, too wishy-washy, too vague-hearted to be taken seriously in the real world where people work, compete, abuse each other, and eventually die—often without much dignity."[1] Such a god resembles the Cheshire cat's fading smile—happy but ethereal and unreal to the vanishing point.

Nothing could be further from the love of God as the Bible describes it. God's love is, by definition, holy love. It is so zealous for the good of the loved one, so consumed with passion for a sin-ravaged creation, that it blazes out in fiery wrath against everything that is evil. This love, this holy love, is what we see most clearly in the cross of Jesus Christ, punishing sin and rescuing sinners.

The Revelation of Glory

In the cross God reveals his glory. On the night he was betrayed our Lord told the remaining disciples, "Now is the Son of Man glorified and God is glorified in him" (Jn 13:31). He was speaking, of course, about his death. Just six days earlier Jesus had spoken of his passion with an urgent immediacy:

"The hour has come for the Son of Man to be glorified. . . . Now my heart is troubled, and what shall I say? 'Father, save me from this hour'? No, it was for this very reason I came to this hour. Father, glorify your name!"

Then a voice come from heaven, "I have glorified it, and will glorify it again.". . .

"Now is the time for judgment on this world, now the prince of this world will be driven out. But I, when I am lifted up from the earth, will draw all men to myself." He said this to show the kind of death he was going to die. (Jn 12:23, 27-28, 31-33)

Fasten your mind firmly on this fact: this painful death was not the pathetic end of a noble martyr. This death was the glorious triumph of the Holy One. Glory blazes out from this mighty sacrifice. When Jesus was lifted up on the cross, he was lifted up in glory. From this place of elevation the great enemy of God was dealt a mortal blow, his evil power broken beyond repair. Sin itself, the evil one's destructive weapon, was overcome. As Moses had lifted up the brass serpent for the healing of Israel, so Jesus was now lifted up for the healing of all the nations (Jn 3:14). Sin's penalty is paid, its grip is broken, its devastation begins to be reversed by the healing power of the Lord Christ as he draws all sorts of broken people to himself. So it is that the Holy One is shown to be all in all.

What a wonderful irony: the Roman instrument of pain and shame and defeat has become the place and the symbol of holy gladness and rejoicing and victory. There is enough noble mirth here to set the whole world laughing on into the endless reaches of eternity. For the Holy One will have the last word, and that word is *joy,* the joy that has been his eternally, and that he shares with his blood-bought friends. So it is that the worship of the myriad hosts of heaven focuses on "the Lamb who was slain" (Rev 5:1-14; 7:9-17).

"All in all" here is perhaps wider in its reach than we are normally accustomed to think. Characteristically we focus on the redeeming and healing power of the cross of Christ for individual sinners. And in all sober truth this is wonderful beyond words. So we sing, rightly and joyfully:

Bearing shame and scoffing rude,
In my place condemned He stood;
Sealed my pardon with His blood:
Hallelujah! what a Savior! (Philip Bliss, "Man of Sorrows")

But Scripture bids us think and rejoice in a wider frame of reference, for the glory revealed in the cross is the glory of the Creator of all reality. Christ's atonement ultimately extends redemption and healing to the whole of creation, releasing it from the alienation and the curse of sin. So the death of Jesus destroys the wall of hostility that separated Jew from Gentile and makes those who were aliens and foreigners into fellow citizens with God's people and members of God's household (see Eph 2:11-22).

If this most basic alienation among people is overcome in the cross, all other causes of estrangement and hostility will be overcome in the cross as well. "There is neither Jew nor Greek, slave nor free, male nor female, for you are all one in Christ Jesus" (Gal 3:28). And, more widely still, the peace that flows from Jesus' death will embrace the whole sin-scarred creation (see Rom 8:18-25; Col 1:18-20). The whole originally good creation of God has fallen under the curse of judgment. It is—to one degree or another, but in every part—twisted and ravaged as a consequence of human sin and rebellion. But in the cross is its release from bondage.

So it is that Jesus' atonement has individual, corporate and cosmic application. In the cross we look for the Holy One to make all things new.

The Revelation of God's Pleasure

From this perspective of glorying in the cross we can see, finally, that *in the cross God reveals the sort of life that he takes pleasure in: a life marked by glad self-abandon.* Jesus, speaking of the cross, said,

> The hour has come for the Son of man to be glorified. I tell you the truth, unless a kernel of wheat falls to the ground and dies, it remains only a single seed. But if it dies, it produces many seeds. The man who loves his life will lose it, while the man who hates his life in this world will keep it for eternal life. Whoever serves me must follow me; and where I am, my servant also will be. My Father will honor the one who serves me. (Jn 12:23-26)

The cross not only purchases our redemption but also provides us a pattern. Life in the light of the cross involves the central gospel paradox of losing life to find it. Says the Holy One to those delivered from his wrath by his grace in the cross:

> You are not your own; you were bought at a price. Therefore honor God with your body. (1 Cor 6:19-20)

> I appeal to you therefore, brothers and sisters, by the mercies of God, to present your bodies as a living sacrifice, holy and acceptable to God, which is your spiritual worship. (Rom 12:1 NRSV)

> Since you call on a Father who judges each man's work impartially, live your lives as strangers here in reverent fear. For you know that it was not with perishable things such as silver and gold that you were redeemed from the empty way of life . . . but with the precious blood of Christ, a lamb without blemish or defect. (1 Pet 1:17-19)

If anything of the majesty and wonder of the cross has gripped you, these words will burn in your minds and move you to renew your devotion to the Holy One. As someone has wryly remarked, "The problem with a living sacrifice is that it keeps on crawling off the altar." So turn aside now to glory in the cross by giving yourself to the Lord without reservation. Make the words of the Passion Chorale your prayer of devotion:

What Thou, my Lord, hast suffered,
Was all for sinners' gain;
Mine, mine was the transgression,
But Thine the deadly pain:

Lo, here I fall, my Savior!
'Tis I deserve Thy place;
Look on me with Thy favor,
Vouchsafe to me Thy grace.

What language shall I borrow
To thank thee, dearest Friend,
For this Thy dying sorrow,
Thy pity without end?
O make me Thine forever,
And should I fainting be,
Lord, let me never, never
Outlive my love for Thee.
(Bernard of Clairvaux, "Oh Sacred Head, Once Wounded")

What the Cross Reveals: A Summary

What, we might ask in summary, becomes of the Old Testament concept of
sacrifice in the New Testament, given the fullness and finality of Jesus' mighty
sacrifice on the cross? Remembering the theological themes that run through
the Old Testament teaching about sacrifice, we see, first, that the cross underscores and deepens our appreciation of the holiness of God. Focusing on
the cross, we see more deeply the blazing, inescapable justice and the amazing, overflowing goodness of the Holy One. God provided the lamb for
sacrifice in a way that answered to the deepest longing and need of sinners.
God the Son became man to seek sinners and die for them. We are stirred
to wonder and confidence, for "who can be against us? He who did not spare
his own Son, but gave him up for us all—how will he not also, along with
him, graciously give us all things?" (Rom 8:31-32).

Second, the structure of priesthood is transformed. Jesus is our high priest,
the one mediator between God and humanity. Because of his priesthood, all
of God's people enjoy freedom of access to the holy presence of God. In
ancient Israel the high priest—to say nothing of other Israelites—could only
dream of this freedom of access. We come boldly to the Holy One, where
he entered with terror. We come freely as the Spirit leads us, where he
approached only through a meticulously performed ritual. We come often, as
often as we wish, where he entered only yearly. For this reason the New
Testament abolishes the priestly caste among God's people and teaches that
all God's people are priests to one another under the Lord Jesus, our glorious
high priest.

Third, the cross achieves the atonement with the Holy One that the Old Testament sacrifices could only point to in hope. Jesus, in the infinite value of his deity, bears the just wrath of the Holy One against our sin in our place ("my God, my God, why have you forsaken me?") so that no wrath is left for me, but only the love of the Father ("it is finished!"). So it is that the New Testament rejects anything that suggests either repetition of Jesus' sacrifice or addition to it.

Finally, the New Testament speaks of continued sacrifice only as costly consecration and worship. Because of the fullness and finality of Jesus' mighty sacrifice, we are claimed completely by the Holy One. In profound thankfulness we offer all to him in a continual sacrifice of praise and worship (Heb 13:15), a life of active sacrificial service to others (Heb 13:16) and a costly giving of our material and financial substance in the service of the gospel of grace (Phil 4:18). Indeed, we offer up the sacrifice of our very selves (Rom 12:1-2).

I have drawn heavily—perhaps too heavily for some—on the tradition of evangelical hymnody to illuminate and drive home the message of the grace of the Holy One in the cross of Jesus. Unfortunately, more contemporary songs and hymns seem much less focused on the cross. This is a strange state of affairs for those whose rule of life and worship is "May I never boast except in the cross of our Lord Jesus Christ, through which the world has been crucified to me, and I to the world" (Gal 6:14). Here, then, is a place for a fresh outpouring of contemporary praise. May the Holy One send us poets and composers to sing as a new song to the Lord the old, ever-new glories of the cross.

Until then, perhaps we can still tune in to an old song of praise and devotion. The words of Isaac Watts's majestic hymn are the heartbeat of those who contemplate Jesus' mighty sacrifice. As you read them, pause to offer them as your own heartbeat to the Holy One.

When I survey the wondrous cross
On which the Prince of glory died,
My richest gain I count but loss,
And pour contempt on all my pride.

Forbid it, Lord, that I should boast,
Save in the death of Christ, my God;
All the vain things that charm me most,
I sacrifice them to His blood.

See, from His head, His hands, His feet,
Sorrow and love flow mingled down;
Did e'er such love and sorrow meet,
Or thorns compose so rich a crown?

Were the whole realm of nature mine,
That were a present far too small;
Love so amazing, so divine,
Demands my soul, my life, my all.
("When I Survey the Wondrous Cross")

11

THE FEAR
OF THE LORD

CAN YOU RECALL HOW YOU FELT WHEN YOU HAD THE OPPORTUNITY TO MEET A
Very Important Person? The thought takes me back to high-school days. Having won an essay contest, I was to attend the inauguration of the governor
of our state and be introduced to him and our two U.S. senators. You can
imagine that the whole affair was a "big deal."

I joked with my friends about the witty, irreverent and even insulting things
I might say to these "two-bit politicians." When it came right down to standing
in the receiving line, however, I fear I was feeling pretty nervous. My palms
were sweaty, my mouth full of cotton. I was afraid they would ask me some
question about my essay and I would proceed to make a fool of myself. Right
then I would rather have been somewhere else, though I wanted to be there
and was thrilled by the privilege that was mine.

Of course I was flattering myself outrageously to think these men would
know anything about my essay, let alone spend any time conversing with me
about it. After three hurried and rather perfunctory shakes of the hand, I was
whisked off to my proper station in life. But I will never forget the contradictory feelings the experience aroused. It was my first introduction to what
the Bible means by *fear*.

The Permutations of Fear

Perhaps, in order to understand the fear of God, it will help you to imagine receiving a gold-embossed invitation to visit privately with the president of the United States. Picture yourself flying to Washington, being whisked from the airport to the White House in a presidential limo, and accompanied by Secret Service agents to the door of the Oval Office. The door of the office is opened.

How do you feel? A little shaky, certainly. Thrilled by the privilege, wanting to be where you are more than anything. But also nervous, scared to death, wanting to run away as fast as your now-rubbery legs will carry you.

Perhaps this exercise in imagination can give you some inkling of what *fear* is in the Bible. It is that jumbled-up combination of thrilling privilege and appalling apprehension that we tamely call *awe*. And if we feel it upon encountering famous or powerful fellow humans, how much more ought this to be our most basic response when we encounter the LORD, the Holy One, the One who is truly awesome?

How awesome is the LORD Most High,
the great King over all the earth! (Ps 47:2)
Let them praise your great and awesome name—
he is holy. (Ps 99:3)

But we must not stop here, for we need to grasp two other aspects of "the fear of the LORD" if our understanding is to begin to be adequate. Another exercise in imagination may help. Picture yourself in relationship to the president of the United States again. But this time you are his personally selected emissary. He has entrusted you with very broad powers to represent both the country and himself. In the course of these privileged duties, however, you have become disillusioned with him and cynical about your responsibilities. You know that he isn't all the media makes him out to be. Really you deserve much more credit than you are receiving. He seems so unappreciative of the loss in income that this government service is costing you.

In a foolish act of deceit and rebellion, you give your loyalties to an enemy intelligence service, becoming a key player in a plan to discredit the president. At first this new way of life is even more fast-paced and exciting. It promises some vindication for underappreciated you. All it requires is constant deceit. The payoff promises to be first-rate. But ultimately you are caught in the web of deceit. And the proper penalty for treason is death.

Again Secret Service agents whisk you off to the White House, this time wearing handcuffs. Again the door to the Oval Office swings open and you march in to face the president. How do you feel under these circumstances?

Again the proper word is *fear,* but its connotations are very different. There is still an element of awe. But now the central feelings are guilt, shame and stark terror. All is hopeless. If the roof could cave in and cover you from his justified anger and your justified punishment, you wish it would.

The Bible does not shy away from this sort of fear. How could it, given its central conviction about the holiness of God and the horror of human sin? Jesus points to this awful reality when he warns us to "be afraid of the One who can destroy both soul and body in hell" (Mt 10:28). Clearly our Lord is not speaking about Satan, who has no such final authority. He is speaking of his Father, whose perfectly righteous judgment is a fearful threat to all sinners.

The writer to the Hebrews raises a similar warning when he reminds sinners who persist in their waywardness that what awaits them is "only a fearful expectation of judgment and of raging fire that will consume the enemies of God. . . . It is a dreadful thing to fall into the hands of the living God" (Heb 10:27, 31).

Pagan Fear Versus Biblical Fear

Some people attempt to ignore this aspect of the fear of God, insisting that it is just a holdover from primitive, pagan concepts of religion. But this will not do. Perhaps it would be instructive to examine the contrast between the pagan and the biblical concepts of fear.

In pagan religion the gods or spiritual beings were personified powers, the controlling essence of the forces of nature. As such, they were very potent. But they were also fickle, changeable, unpredictable and in constant need of appeasement. The root cause of the fear they engendered lay in this combination of power and unpredictability. You couldn't be too careful around these "sacred" beings, and it would be best not even to come too close. Notice that in this "fear," then, there was no moral content. The gods and spirits had no predictable moral character. Fear was human beings' spooky reaction to unknown, unpredictable potencies.

Now consider the biblical account of fear. It shares some of the sense of terror, but on a totally different foundation. This terror arises not from what is unknown and unpredictable, but from the known, absolute predictability of God's character. God is holy, unchanging in his judgment of sin and sinners. The central determinant of the fear of God is moral. Fear is not "spookiness" but terror in the face of God's just punishment of our sin, of our disloyalty and proud rejection of God himself.

These two kinds of fear, pagan and Biblical, are miles apart. One is the seedbed of superstition, the other the foundation of a moral universe.

Wail, for the day of the LORD is near;
  it will come like destruction from the Almighty.
Because of this, all hands will go limp,
  every man's heart will melt.
Terror will seize them,
  pain and anguish will grip them;
  they will writhe like a woman in labor.
They will look aghast at each other,
  their faces aflame.

See, the day of the LORD is coming
  —a cruel day with wrath and fierce anger—
to make the land desolate
  and destroy sinners within it. . . .
I will punish the world for its evil,
  the wicked for their sins.
I will put an end to the arrogance of the haughty
  and will humble the pride of the ruthless. (Is 13:6-9, 11)

While this is an unavoidable and even central aspect of the fear of God, it is not the last word. Let's return to our exercise of imagination. You, the traitor to president and country, have been exchanged for agents held by the enemy. After a long, draining interrogation, you have been left to rot in the enemy gulag. After all, who really has use for a traitor?

Suddenly one day, your guards clean you up and prepare to ship you back to the United States. En route you discover, to your amazement, that you have been ransomed from prison and given a presidential pardon. In fact, the president wants to talk directly to you.

As you wait outside the Oval Office, one of the Secret Service guards shakes his head in disbelief and informs you that in order to obtain your release the president has turned over his only son, a rising young military officer, to the enemy.

Just then the door to the Oval Office opens, and you face the president. Now how do you feel?

Certainly the old awe has not completely disappeared. And shame at the enormity of your treason has also not disappeared, even though the old terror at facing the one you betrayed could be set aside. But what must flood over you is overwhelming gratitude, love, trust and willingness to do anything you are asked to do. Nothing you can give in the way of gratitude and renewed loyalty could ever be enough, nor would you hesitate to give it.

This combination of emotions and commitments the Bible also calls "the fear of the LORD."

> If you, O LORD, kept a record of sins,
>   O Lord who could stand?
> But with you there is forgiveness;
>   therefore you are feared. (Ps 130:3-4)

> They will be my people, and I will be their God. I will give them singleness of heart and action, so that they will always fear me for their own good and the good of their children after them. I will make an everlasting covenant with them: I will never stop doing good to them, and I will inspire them to fear me, so that they will never turn away from me. (Jer 32:38-40)

> Since you call on a Father who judges each man's work impartially, live your lives as strangers here in reverent fear. For you know that it was not with perishable things such as silver and gold that you were redeemed . . . but with the precious blood of Christ, a lamb without blemish or defect. (1 Pet 1:17-19)

The fear of God, then, is a response of heart and life to God's revealed character that takes God with absolute seriousness. It is an unconditional reverence for and submission to his authority, majesty and goodness. Other self-serving considerations must be set aside; to fear God is to be absorbed with his holiness.

Do not call conspiracy
  everything that these people call conspiracy;
do not fear what they fear,
  and do not dread it.
The LORD Almighty is the one you are to regard as holy,
  he is the one you are to fear,
  he is the one you are to dread,
and he will be a sanctuary. (Is 8:12-13)

Abraham the God-Fearer
The greatest Old Testament exemplar of the fear of God is Abraham. His whole life was marked by a growing, reverent submission to the will and ways

of God. Of course Abraham was and remained a sinner all his life long. He sometimes fell into particularly cowardly and selfish sin. Not once but twice he lied about his relationship with Sarah, his wife, insisting she was his sister and exposing her to great risk to save himself (Gen 12:10-20; 20:1-17). Nor was he above trying to help God's promise come true by conceiving a child by his wife's servant Hagar. Then he compounded his error by allowing Sarah to treat Hagar ruthlessly.

Nor was Abraham always a model of reverence and faith. When God reiterated his covenant promises after Ishmael's birth and clearly specified that the promise of innumerable descendants would be fulfilled through Sarah, how did Abraham react? He laughed out loud! How could a one-hundred-year-old man with a ninety-year-old wife bear children (Gen 17:17)? Sarah was no better. When God repeated his promise to her, she also laughed to herself (18:12) and then denied that she had done so (18:13-15). When the baby was finally born, he was called Isaac, which means "he laughs." The Lord, who had said to the unbelieving parents, "Is anything too hard for the LORD?" (18:14), made it clear to Abraham and Sarah—and to you and me—who had the last laugh.

To Abraham's credit, he saw the wonderful good humor of God's grace and joined in the laughter. But the point stands: Abraham was no angel. He was a struggling sinner like you and me, declared righteous by God's grace (Gen 15:6) and through faith in God's promise, learning to live his life for God.

But what remains a wonder about this very ordinary man was his extraordinary God-centeredness. Consider the record of his life. We first find him living in Ur of the Chaldeans (Gen 11:31), a sophisticated, wealthy city-state. His life was obviously very comfortable materially, for he appears through the account in Genesis as a wealthy man. He was surrounded by the impressive kaleidoscope of pagan gods and worship practices, which in Ur centered on the great temple of the moon goddess. Into his comfortable, safe environment, an unknown God hurled the thunderbolt of his word to explode in Abraham's mind and heart: "Leave it all and go to a land I will show you, and I will bless you, make you great and through you bless all the nations" (see Gen 12:1-3).

Recall that Abraham had no Bible in his hand, no church gathered round him for support. He had no notion of where he was to go. His whole environment doubtless shouted out against the foolishness of God's call. All Abraham had was the command and the promise. And wonder of wonders, he moved out. He packed up his family and possessions and took up the life of a stateless alien. For such a man, can there be any doubt about what matters most in life?

The same spirit shines out in Abraham's relationship with his young cousin Lot. He settled a dispute between his herdsmen and Lot's by offering the younger man the choicest land with its notorious neighbors in Sodom and Gomorrah (Gen 13). Immediately he was forced to rescue Lot from the grip of an invading alliance of kings (Gen 14). And finally he interceded for Lot and the cities of the plain, pressing God to show mercy (Gen 18) and ultimately securing Lot's deliverance (Gen 19). Abraham showed himself in all these events to be a man who lived to and for his God.

The climactic point of Abraham's life before the Holy One came later, when God tested him. Abraham was commanded to take Isaac, his only beloved son, the child of laughter and delight, and slay him as a burnt offering (Gen 22). *Immediately* (v. 3) he set out to obey. Can you even begin to imagine the raging flood of emotion that this man experienced? As the two of them trudged up Mount Moriah, Isaac innocently asked, "Father, I see we have fire and wood, but where is the lamb for the burnt offering?" That question must have gone through Abraham's heart like a knife. "God himself will provide the lamb," was his answer (see vv. 7-8).

No one who has looked in his or her own son's face can fail to be overwhelmed by the unfolding of this incredible event. But this is not just a son. This is the miracle child, the child of promise, the child of divine laughter. How hollow and even bitter was the gall of that laughter on this black day.

On they plodded together. With each step Abraham's feet must have felt more and more leaden. The summit was reached. Father and son together built the altar and arranged the wood. The knots in Abraham's stomach must have been tighter than those in the cords with which he bound his boy to the altar. With a thought very much like "the Lord gives and the Lord takes away; blessed be the name of the Lord" screaming in his brain, this amazing man laid hold on the knife, ready to plunge it into the boy, the sacrifice that God had supplied and demanded.

And against all hope, God intervened. The angel of the Lord stopped Abraham's hand in midair and then pronounced God's approval: "Now I know that you fear God, because you have not withheld from me your son, your only son" (v. 12).

This, then, is the fear of God: to cherish nothing, not those dearest to us, not even God's gifts and blessings, above the Lord himself. Again, the fear of God is unconditional reverence and submission to God's authority, majesty and goodness. The confrontation between Abraham and God on Mount Moriah gives clear expression to this wonderful reality. Each of us must allow ourselves to be interrogated by this event. Are you a stranger to this kind of experience? Have you ever allowed yourself to stand thus before the Holy One? Do you know what it is to tremble before him? Have you climbed up your personal Mount Moriah with your most cherished things and relationships, and bound them to the sacrificial altar in the fear of the Holy One?

Slavish Fear and Reverent Fear

Some would seek to blunt the force of these questions by observing that the New Testament mentions "the fear of God" much less frequently and seems to make it a much less central concept than does the Old. Indeed, some people quote the apostle John, "Perfect love drives out fear" (1 Jn 4:18), to settle the matter. They assume that fear is a dark, primitive stage of religious consciousness that disappears when the light of the love of God shines into our lives.

But look more closely at what John actually says: "There is no fear in love. But perfect love drives out fear, because *fear has to do with punishment.* The one who fears is not made perfect in love." The key phrase for understanding what John has to say about fear in this verse is the one italicized. Fear has to do with punishment, with the righteous judgment of God. God in love has sent his Son into the world to bear that punishment in our place (1 Jn 4:9-10). No punishment remains for us when we trust in Jesus. He has borne it all, demonstrating the love of God for us. When we understand and trust that perfect love, we need never fear punishment. The fear of punishment is swallowed up in the perfect love of God. What a marvelous, liberating truth.

Frequently *fear* means this slavish fear of punishment. This sort of fear is strictly a natural consequence of sin. Adam, after the Fall, answered the Lord's question by explaining, "I heard you in the garden, and I was afraid because I was naked; so I hid" (Gen 3:10). Before he sinned, Adam had walked with the Lord in the cool of the day, but now he felt shame and fear. In the same way Hebrews speaks of "a fearful expectation of judgment and of raging fire that will consume the enemies of God," and adds, "It is a dreadful thing to fall into the hands of the living God" (Heb 10:27, 31).

Often this slavish fear and terror comes as a part of the punishment of sin. Says the writer in Proverbs, "The wicked man flees though no one pursues" (28:1), picturing the self-imposed torture of the guilty conscience. Thanks be to the Holy One for swallowing up this humble, slavish fear in the cross of the Lord Jesus.

But the fear of God does not have to do only with fear of punishment. It is also, most basically, an unconditional reverence for and submission to God's person, to his majesty, authority and goodness. In this sense the fear of God is *intensified* by the deeper knowledge of the love and grace of God that we enjoy because of Jesus' coming.

Fear played an important place in the life of Jesus himself, though he obviously had nothing to fear in the way of punishment for sin. Says Hebrews, "During the days of Jesus' life on earth, he offered up prayers and petitions with loud cries and tears to the one who could save him from death, and he was heard because of his reverent submission [literally, heard in that he feared]" (Heb 5:7). Thus the fear of God, as reverent submission to the will and ways of the Father, was a central reality in the life of the incarnate Son.

It is also to be a central reality in our lives. Meditation on the finished sacrificial death of our Lord drives out slavish fear of punishment, but it also motivates a holy fear of our majestic and gracious God. The words of the spiritual are deeply true:

Were you there when they crucified my Lord?

Oh, sometimes it causes me to tremble, tremble, tremble.

Were you there when they crucified my Lord?

The distinction between slavish fear and reverent fear and their connection to the work of the Lord Jesus also help us to understand why the New Testament speaks less frequently of fear. Generally speaking, Old Testament fear becomes New Testament faith. Coming to Christ, taking his yoke, learning from him, receiving the Spirit from God can be summarized in the word *faith.* And this is the equivalent of fearing the Lord.

All true faith, when its object is the Lord of all reality and glory, necessarily contains the elements of reverence and submission. And when this Lord of faith is come down from heaven, a humble-hearted man obedient to death on the cross, when faith is in Jesus crucified, it pours contempt on all our pride and calls forth from us an unconditional devotion. Not for nothing did Jesus instruct us that to save our life we must lose it for his sake (Mk 8:35).

This is how in the New Testament the fear of the Lord is faith in Christ. So the questions raised earlier stand, magnified now through the greatness of the cross. The Holy One has indeed supplied the Lamb and thereby presses on us the issue of the fear of God. Could he say of you, "Now I know that you fear me"?

To answer this question, it will help to look at the characteristics of the lives of people who fear God. Four qualities mark those who live in the fear of the Holy One: humility, obedience to the Lord, radical avoidance of evil and exclusive loyalty to the Holy One.

Humility

Notice how Proverbs links the fear of the Lord and humility:

The fear of the LORD teaches a man wisdom,
and humility comes before honor. (15:33)

Humility and the fear of the LORD
bring wealth and honor and life. (22:4)

Paganisms of all sorts, even the noblest sort, view humility as a vice rather than a virtue. The Greek word for humility in the New Testament was used to describe a vice associated with weaklings. Humility involved what we might describe as "having a poor self-concept." The reason for this attitude toward humility is not hard to understand. Lacking a supreme God, paganism always gravitates toward a humanism that glorifies the exploits of the wise and powerful. Human achievement, self-realization and advancement become the supreme marks of greatness. Meekness, self-sacrifice and humility are only barriers to the good life. They are the characteristics of "losers."

The paganism of our outlook is as clear as that of the ancients. We are convinced that pride is no problem for us. What everyone wants to avoid at all costs is a poor self-concept. We are into self-help and self-fulfillment. The Christian media moguls have discovered and proclaimed that really original sin is not pride but a low self-concept, and that God wants to restore us to high self-esteem and to feeling good about ourselves. Thus does a self-absorbed culture spawn a narcissistic religion.

Notice, it becomes a religious right and duty to feel good about yourself and strive for self-fulfillment. I wonder what Abraham might be muttering under his breath if he lived in our day. For the first casualty of this outlook is humility, and with it the fear of God. Hidden from us in our militantly "selfist" culture is the soul-deadening sin of pride.

Do you doubt that we have blinded ourselves by a proud spirit? Do you think that pride is no problem for us? We all need to think again. Consider the evidence being amassed in social psychologists' study of the phenomenon of "self-serving bias." David G. Myers has collected and synthesized this data in his important book *The Inflated Self*.[1] For example, most people see themselves as better than average in any trait that is personally or socially desirable. The College Board recently asked the nearly one million high-school seniors taking its aptitude exam to rate themselves in certain qualities compared to their peers. Sixty percent rated themselves as better than average in "athletic ability," and only 6 percent as below average. Seventy percent rated themselves above average in "leadership ability," and 2 percent as below average. In "ability to get along with others," 60 percent considered themselves to be in the top 10 percent, and a staggering 25 percent reckoned themselves to be in the top 1 percent. Less than 1 percent who responded rated themselves below average. Life in United States high schools must now be more wonderful and harmonious with all this leadership and ability to get along than what I recall and than the reports of school administrators suggest! These self-ratings, which are comparable to those of older people in other life situations, hardly reflect a plague of low self-esteem.

We also consistently overestimate how desirably we would act. For example, when residents of Bloomington, Indiana, were asked to volunteer three hours to an American Cancer Society drive, only 4 percent agreed to do so. But when a comparable group was contacted and asked to *predict* how they would react if called on, almost half predicted they would help. Many other streams of evidence could be added. We accept more responsibility for success than for failure. We engage in self-deceptive self-justification, believing that "if I did it, it must be good." We more readily believe flattering than self-deflating descriptions of ourselves. We remember our past in self-enhancing ways. We guess that physically attractive people have personalities more like our own than do unattractive people. David Myers and Martin Bolt conclude:

> It's true that high self-esteem and positive thinking are adaptive and desirable. But unless we close our eyes to a whole river of evidence, it also seems true that the most common error in people's self-images is not an unrealistically low self-esteem, but rather a self-serving bias; not an inferiority complex, but a superiority complex.[2]

> For centuries pride has been considered the fundamental sin, the deadliest of the seven deadly sins. If I seem confident about the potency of pride, it is not because I have invented a new idea but because I am simply assembling new data to reaffirm an old, old idea.[3]

If pride is, in its destructive essence, a distorted, inflated view of self, humility involves an accurate, realistic self-estimate. Gone are flattering half-truths and self-serving, self-advancing outlooks. At the heart of an accurate self-understanding is the capacity to see the self in relation to the Holy One. In that relationship one knows oneself to be a creature made in the image of God, a bearer of the divine glory. There are no false putdowns here. But one remains a creature nonetheless, a copy in finite dimensions of the great original and originating infinity of the Holy One. And, alas, the light of God's reality exposes evil, rebellion, moral and spiritual failure at every point in our life's journey.

As we seek humility, we need to be aware of two counterfeits. True humility does not involve false modesty. True humility does not mean that bright people must try to believe that they are really quite stupid or that handsome people must try to convince themselves that they are really ugly. Ironically, this sort of doublethink usually leads to pride in our better-than-average humility! True humility leads us to regard our talents and advantages as gifts to be placed at God's disposal for the service of others.

Still less does true humility involve self-contempt and self-hatred. It reckons with the twisted greatness of our human constitution, with the morally odd and monstrous turning into ourselves that is the fruit of pride. In fact, self-contempt leaves us still caught up with our own self, even if that self-involvement is characteristically too negative. Humility involves owning feelings of guilt and shame as real indicators of our moral and spiritual condition, like the warning lights on the dashboard of a car. To sit staring at the warning lights would lead to breakdown and destruction. The purpose of a warning light is to tell us to stop for repair. True humility, seeing our sin-ravaged condition, looks outward to God for mercy and, finding it, continues to look outward to serve God and others.

Thus true humility is more like self-forgetfulness than either false modesty or self-loathing. The great news of the gospel is that we sinners can truly live before the Holy One in awe and love. He frees us not from a low self-concept to love ourselves (Scripture *assumes* that we will love ourselves; it does not *command* us to do so), but from sinful self-obsession to love the Lord supremely and to love our neighbor as we love ourselves. The cross frees us not for the ego trip but from the false, inflated ego.

Obviously humility is no easy thing to acquire, but the two beginning steps are now clear. First we must admit that we are proud. C. S. Lewis notes, "If anyone would like to acquire humility, I can, I think, tell him the first step. The first step is to realize that one is proud. And a biggish step, too." Second, we must see the Holy One and ourselves in contrast to him. Again, Lewis notes, "He and you are two things of such a kind that if you really get into any kind of touch with Him you will, in fact, be humble, feeling the infinite relief of having for once got rid of [the pretensions which have] made you restless and unhappy all your life."[4]

Obedience

People who fear the Holy One are marked by obedience to all he commands. There is the closest possible connection between fearing the Lord and reverencing, taking delight in and keeping the law of the Lord. (See, for example, Deut 4:10; 8:6; Ps 19:9; 119:97, 120 [and throughout]; Eccl 12:13-14; Is 8:12-22.)

And now, O Israel, what does the LORD your God ask of you but to fear
the LORD your God, to walk in all his ways, to love him, to serve the LORD
your God with all your heart and with all your soul, and to observe the
LORD's commands and decrees that I [Moses] am giving you today for your
own good? (Deut 10:12-13)

Jesus replied, "If anyone loves me, he will obey my teaching. My Father
will love him, and we will come to him and make our home with him.
He who does not love me will not obey my teaching." (Jn 14:23-24)

The reason for this close connection is not hard to grasp. If we stand in
genuine awe of the Holy One, remembering the greatness of his majesty and
authority and goodness, the words he speaks to us will be of particularly great
importance to us. Indeed, we will tremble at his word just because it is *his*
word. We will honor those words as his guidance to us so that we can live
in his ways, obeying his commands, trusting his promises, believing his witness about himself and his ways with men and women.

The obedience we offer will not be legalism. There will be no thought of
bribing God with our self-achieved goodness. Rather, we will be responding
in gratitude (his goodness abounded to us in grace before we could even
think of obeying him) and humility (we do not know better than he does
how his creatures can live most fruitfully and joyfully).

Indeed, obedience under the fear of the Holy One will have a totally
different quality. It will not be marked by the foot-dragging reluctance that
so often dogs us. If we delight in his Word (see Ps 119:97, for example),
making it the object of our meditation and knowing the One from whom it
comes, we will see it as his fatherly instruction and guidance to his beloved
adopted children. After all, one of life's greatest joys is to know God's will,
to desire that will from the depths of our being and then to do it with all our
heart. If obedience is completely joyless and duty-bound, it suggests just what
strangers we are to the fear of God.

The life of reverent obedience to the Holy One, however, is no easy calling.
We are repeatedly told that the fear of the Lord is something we must *learn*
(Deut 4:10; 14:23; 17:19; 31:12-13; Ps 34:11). Reverent obedience does not
come naturally to fallen men and women. There are aspects of the fear of the
Lord that run counter to our instincts and social condition. So obedience is
often a very costly struggle. Like any new discipline, it is painfully difficult and
highly unnatural. We must unlearn old ways that seem very normal and appropriate. We must learn new ways, building up new moral muscle, strength-
ening what has atrophied. The pain and stiffness that accompany such moral
training should come as no surprise. To endure it all, we must keep our eyes

on the Trainer, reaffirming his wisdom and goodness.

Says the writer to the Hebrews: "No discipline seems pleasant at the time, but painful. Later on, however, it produces a harvest of righteousness and peace to those who have been trained by it. Therefore, strengthen your feeble arms and weak knees. 'Make level paths for your feet,' so that the lame may not be disabled, but rather healed" (Heb 12:11-13).

Radical Avoidance of Evil

People who fear the Holy One are marked by a radical avoidance of evil. Because evil is the very antithesis of all their God is and stands for, they give it a very wide berth. Indeed, they hate evil, seeing in it the destructiveness that brings upon evil and evildoers the judgment and wrath of the Holy One. Proverbs says, "Through the fear of the LORD a man avoids [literally, hates] evil," and "To fear the LORD is to hate evil; I hate pride and arrogance, evil behavior and perverse speech" (Prov 16:6 and 8:13; see also Job 1:1, 8; 2:3; 28:28; Ps 34:11, 14; Prov 3:7; 14:16).

Needless to say, the evil we need to set our face against most rigorously is not the evil that besets others, but the evil we find lurking in our own hearts and lives. We are called to "put to death" all sin (Col 3:5), to deal with it as a particularly vicious and deadly enemy. To speak of killing it suggests something of the difficulty of this task.

Jesus comments on the rigor with which we must resist the sin that besets us in Matthew 18:7-9:

> Woe to the world because of the things that cause people to sin! Such things must come, but woe to the man through whom they come! If your hand or your foot causes you to sin, cut it off and throw it away. It is better for you to enter life maimed or crippled than to have two hands or two feet and be thrown into eternal fire. And if your eye causes you to sin, gouge it out and throw it away. It is better for you to enter life with one eye than to have two eyes and be thrown into the fire of hell.

The vivid figurativeness of Jesus' teaching should not cause us to react against what he is saying. Notice the three issues he raises.

1. Because we live in a fallen world, there will be situations, events or objects that will cause us to sin. They will represent temptations that we do not have the capacity to overcome.

2. These "causes to sin" will vary from person to person. Our responsibility is to realistically and honestly identify what they are for ourselves. The issue here is personal honesty and integrity before the Holy One. We are not called to legislate for everyone on the basis of our own weaknesses, but to be vitally

aware of just those places where we are apt to sin.

3. Those things that cause us to sin are to be eliminated from our lives with the utmost severity. Jesus' language here is not to be taken literalistically; chopping off one's limbs actually would not stop the temptation or deal with its source. But that does not mean that there is nothing to be done, no radical surgery to be performed. Some will need to eliminate certain activities, drop relationships or avoid situations for the sake of their integrity before the Holy One. These things are not necessarily evil in and of themselves. Certainly hands and eyes are a part of the Holy One's good creation. But their effect on us is to cause us to slip into evil and away from our good Creator. What troubles us may be no problem for others. They may even ridicule us as zealots or fools. But mark it clearly, integrity before the Holy One is what matters most to the man or woman who fears the Lord. It alone is of eternal consequences.

In these days of easy relativism and the worship of personal "wholeness," such radical severity and self-denial seem bizarre and extreme. Rather than "fleeing lust" (1 Tim 6:6-12; 2 Tim 2:2), we stand around and seek to negotiate some acceptable compromise that preserves our wholeness. Then we are amazed to find ourselves trapped in a raging fire, as lust burns and consumes us.

Most notably in our culture, the lusts that threaten to consume us are easy sexual gratification and an insatiable desire for material possessions. The extent to which we are barraged by sexually explicit and titillating materials, particularly in advertising media, is dismaying. But despite this frightening pressure, Christian people seem relatively well prepared to resist sexual temptation, compared to their resistance to lust for wealth, possessions and comfort. In our world we are more likely to lose our soul because of greed, forgetting that Scripture warns us of its danger in the clearest of terms:

People who want to get rich fall into temptation and a trap and into many foolish and harmful desires that plunge men into ruin and destruction. For the love of money is a root of all kinds of evil. Some people, eager for money, have wandered from the faith and pierced themselves with many griefs. But you, man of God, flee from all this. (1 Tim 6:9-11)

In any case, our task is the difficult one of honesty before the Holy One. We must identify our besetting weaknesses and deal with them radically and severely in order to shun evil. Only the fear of the Holy One will give us the required spiritual and moral energy for this exacting task.

Exclusive Loyalty

People who fear the Holy One are marked by an exclusive loyalty to the Lord alone. Only clear awareness of and absolute submission to the majesty, authority and goodness of the Holy One—that is, only the fear of the Lord—allows us to love and serve the Lord with all our heart and all our soul (Deut 10:12-13). The fear of the Lord makes us able to fulfill the first and greatest commandment and to honor the central demand of our relationship with our God.

Moses reminded Israel (in Deut 8:1—10:11) that two impulses would cause them to desert their loyalty to the Lord. First is the impulse to declare independence from God, thinking that our efforts have brought us life and all its blessings. The Lord warns,

> When you have eaten and are satisfied, praise the LORD your God for the good land he has given you. . . . Otherwise, when you eat and are satisfied, when you build fine houses and settle down, and when your herds and flocks grow large and your silver and gold increase and all you have is multiplied, then your heart will become proud and you will forget the LORD your God. . . . You may say to yourself, "My power and the strength of my hands have produced this wealth for me." But remember the LORD your God, for it is he who gives you the ability to produce wealth. (Deut 8:10, 12-14, 17-18)

Surely we can see ourselves, given our time and our culture, as appropriate objects of this warning.

Self-reliance always engenders pride, a haughty self-absorption that makes us strangers to the fear of God and causes our ultimate loyalty to be placed elsewhere than in the majesty, authority and goodness of the Holy One. Over against this trap of self-reliance, Moses set the lesson of God's provision of manna during Israel's wandering in the wilderness. Daily God fed his people when they could not feed themselves, so that they and we might know that "man does not live on bread alone but on every word that comes from the mouth of the LORD" (Deut 8:3). At all times we are no less dependent than they were as they wandered through the wilderness.

Exclusive loyalty to the Holy One moves us to respond to the way things are in all sober reality. In this way the fear of the Lord causes us to live in reality rather than in the false world of self-flattering illusion.

The impulse toward self-righteousness also leads us away from a properly exclusive loyalty to the Holy One. Moses warned Israel against thinking that it was because of their integrity and righteousness that the Lord was giving them the land of Canaan. Not so! It was because of the wickedness of the nations of the land and *in spite of* their own proud and stubborn unrighteousness that they were to receive the blessing. Israel's history, like our history, was marked by rebellion and resistance to the ways of the Holy One. "He saved us, not because of righteous things we had done, but because of his mercy" (Tit 3:5). Self-righteousness always engenders a preoccupation with our own supposed achievements in goodness. So we are blind to our actual needy unrighteousness. We become strangers to the majestic, perfect goodness of the Holy One. Unable to see his blazing purity and ourselves in its blinding light, we transfer ultimate loyalty from him to ourselves.

Over against this trap of self-righteousness Moses set the lesson of the golden calf. Having just been delivered from abject, degrading slavery in Egypt by the mighty and gracious hand of God, Israel immediately yearned for return to Egypt and erected an idol in direct defiance of God's law. But for the intercession of Moses and the free, sovereign mercy of the Holy One, the people of Israel would have been consumed.

The same pattern of unthankful rebellion and restoration by grace was repeated at Kadesh Barnea, when Israel in fear and forgetfulness refused to enter the land. Said Moses to them, and no less to us, "You have been rebellious against the LORD ever since I have known you" (Deut 9:24). At all times we are no less dependent than they on the overflow of the goodness of the Holy One in grace.

O to grace how great a debtor
Daily I'm constrained to be!
Let Thy goodness, like a fetter,
Bind my wandering heart to Thee.
(Robert Robinson, "Come, Thou Fount of Every Blessing")

Seeing the Holy One in the brilliance of his goodness and ourselves as guilty rebels prompts exclusive loyalty to our God. In this way the fear of the Holy One enables his people to resist the pressure exerted by an alien surrounding culture.

Cognitive minorities are always threatened with extinction by cultural absorption. Israel was a tiny island of covenantal theism in a vast ocean of magical, mystical, powerful polytheism. The infant Christian movement was an even tinier island of messianic Hebraism in the confusing polytheistic world of the late Greco-Roman era. Almost every interaction with the wider social world tended to disconfirm these "minority" views. Doubtless they appeared narrow, provincial and hopelessly particularistic to their cultured and powerful neighbors. What keeps a person in the faith under these conditions? Nothing less than a vivid awareness of the mystery, authority and goodness of the Holy One, nothing less than the reality of the fear of God.

Moses pressed this on the Israelites as they were poised to enter Canaan in Deuteronomy 13. His basic thesis was "It is the LORD your God you must follow, and him you must revere [fear]. Keep his commandments and obey him; serve him and hold fast to him" (v. 4). He envisioned three very difficult test cases that would arise to threaten the fear of the Lord, and with it Israel's unconditional loyalty to God. A false, wonder-working prophet, a beloved family member (including even one's spouse or children) or a whole neighboring town might call God's people to worship other gods. In each case, Moses warned, this evil must be purged via capital punishment when those who were leading God's people astray did not manifest repentance.

Similarly, in the New Testament it is an offense of the utmost seriousness to rebelliously defect from the gospel by taking up the idea and ways of the surrounding world. The penalty is no longer capital, but the guilty party faces both removal from the fellowship of God's people and the threat of a more serious and long-lasting loss. At stake is eternal judgment. Paul says to the wayward Galatians,

> I am astonished that you are so quickly deserting the one who called you by the grace of Christ and are turning to a different gospel—which is really no gospel at all. Evidently some people are throwing you into confusion and are trying to pervert the gospel of Christ. But even if we or an angel from heaven should preach a gospel other than the one we preached to you, let him be eternally condemned! As we have already said, so now I say again: If anybody is preaching to you a gospel other than what you accepted, let him be eternally condemned! (Gal 1:6-9)

(See also 1 Cor 5:1-12; 2 Tim 3:1-9; Heb 5:11—6:12; 2 Pet 2:1-22; 1 Jn 4:1-6; 2 Jn 7-11; Jude 3-16; Rev 22:18-19.)

The Lord, the Holy One, will tolerate no rivals. Neither will his people if they fear him.

For His Sake and for Ours

These, then, are the qualities of the life of the man or woman who fears the Holy One: humility, obedience, hatred of evil, and exclusive loyalty to the Lord. Each of these qualities arises from the foundational reality of the fear of the Holy One. But notice, as well, that when we enter into and learn and thoughtfully practice these qualities of life, we are led more deeply into the fear of the Lord. So if we would deepen our reverence for the majesty, authority and goodness of the Holy One, we must both seek to meditate on his holiness and cultivate these qualities in the day-in-and-day-out business of living.

As I noted earlier, living in the fear of the Lord is no easy thing for sinners like us, living in a culture like ours. It can be painful personally, and it constantly exposes us to the further pain of being misunderstood. Why then should we practice the fear of the Holy One? Why not simply trim our sails and run with the prevailing social winds? What motivates and sustains us in the struggle?

Foremost in our thinking must be the blazing reality of the Holy One. It is true, whether we acknowledge it or not, that he is holy. The fear of the Lord is nothing other than the manner of life that arises consistently from this most basic reality of all realities. Any other way of life is an illusion, the opiate of the masses in our wayward, God-denying culture. Such an illusion is very dangerous. It whispers in our ear, "Relax. Don't be so uptight. All will be well." These comforting words are a lie, not least because no reality under-girds them. Over and over again we must remind ourselves, "He is holy!" We practice the fear of the Lord *for the Lord's sake.*

To reinforce this truth dimension, the Lord adds another, wonderfully encouraging factor. The Holy One promises to confirm the truth by rewarding our faithfulness with his tangible approval. When we apply our lives to living in the fear of God, we come to know more and more deeply the blessing of the Holy One. This blessing is wonderful. It makes the cost and pain of learning the fear of God seem like nothing at all. The psalmist encourages us:

Fear the LORD, you his saints [chosen people],
    for those who fear him lack nothing.
The lions may grow weak and hungry,
    but those who seek the LORD lack no good thing. (Ps 34:9-10)

So we practice the fear of the Lord for *our* sake as well! Wonderfully, truth and blessedness are coordinate realities. Psalm 112 in its entirety is a meditation on the blessedness that befalls the person who lives in the fear of the Lord. It summarizes its theme with these words: "Praise the LORD [hallelujah!]. Blessed is the man who fears the LORD, who finds great delight in his commands" (v. 1).

As we analyze the particular aspects of the blessing the Holy One pours out on those who fear him, we see joy, wisdom and justice. Each bears careful consideration and will require extended analysis so we can clearly grasp its connection to the fear of the Holy One.

The Way to Joy
Paganism boasts falsely that it brings joy: "Don't worry, be happy." This kind of happiness, like the word itself, is rooted in "happenstance" (the Old Eng-

lish word *hap,* or "chance"). Pagan happiness is a crapshoot, a random, superficial moment of pleasure, so it fades as circumstances change. And change they must. The dizzy, maddening pursuit of passing pleasure creates a tremendous din all around us. "Put a little weekend in your week," the commercial exhorts us. What it actually means, as all too many quickly discover, is "work a little harder for decreasingly satisfying pleasures."

Joy, by contrast, arises from within us and persists through all the changing circumstances of life. It is the inner quality of a life worth living. It is the quiet, confident possession of those who fear the Holy One. Consider the following statements about life and the fear of the Lord from Proverbs:

The fear of the LORD adds length to life,

  but the years of the wicked are cut short. (10:27)

The fear of the LORD is a fountain of life,

  turning a man from the snares of death. (14:27; compare 13:14)

The fear of the LORD leads to life:

  Then one rests content, untouched by trouble. (19:23; compare 2:19; 5:6; 10:17; 15:24)

Humility and the fear of the LORD

  bring wealth and honor and life. (22:4; compare 3:18; 11:30, 13:12; 15:4)

These promises should come as no surprise. Moses had promised, in a similar vein, that obedience to the Lord would yield a rich and fruitful life in the promised land of blessing. Conversely, disobedience was the way to loss and destruction under God's just hand (Deut 8:1, 19-20). Jesus asserted in like fashion to those being trained in the fear of the Lord that he had come to give them "life, life in all its fullness" (Jn 10:10 TEV). Indeed, our Lord struck his more fussy contemporaries as a person who was having just too good a time and was much too free about sharing real enjoyment with notorious sinners (see Mt 11:16-19). After all, his first miraculous sign was to bless a wedding celebration with outrageous quantities of the best wine (Jn 2:1-11).

No book of Scripture helps us understand the connection between joy and the fear of the Lord better than Ecclesiastes.[5] This statement will strike some as more than a little wide of the mark. How can a book that talks about life as "meaningless" ("vanity," 1:2) be about enjoyment? But perhaps we have not heard the Teacher's message on its own terms. Throughout, he is concerned to commend "the fear of the LORD" to his readers (3:14; 5:7; 7:18; 8:12-13), and his overall conclusion is particularly clear:

Remember your Creator

  in the days of your youth. . . .

Now all has been heard;

● here is the conclusion of the matter:
Fear God and keep his commandments,
   for this is the whole duty of man.
For God will bring every deed into judgment,
   including every hidden thing,
      whether it is good or evil. (Eccles 12:1, 13-14)

These are not the words of a cynic who believes in the meaninglessness of life.

How, then, should we understand what the Teacher has to say about "meaninglessness" and the enjoyment of life? Meditate on the key passage in the book:

● [God] has made everything beautiful in its time. He has also set eternity in the hearts of men; yet they cannot fathom what God has done from beginning to end. I know there is nothing better for men than to be happy and do good while they live. That everyone may eat and drink, and find satisfaction in all his toil—this is the gift of God. I know that everything God does will endure forever; nothing can be added to it and nothing taken from it. God does it so men will revere [fear] him. (3:11-14)

Notice the glory and plight of humanity in this text. God has made us with eternity in our hearts, with a spiritual hunger to understand the meaning of all things, to know and understand the ways and work of our Maker. Yet at the same time, such comprehensive vision is beyond us. We can never comprehend the entirety of God's ways and works. "Meaninglessness" or "vanity" is not a statement of either the futility of life or the Teacher's conclusion that nothing is worth living for. "Vanity" is the humbling truth that life in and of itself cannot provide the key to its own meaning, nor can it free us for real and lasting joy.

A fashionable and proud secularism that "brackets off" the God question in order to attend to the immediate concerns of life, has demonstrated the truth of the Teacher's insight. Starting from the transient flux of our life and times, we can never put life together meaningfully. We can only tranquilize ourselves with decreasingly pleasurable pastimes. Thus we avoid the question of eternity, which our own hearts press on at every turn. Apart from relationship to the Holy One nothing will ever make sense, and we find ourselves strangers to joy.

At this point, sadly, believers seem often to fall into the proud temper of our times. Knowing something of God, we begin to feel that our privileged place gives us access to more knowledge than we actually are able to possess. We dupe ourselves into thinking that now we *can* "fathom what God has done from beginning to end." So we abuse our minds and our relationship with the Holy One, making for futility.

The realities of life and death press upon us and destroy our illusion that we know what God is doing at any and every point in his sovereign plan. Yes, we may be assured that he is working out a plan, a plan for good ("everything God does will endure forever"; compare Rom 8:28). But *what* exactly he is up to, *how* precisely he is working for good in a given circumstance—these things are characteristically beyond us. The Teacher rubs our noses in the disappointments and perplexities of life (its "vanities") to show us our pride and lead us to the more modest stance of fearing the Lord.

From the perspective of "the fear of the LORD," we can affirm God as Maker and Ruler and Judge over all of life. Enjoyment of food, sex, family and work require proper relationship to him and obedience to his revealed will, because these things are parts of his wise plan and matters for his just judgment. Ultimately, "this is the gift of God." The capability to enjoy eating, drinking, riches, wealth and marriage is, in the Holy One's scheme of things, a gift from above given to those who live before him in humility, obedience and faithfulness (Eccles 2:10; 3:22; 5:17-18; 8:15).

This enjoyment does not disappear in the face of perplexity, disappointment and pain. These hard things too are under his good management. Joy does not arise from circumstances. It comes down from the Holy One himself. So it is that rejoicing in the face of adversity is the characteristic lot of those who fear the Lord.

The Path of Wisdom

The second blessing that the writer of Psalm 112 claims will characterize those who fear the Holy One is wisdom. Wisdom is skill, expertise, competence in the art of living. Above all, it is the requirement of a ruler or a leader: the ability to govern people, to judge and to plan. Wisdom consists of the ability to select both the best ends and the best means to achieve those ends. Given this "real world," everyday orientation, it is not hard to see why it is such an important quality.

This essentially practical bent of wisdom is not the whole story, though. The advice and generalizations of the wise entail confidence in the predictability of life. Wise sayings demand a basic confidence in the consistency of the physical and moral order. So there is an inevitable theoretical and theological dimension to wisdom.

Wise sayings that arose in the pagan cultures around Israel and that arise around us are often framed against the background of an impersonal fate and destiny. Or they may be expressions of a cynical rejection of any order or stability in life. One thinks, for example, of the definition of history attributed to Henry Ford: "the succession of one darn thing after another." But for a believer in the Holy One, it is impossible to speak of true wisdom and ignore the realities of God's creation and providence. So the Scripture speaks of wisdom as the source of harmony and coherence in God's work of creation:

> By wisdom the LORD laid the earth's foundations,
>> by understanding he set the heavens in place;
> by his knowledge the deeps were divided,
>> and the clouds let drop the dew. (Prov 3:19-20; compare 8:22-31)

> Who has measured the water in the hollow of his hand,
>> or with the breadth of his hand marked off the heavens?
> Who has held the dust of the earth in a basket,
>> or weighed the mountains on the scales
>> and the hills in a balance?
> Who has understood the mind of the LORD,
>> or who instructed him as his counselor?
> Whom did the Lord consult to enlighten him,
>> and who taught him the right way?
> Who was it that taught him knowledge
>> or showed him the path of understanding? (Is 40:12-14)

> But God made the earth by his power;
>> he founded the world by his wisdom
>> and stretched out the heavens by his understanding. (Jer 10:12)

So wisdom, above all, is an attribute of the Holy One displayed in his creation of the world and in his ongoing rule over all creatures. Human beings, as his image-bearers, are expected to live in wisdom, coming to understand, in a way consistent with their finiteness, the wisdom of their Maker. Both the physical creation and human life are to be observed and enjoyed and understood because they are the work of the Holy One. Faithfulness to him demands that we seek wisdom and order our lives by it.

But there is another side to this privilege and responsibility. If the whole of reality comes from and is ordered by the one wise and sovereign Lord, nothing is independent of him and nothing can be truly interpreted apart from him. After the rebellion of the Fall, however, we became all too prone to obscure this truth. As a result, there are two kinds of wisdom. On the one hand there is "worldly" wisdom. It ignores God and turns out, despite its attractive appearance, to be foolishness. On the other hand there is true wisdom. It comes ultimately from God.

So over and over again, in a variety of ways and vocabularies, Scripture presses on us that true wisdom has its foundations in a proper relationship to the Holy One (Deut 4:6; 29:29; Job 28:28; Ps 111:10; Prov 1:7; 3:5-6; 9:10; Jer 8:8-9; 9:23-24; 1 Cor 1:26—2:16; Jas 1:5-8; 3:13-18). True wisdom involves a rejection of false autonomy and a trusting acknowledgment of the Holy One at every step of our practical and intellectual pilgrimage. Whether our quest for insight and understanding is of a very practical, everyday kind or a more intellectual, theoretical sort makes no basic difference. Wisdom is to be found with the Holy One alone.

Where then does wisdom come from?
Where does understanding dwell?
It is hidden from the eyes of every living thing,
concealed even from the birds of the air.
Destruction and Death say,
"Only a rumor of it has reached our ears."
God understands the way to it
and he alone knows where it dwells,
for he views the ends of the earth
and sees everything under the heavens.
When he established the force of the wind
and measured out the waters,
when he made a decree for the rain
and a path for the thunderstorm,
then he looked at wisdom and appraised it;
he confirmed it and tested it.
And he said to man,
"The fear of the LORD—that is wisdom." (Job 28:20-28)

Everyone wants to excel in the art of living well. But unless the quest for wisdom brings us to our knees in awe and reverence before the only wise God, unless we acknowledge our helplessness to make ourselves wise and commit ourselves unreservedly to life in the fear of the Holy One, we will only show ourselves to be fools.

"The fear of the LORD is the beginning of knowledge." This motto of the wise man or woman appears in three different settings in the Old Testament wisdom writings, opening to us three different facets of the way of wisdom.

In Proverbs (1:7; 9:10) it stands at the introduction and climax of a profound meditation on the substance and importance of wisdom. Here it is a foundational and programmatic thesis that introduces and underwrites all of the subsequent bits of practical guidance. It protects wise counsel from slipping into mere shrewdness or unprincipled pragmatism.

In Job (28:28) this motto opposes the superficial wisdom of false comforters with true wisdom. This true wisdom—as James, the New Testament wisdom book par excellence, says (3:17)—"comes from heaven." More valuable than anything discovered by the art, science or technology of humankind, this beautiful jewel shines the more brightly for its startling contrast to mere human-made imitations.

Finally, in Psalm 111:10 the motto of the wise is quoted in the spirit of praise. With the psalmist, we marvel at the wideness of God's mercy and the bounty of his benefits. His revelation reverently received makes his people truly wise. So we join the cry, "Hallelujah! To the Holy One belongs eternal praise."

Marked by Justice
Third, Psalm 112 indicates that justice will be a mark of those who fear the Holy One. Justice is the most important quality of our lives in social relationships. Justice is characteristic of a society that God approves. Its lack calls down the judgment of the Holy One.

But what do we mean by this important word? In the Old Testament the Hebrew word characteristically translated "justice" *(mišpāṭ)* is taken from the legal world and refers to the declaration of a judge that accords with what is "right" and true. The Holy One, as Judge of all the earth, is the ultimate source and standard of justice. No amount of political or military influence or force can make just an injustice, a violation of his standard. Justice, then, is action that accords with the declarations and character of the Holy One.

A further element is inevitably bound up with justice: equity. Because the standard of justice transcends social status and cultural identity, all people must be treated by the same standard. There are to be no privileged or sentimental exceptions.

The people most at risk in any society are those who are weak and powerless. In the Old Testament those persons were the widows, the orphans, the resident aliens, the poor and the slaves. Such people are always at risk. For this reason, justice is most clearly tested when the weak and powerless are involved. The Holy One was particularly concerned for their welfare, that justice be done for them. He was their advocate as they faced the powerful.

So biblical justice involves a special concern for the weak and the powerless.

Note that both these elements—a transcendent, true standard and equity before that standard—are necessary to justice. Equity without a standard degenerates into the arbitrary tyranny of majority moral tastes. In such a situation, there can be no appeal beyond the social conventions we call laws. Law itself can be, and inevitably is, manipulated in the interest of the powerful. Meanwhile the whole social order slides into relativism and selfishness, and there is no social conscience to check the slippage. All have opportunity to practice injustice. On the other hand, a true standard without equity is hypocrisy. Unless the ultimate standard applies to all, paying lip service to it is the worst kind of rationalization. It is injustice, plain and simple.

The fear of the Holy One undergirds and reinforces both of these aspects of justice. The transcendent standard of God's law stands despite intense social, political or even military pressure for the person who reverences the majesty, authority and goodness of God. Consider the test case of the Hebrew midwives Shiphrah and Puah during the most oppressive time of Israel's slavery in Egypt. Pharaoh, the demigod sovereign of the ancient superpower, decreed that all Hebrew boys were to be put to death at birth. These women of God, however, defied his decree. Where did they summon such courage to act for justice? They feared God (Ex 1:17, 21), and thus they did not fear Pharaoh and his unjust power.

Equity before God's law is mandated by God's law. Consider, for example, the laws of neighborliness in Leviticus 19. This chapter treats a wide variety of cases under the general principle "Love your neighbor as yourself. I am the LORD" (v. 18). "Neighbors" here include the socially weak and disadvantaged. They are to be treated with dignity, respect, concern and justice. For example: "Do not curse the deaf or put a stumbling block in the way of the blind, but fear your God. I am the LORD. Do not pervert justice; do not show partiality to the poor or favoritism to the great, but judge your neighbor fairly" (vv. 14-15).

What prevents the cheating of the weak, the cursing of the deaf, the tripping up of the blind? Notice the majestic repetition of the phrase "I am the LORD" (vv. 3, 4, 10, 12, 14, 16, 18, 25, 28, 30, 31, 32, 34, 36, 37). And lest we miss this, the laws are introduced with this heading: "Be holy because I, the LORD your God, am holy" (v. 2). Even when no government official or neighbor sees, the Holy One does. When we fear our God, all people are treated with equity. Justice flowers in this soil.

The same picture emerges from the description of the blessings of the man who fears the Lord in Psalm 112. He is wealthy and living securely, in the joy of his Maker. But that does not lead him to cut corners or exploit others. Rather, he "conducts his affairs with justice" (v. 5). He is "generous and lends freely" (remember, no interest was exacted!—v. 5); "he has scattered abroad his gifts to the poor" (v. 9).

Boaz (in the book of Ruth) was just this sort of man—wealthy, contented, secure. But no hint of injustice or exploitation tarnished his prosperity. He enjoyed honorable and just relationships with his workers. His greeting to them, "The LORD be with you!" and their response to him, "The LORD bless you!" are no mere formality; rather, they evidence the respect, concern and fairness of God-centered relationships that transcend barriers of social class (see Ruth 2:4). And Boaz shows great generosity to the impoverished Naomi (a widow) and Ruth (a resident alien), going beyond the exact dictates of the law (Ruth 2:15). Justice is a fruit of the fear of the Holy One.

The Transforming Fear
We have covered a great deal of ground. That in itself should help us to see that fear is basic to the whole of life before the Holy One. We have seen what the fear of the Lord is: an unconditional reverence for and submission to God's authority, majesty and goodness. It is simply an appropriate response to who the Holy One actually is. We have looked at the marks of the fear of God—humility, obedience, hatred of evil, and exclusive loyalty. We have considered the very desirable fruits produced in the lives of those who fear the Holy One—joy, wisdom and justice.

These matters are obviously important. They are desirable and impressive. They inspire us to return with even deeper earnestness to my earlier questions: Are you a stranger to the fear of God? Have you ever allowed yourself to stand like Abraham, or Shiphrah and Puah, or Boaz, before the Holy One? Do you know what it is to tremble before him? Have you climbed your personal Mount Moriah and bound your most valued possessions or relationships to the altar of sacrifice? Have you looked the powerful defiantly in the eye in the name of the Holy One, trusting to his blessing? Have you treated your employees or those less fortunate than you with dignity, compassion and justice? Could the Holy One say of you, "Now I know that you fear me"?

No questions seem more pressing to me in our day than these. May God grant, in mercy, a return in our time to the fear of his mighty, sovereign, gracious name.

12

GLORY

AN INTERESTING AND HIGHLY SIGNIFICANT TRANSFORMATION IN MEANING OCCURS to the Greek word *doxa* in Scripture. In ordinary Greek its basic meaning is "opinion," "view" or "conjecture." From this root we get our English word *orthodoxy,* literally "right opinion." From this basic meaning, *doxa* came over time to mean "high regard or esteem," and its synonyms are *reputation, praise* or *fame.* Now, it is this Greek word that the translators of the Hebrew Old Testament chose to render the Hebrew word *kābôd,* "glory." And as a result *doxa* is also the New Testament word for "glory." From it we get the word *doxology.*

The transformation in meaning that occurs becomes clear when we look at the Old Testament's usage of *glory.* It never means mere "opinion" or "esteem," though that is the basic, secular Greek meaning. It is almost never used for the honor or praise shown to human beings. Another Greek word *(timē)* has that function. More frequently *doxa* is used for the honor given to God. But characteristically it is used to translate "God's glory." The meaning of *glory* in the New Testament is based on this Old Testament concept. So the meaning of *doxa* in the Bible shifts dramatically away from its meaning in secular Greek.

The reason for this shift in meaning becomes apparent when we investigate what the Old Testament means by "the glory of God." *Glory* (Hebrew *kābôd*) apparently had the original meaning of "heavy" or "weighty." "Heavy, man, heavy!" the beatniks of the late 1950s would intone in response to some striking or significant poetic utterance. *Glory* means something like our English *gravity*, literally "weighty" and figuratively "profoundly important or impressive."

The Weight of Glory

When we confront the glory of God, we are faced with a thing of literally overwhelming gravity. It was the glory of God that Ezekiel saw in a vision that inaugurated and continued to inspire his prophetic ministry. What exactly he did see remains a matter of considerable mystery. A movable throne arose out of a violent thunderstorm. The throne was supported by strange living creatures and amazing wheels that allowed it to move in all directions. Burning fire and flashes of blinding lightning surrounded the wheels, creatures and throne. Seated on the throne was a figure like a man, full of fire, glowing like metal, surrounded by brilliant light and a rainbow.

Obviously Ezekiel is groping to describe the indescribable. In the final analysis, words fail to provide an adequate statement of this reality. Thirteen times in these few verses he says *appearance* or *likeness* or *like*. But he makes it clear to us what he is describing: "This was the appearance of the likeness of the glory of the LORD." And its overwhelming "gravity" is also clear: "When I saw it, I fell facedown, and I heard the voice of one speaking" (1:28).

Ezekiel's experience is typical of the Old Testament portrayal of the glory of God. It is an objective reality that characteristically manifests itself visibly. It appeared in the pillar of cloud and fire that led Israel from the Red Sea to Sinai and on into the wilderness (Ex 16:10; 24:16-17). It came to fill the tabernacle (Ex 40:34-35) and temple (1 Kings 8:11; 2 Chron 5:14; 7:1-3) as a cloud and as a bright light. Specifically, the glory was visible in the Most Holy Place hovering above the ark of the covenant. This was the place of atonement, which established the foundation for harmonious relations between sinful Israel and the Holy One (Lev 9:23; Num 14:10; 16:19, 42). Sadly, Ezekiel also saw this glory depart from the temple (Ezek 10:4, 18-19; 11:22-23) and was left waiting, along with the rest of the prophets, for the day of future restoration when "the earth will be filled with the knowledge of the glory of the LORD, as the waters cover the sea" (Hab 2:14). (See also, for example, Is 11:9-10; 35:2; 40:5; 59:19; 60:1-2; Ezek 43:2-5.) The glory of God, then, is something we are to be aware of; it is meant to be "seen."

But these biblical accounts of the glory of God as a visible reality require some biblically based qualifications. The glory of the Lord is not to be seen in a casual glance. Indeed, it is not characteristically visible at all. Rather, it is made visible as the Holy One manifests his reality to his creatures. *Glory* belongs to the biblical vocabulary of revelation. We see the glory of the Holy One as he manifests his towering majesty to our sight.

Further, these wonderful visible manifestations of glory are invariably accompanied by words of explanation. The Holy One not only impresses his majesty on us but also explains the meaning and significance of what he shows us of himself. Not only does he impress us visibly with his greatness, but he also invites us into a significant measure of understanding by explaining himself to us.

What is seen is never the Holy One himself, nor an image of the Lord to be reproduced, but the impress and effects of his majestic greatness accompanied by his word of explanation and direction. So the visible manifestation of the glory of the Lord is not designed to suggest that we can trust our sense of sight more than our other senses. Nor are we to think that vision somehow puts us in touch with fundamental reality in some superior way. Rather, the tangible manifestation of the reality to our creaturely senses, along with the understanding that flows from the Holy One's words of explanation, constitutes the full wonder of the revelation of the glory of God.

Consider the towering manifestation of the glory of the Holy One that was given to Israel on Mount Sinai. As the Lord ratified his covenant friendship with his people, a visible display of divine holiness was given to the people in peals of thunder, lightning and a pillar of cloud and fire. The mountain blazed with fire to the very heavens. Here was a reality to be reckoned with—vast, beautiful, overwhelming and even frightening, the living God himself. Indeed, the mass of Israel was paralyzed with fear, and Moses' role as mediator was an obvious necessity. But what did the Lord want the Israelites to remember as they later recalled this display of the glory of God? Certainly they were to remember the greatness of God's holiness. But they also were to recall that they saw no form or image to be reproduced. And above all, they heard his voice, which declared to them the way they were to live before the Holy One (Deut 4:9-14).

As we consider what it means to live for the glory of the Holy One, it is very important to stress these twin ideas of *objectivity* and *manifestation.* The glory of God is awesomely, blindingly real, quite independent of our perception or orientation toward or against it. It is meant, above all, to be revealed. To live for the glory of the Lord is to act so that his glory may be manifested and made tangible. To glorify the Lord, then, is to draw attention to him, to act so that his inherent, towering majesty, authority and goodness become visible. To glorify the Lord is to think and act so that something of the pillar of cloud and fire that fell on Sinai in a blazing display of majesty will rest in perceptible reality on our lives. Clearly, this will be wonderful for us. But better still, it will point beyond us to the sheer wonder of our God.

What a contrast this is to what we call "values." Glorifying God is not what we characteristically mean by "valuing" God or having God as a "value." Values are our subjective view of what is important in life. Like the classical Greek meaning of *doxa,* values center on our opinions. The key thing is our personal act of evaluation and choice. So we clarify our values and make them visible in reports on the latest public-opinion polls. One characteristic respondent to such a study said, "What I think the universe wants from me is to take any values, whatever they might happen to be, and live up to them as much as I can."[1]

Small wonder, then, that in our highly individualistic society, everyone is awash in a trackless sea of relativism. Those of us who seek to live before the Holy One must resolutely set our face against the power of polls. Unlike the social world around us, we may not swallow the latest public-opinion poll, with all the moral and spiritual indigestion and malnutrition such foolishness entails. We must live instead by a compass that constantly orients us toward the true north, toward the blazing, overpowering glory of the Holy One.

The Excellence of God's Being

Look more closely at the precise nature of this compass we propose to adopt. What exactly is "the glory of God"? In the Old Testament, which gives us the basic biblical meaning, two central concepts are expressed. Sometimes one or the other is emphasized, but both are usually present in some measure.

First, the glory of something manifests the characteristic excellence of that thing. The cases where *glory* is used in reference to people or places make this aspect clear. So the "glory" of the rich man is his wealth (Ps 49:16-17; note the parallelism) or the "glory" of a human being is her "soul" or "heart" (Ps 16:9; 57:8), or again, the "glory" of Lebanon is its forests of pine, fir and cypress (Is 60:13).

The glory of God, then, is a manifestation of the characteristic excellence of God, his holiness, his overwhelming majesty, authority and goodness. This glory is to be seen in both his being—what he is in himself—and his works— what he does. His works include both his work of creation, so that "the whole earth is full of his glory" (Is 6:3; also see Ps 19; 29) and his mighty deeds of deliverance—in the exodus, God said, "the Egyptians will know that I am the LORD when I gain glory through Pharaoh, his chariots and his horsemen" (Ex 14:18). So all the nations will "ascribe to the LORD the glory due his name" (Ps 96:8).

Because God in his holiness is in a class by himself, the glory due his name is also utterly unique. His glory simply is not transferable to any other. Says the Holy One, "I am the LORD; that is my name! I will not give my glory to another" (Is 42:8). Or again, speaking of his work of redeeming and purifying his people, he says, "For my own sake, for my own sake, I do this. How can I let myself be defamed? I will not yield my glory to another" (Is 48:11). Indeed it is necessary for us to realize that in all his works the Holy One aims to display his glory, to open our eyes wider and wider to the utterly unique, supremely "weighty," blindingly brilliant nature of our one true and living God.

For some this biblical emphasis on the uniqueness and centrality of the glory of God strikes a discordant note. It is more of a liability than an asset, because it seems to smother all human concern for happiness and fulfillment. But consider again the question, What higher aim is there for the Holy One to realize than his own glory? "Nothing!" we must answer in all sober reality. All other answers amount to saying that our welfare or exaltation is somehow greater and more central to reality than God. Thankfully, because of his overflowing goodness, the well-being of his creatures is bound up inextricably with his glory. But mark it clearly in your own mind and heart: to elevate our happiness or blessedness or welfare above the glory of the Lord is to engage in a very subtle and insidiously destructive form of idolatry.

As a corrective, consider the concern for the glory of God expressed in the first half of Psalm 115:

> Not to us, O LORD, not to us
>> but to your name be the glory,
>> because of your love and faithfulness.
>
> Why do the nations say,
>> "Where is their God?"
> Our God is in heaven;
>> he does whatever pleases him.
>> But their idols are silver and gold,
>> made by the hands of men.
> They have mouths, but cannot speak,

eyes, but they cannot see;
they have ears, but cannot hear,
   noses, but they cannot smell;
they have hands, but cannot feel,
   feet, but they cannot walk;
   nor can they utter a sound with their throats.
Those who make them will be like them,
   and so will all who trust in them. (vv. 1-8)

Derek Kidner, commenting on this psalm, goes to the heart of the matter:

> The pagan's pride in what he can see, and his contempt for what he cannot (which are modern attitudes as well as ancient), are flung back at him. A God too great to tie down to any image or even to earth itself, who is not the prisoner of circumstances but their master, is a God to glory in. And He is *our God,* not in the petty sense in which the heathen have *their idols*—all their own work!—but in the personal bond of "steadfast love and . . . faithfulness" (*cf.* verse 1).
>
> The caustic catalogue of 4-7, like the work-study on god-making in Isaiah 44:12ff., or on god-transport in Isaiah 46, needs no sermonizing to make its point: the facts are enough. It is one of the places where Scripture, like the child in the story of the Emperor's New Clothes, takes a cool stare at what the world does not care to admit.[2]

Reflecting soberly and deeply on these things has a way of turning reality right-side up. Uniquely and supremely, the Holy One is "the God of glory" (Ps 29:3). "The LORD Almighty—he is the King of glory" (Ps 24:10). God's glory, then, manifests his characteristic excellence, his holiness.

God's Holy Presence

There is a second aspect associated with the Old Testament concept of the glory of God: the presence of the Holy One with and in the midst of his people. The Lord is "the Holy One of Israel" (Is 41:16). The personal presence of the Lord himself is most centrally what the tabernacle was all about. Nowhere is this stated more clearly than in Exodus 29:42-46, where the Lord says of the tabernacle, "There I will meet you and speak to you; there also I will meet with the Israelites, and the place will be consecrated by my glory. . . . Then I will dwell [tabernacle] among the Israelites and be their God. They will know that I am the LORD their God, who brought them out of Egypt so that I might dwell among them. I am the LORD their God."

Interestingly, one of the Hebrew names for the tent sanctuary of God was *mĭškān,* taken from the verb *šākan,* "to tent, dwell, tabernacle." The normal Hebrew verb used to speak of a permanent dwelling was *yāšab,* "to sit or dwell." This verb is used whenever the Old Testament speaks of the Lord dwelling in heaven. But invariably when the text speaks of the Lord's dwelling with humankind on the earth or in the tabernacle, the verb used is *šākan.* These two verbs thus seem to contrast God's transcendence *(yāšab),* the permanent, more basic truth about the Holy One, with God's immanence *(šākan),* his gracious coming to his people. In this way a deeper sense of the closeness and active presence of God was given to his people.[3]

One exception to this distinction should be noted. The verb *yāšab* and its derivatives were used to express the fact that God "is enthroned [seated] between the cherubim" (1 Sam 4:4; 2 Sam 6:2; 1 Chron 13:6; Ps 99:1; Is 37:16). This phrase refers to the ark of the covenant, which was overshadowed by carved statues of two cherubim. Here was the mercy seat, the place of atonement, where the Holy One in grace had made provision for the sins of his people. At this place was to be found the most intimate and enduring expression of God's nearness and dynamic presence.[4]

When the Holy One draws near to manifest his holiness to his people, there are three characteristic consequences. First his people are overwhelmed. What they "see" is often fascinating and incredibly beautiful. But initially they are shattered and find themselves on their face. Ezekiel, for example, "saw the wheel, way up in the middle of the air," as the spiritual says. It was a sight, as he recalls it, of great complexity and beauty. But his immediate response was not fascination. He found himself prostrate before the glory: "when I saw it, I fell facedown" (Ezek 1:28). Similarly, when the fiery glory-cloud descended on Mount Sinai as the Holy One ratified his covenant with Israel, the people did not respond with an enchanted "Wow!" "They trembled with fear" (Ex 20:18).

Second, God's people are challenged to know and obey the Holy One. The visual phenomenon never stands alone. It is always accompanied by a word from the Lord of explanation and instruction designed to establish relationship and fellowship. For example, recounting the shattering events at Mount Sinai, Moses says,

> You came near and stood at the foot of the mountain while it blazed with fire to the very heavens, with black clouds and deep darkness. Then the LORD spoke to you out of the fire. You heard the sound of words but saw no form; there was only a voice. He declared to you his covenant, the Ten Commandments, which he commanded you to follow and then wrote them on two stone tablets. (Deut 4:11-13)

The glory-cloud above the ark of the covenant in the tabernacle was not principally for a show of beauty or to attract attention. "There," says the Holy One to Moses, "I will meet with you and give you my commands for the Israelites" (Ex 25:22). Ezekiel's experience follows the same pattern. Having fallen on his face before God's movable glory-throne, he says, "I heard the voice of one speaking" (Ezek 1:28). There follows a dialogue in which his prophetic ministry is commissioned (2:1-8) and his prophetic message is imparted (2:9—3:27).

It is impossible to overemphasize the importance of this pattern. When the Holy One draws near, it is never just to leave an overwhelming impression. Rather, he seeks the friendship and fellowship of sinful men and women. To that end he instructs us, extending himself in grace to establish a relationship based not on our impressions and intuitions, but on understanding and rational clarity. He genuinely wants us, within the limits of our creatureliness, to understand what he is like so that we may enjoy a genuine person-to-person intimacy. In addition, his words on these occasions where he manifests his glory contain an element of challenge, command and commissioning. The Holy One invites us not only to *understanding* but also to the kind of *living* that sustains a deepening fellowship. In the display of his glory, the Holy One always gives us understanding of who he is and what his will is, to further his gracious friendship with us. So it is that knowledge and obedience are bound together with the glory of God.

Third, his people recognize that God's glory (the holy nearness of the Holy One) is their own glory (their characteristic excellence). By the display of his glory, the Holy One in sovereign goodness draws near his people to lead them and bless them. The glory-cloud and fire, which attested to the presence of the tabernacling God, became the glory of the people of God.

Moses recognized this from the very beginning. After the disaster of the golden calf, the Lord promised him, "My Presence will go with you, and I will give you rest" (Ex 33:14). Moses responded, "What else will distinguish me and your people from all the other people on the face of the earth?" (33:16).

When the construction and consecration of the tabernacle were completed, the Lord kept this promise in spectacular fashion.

Then the cloud covered the Tent of Meeting, and the glory of the LORD filled the tabernacle. . . . In all the travels of the Israelites, whenever the cloud lifted from above the tabernacle, they would set out; but if the cloud did not lift, they did not set out—until the day it lifted. So the cloud of the LORD was over the tabernacle by day, and fire was in the cloud by night, in the sight of all the house of Israel during all their travels. (Ex 40:34, 36-38)

Nothing could be more important to God's people than the fact that the Holy One was with them.

The Departure of God's Glory

This same concern for the visible manifestation of the nearness of the Holy One was central to the construction and dedication of the temple in Solomon's day. When the priests concluded their offerings of consecration, the glory-cloud filled the house. Such gravity was upon the place that the priests could not continue their service, "for the glory of the LORD filled his temple" (see 1 Kings 8:1-11). The wonder of the occasion was captured by Solomon in his great prayer of dedication. In an outburst of elevated praise, he cried,

O LORD, God of Israel, there is no God like you in heaven above or on earth below—you who keep your covenant of love with your servants who continue wholeheartedly in your way. . . . But will God really dwell on earth? The heavens, even the highest heaven, cannot contain you. How much less this temple I have built! Yet give attention to your servant's prayer and his plea for mercy, O LORD my God. . . . May your eyes be open toward this temple night and day, this place of which you said, "My Name shall be there." . . . Hear the supplication of your servant and of your people Israel when they pray toward this place. Hear from heaven, your dwelling place, and when you hear, forgive. (1 Kings 8:23, 27-30)

Conversely, the departure of God's glory from his people was a disaster. We need to grasp how deeply sad was the departure of the glory of God that Ezekiel witnessed. Ezekiel was transported in a vision to the temple in Jerusalem (8:2-4). There he witnessed the horrible sins of Judah, committed right in the house where God's glory was to be visible. Visible, instead, were such "utterly detestable things" as "the image of jealousy" (perhaps goddess Asherah poles—see 2 Chron 33:7, 15) erected in the temple (8:3), animal worship (8:7-13), women weeping in sympathetic magic for Tammuz, the Sumerian god of vegetation (8:14-15), and the worship of the sun (8:16-18). These same idolaters also filled the nation with violence and oppression (8:17).

There was only one possible response to such confusion and rejection of the Holy One: judgment. "Therefore I will deal with them in anger; I will not look on them with pity or spare them. Although they shout in my ears, I will not listen" (8:18). This judgment was made visible to Ezekiel: "Then the glory of the LORD departed from over the threshold of the temple" (10:18). For Judah, its government, its religious instructors, its false religion, it was all over. The glory had departed.

But this tragedy of the departure of God's glory in judgment was not to be the final word. During the days of exile, the Holy One himself would be the real temple for the remnant of true believers (Ezek 11:16-20). Men and women would thus realize that the nearness of the Lord was more important than buildings and all the external trappings of religion. And beyond the exile, at some point in the future, the Lord would do a work of inner renewal in his people. So radical a transformation would be effected that Ezekiel referred to it as a "new spirit," "an undivided heart" and a "heart of flesh" as opposed to an old stony heart (11:19). This transformation in spiritual depth would enable God's people to keep his law eagerly and would restore to them the lost nearness of the Holy One ("I will be their God," 11:20).

Thus Ezekiel shares with others of the prophets the hope of a final, triumphant revelation of God's glory. This victorious act of the Holy One would transform his ancient people, gather the Gentiles in to share the blessedness of Israel, judge and punish all people, and usher in the new heavens and earth. Typical of this vision of hope and glory is the conclusion of Isaiah's prophecies:

And I, because of their actions and their imaginations, am about to come and gather all nations and tongues, and they will come and see my glory.

I will set a sign among them, and I will send some of those who survive to the nations . . . to the distant islands that have not heard of my fame or seen my glory. They will proclaim my glory among the nations. And they will bring all your brothers, from all the nations, to my holy mountain in Jerusalem as an offering to the LORD. . . .

As the new heavens and the new earth that I make will endure before me . . . so will your name and descendants endure. From one New Moon to another and from one Sabbath to another, all mankind will come and bow down before me. . . . And they will go out and look upon the dead bodies of those who rebelled against me: their worm will not die, nor will their fire be quenched, and they will be loathsome to all mankind. (Is 66:18-20, 22-24)

(See also Jer 30—31; Ezek 37:15-28; Dan 2; Joel 2:1-2; Amos 9:11-15; Micah 4—5; 7:8-9.)

The Lord of Glory

From this unreached promise and hope, it seems natural to turn to the New Testament. There *glory* has the same twofold meaning of "manifestation" and "presence." But a new orientation is given with the coming of Jesus. He is the "sign" that Isaiah promised would be sent in the midst of Israel, which would transform all things and set off a new epoch in the glory of God. All now revolves around "the Lord of glory" (1 Cor 2:8).

Nowhere is this focusing of the glory of God in Jesus more clearly seen than in the transfiguration (Mt 17:1-18; Mk 9:2-8; Lk 9:28-36). Following Peter's confession ("you are the Christ") and the Lord's first prediction of his passion, Jesus took Peter, James and John up onto a mountain to pray. What happened—though it clearly defies precise description—is that "they saw his glory" (Lk 9:32). Note the similarities to Old Testament accounts of the revelation of God's glory. Jesus' divine majesty shone out in great brightness and splendor. The bright cloud descended over the whole scene, just as the glory-cloud descended on Mount Sinai. Then the voice came from heaven with its word of interpretation ("this is my Son, whom I have chosen") and command ("listen to him"). The presence of two great Old Testament prophetic figures (Moses and Elijah) and their discussion of "his departure [exodus of liberation], which he was about to bring to fulfillment at Jerusalem" (Lk 9:31), stress the connection to the prophetic promise and its centering in the person and work of the Lord Jesus.

Recalling this wonderful event, Peter lays particular emphasis on the voice from heaven (2 Pet 1:17-18) and quite naturally is led to reflect on the foundational importance of the prophetic word for our lives. "We have the word of the prophets made more certain, and you will do well to pay attention to it, as to a light shining in a dark place, until the day dawns and the morning star rises" (2 Pet 1:19).

To Moses' appeal to the Holy One, "Show me your glory" (Ex 33:18), the New Testament responds, "In the beginning was the Word, and the Word was with God, and the Word was God. . . . The Word became flesh and made his dwelling [literally, tabernacled] among us. We have seen his glory, the glory of the One and Only, who came from the Father, full of grace and truth" (Jn 1:1, 14).

Whether speaking of his earthly life (Lk 9:32; Jn 1:14; 2:11; 1 Cor 2:8), his exalted existence (Lk 9:32; Jn 17:5; Rom 8:17; Phil 3:21; 2 Thess 2:14; 1 Tim 3:16), his return (Mt 16:27; 24:30; Mk 8:38; 13:26; Lk 9:26; 21:7; Tit 2:13; 1 Pet 4:13), his preexistence (Jn 12:41; 17:5) or his very being (Jn 17:22, 24; 2 Cor 3:18; 4:4, 6; 2 Thess 2:14), the New Testament pours forth descriptions of Jesus as marked by glory, the glory that is uniquely and specifically the Holy One's alone.

Two further features of the New Testament presentation of glory follow from this focusing of glory in Jesus. First, those who are united to Jesus by grace through faith now share in Jesus' glory. Says Jesus in his great high-priestly prayer, "I have given them the glory that you gave me, that they may be one as we are one" (Jn 17:22; see also Rom 8:30; 2 Cor 3:18). Notice that this possession is a corporate one, realized in the unity of his followers, a unity that includes both Jews and Gentiles in fulfillment of the hope of the prophets. There is no atomic individualism here.

For this reason the community of believers in Jesus becomes the temple, the new place where the glory of God dwells (1 Cor 3:16-17; Eph 2:19-22; 1 Pet 2:4-6). Our present sharing in the glory of God is only partial and anticipatory. But the day is coming when the full extent of the prophetic hope will be realized. That will be the true day of glory for the Lord and his people (Rom 8:17-18, 21; 1 Cor 2:7; 2 Cor 4:17; Phil 3:21; 1 Thess 2:12; Heb 2:10; 1 Pet 5:1, 4, 10). Having been given an anticipatory share in the glory of God, we now live with "the hope of glory" (Col 1:27; see also Eph 1:18; 2 Thess 2:14; 2 Tim 2:10).

Second, the New Testament has a distinct distrust of and distaste for the fame and glory of this world. When the Lord of glory is a man from very humble origins, marked by gentleness, meekness and love for enemies, whose calling is to suffer at the hand of the mighty, something is going on that is strange by normal human standards. Indeed, the whole concept of glory is being restored to its true shape. God is being restored to his proper place at the center of all things. The proud glory-seeking of men and women is seen for the folly and the travesty it truly is. It is vain glory. The Holy One is both the proper object (glory *to* God our Maker as praise) and subject (glory *from* God our Judge as fame and honor) of true glory.

In a dispute with his scribal adversaries, Jesus presses home this point when he says,

> I do not accept praise [glory] from men, but I know you. I know that you do not have the love of God in your hearts. I have come in my Father's name, and you do not accept me; but if someone else comes in his own name, you will accept him. How can you believe if you accept praise [glory] from one another, yet make no effort to obtain the praise [glory] that comes from the only God? (Jn 5:41-44)

Here, then, is the glory of God: it is nothing other than the wonderful, manifested nearness of the Holy One. His holiness is impressed on all he does, so that his whole creation declares that glory. But in a fallen, disjointed creation, that glory is centrally focused in Jesus. The Holy One comes near as a sign of his intention to restore and bless. Those who welcome this gracious initiative of the Holy One are the people of God. As they are one with Jesus and one another, they share in the glory of God, the temple where he dwells by his Spirit. This sign reaches forward to the Holy One's restoration of all things in a new heaven and earth where all will be glory.

Giving Glory to God

What does it mean, then, to *glorify* God? It should be clear by now that a perception of the excellence and the nearness of the Holy One is the soil from which the glorification of God grows. When we reckon deeply with the towering, blazing actuality of the Lord's holiness and presence, two conclusions become inescapable: (1) God's glory is the most important factor in all things, and therefore (2) our central aspiration and consuming passion must be to make that glory visible in every area of our lives.

Depth is added to this passion when we realize that the Holy One, the God of transcendent and boundless power, authority and goodness, not only claims us as our Maker but has also reclaimed us from our rebellion and sin by grace in his Son. So Paul urges the wayward Corinthians, "You are not your own; you were bought at a price. Therefore honor [glorify] God with your body" (1 Cor 6:19-20). Note that he says "with your body." In the immediate context, Paul is urging the decisive avoidance of sexual immorality. But "the body" in Paul's view is our whole person as it operates in God's good (if fallen) creation. It relates not just to distinctly religious or sacred dimensions of life, but to all of life in the creation of the Holy One.

So to glorify God is to live with such a passionate devotion to the Holy One, his person, his purpose and his praise, that his glory will be made apparent in all of life to all people. The classic description of this sort of life was given by J. C. Ryle, when he described *zeal* in the following terms:

Zeal in religion is a burning desire to please God, to do His will, and to advance His glory in the world in every possible way. It is a desire which no man feels by nature—which the Spirit puts in the heart of every believer when he is converted but which some believers feel so much more strongly than others that they alone deserve to be called "zealous" men. . . .

A zealous man in religion is pre-eminently a man of one thing. It is not enough to say that he is earnest, hearty, uncompromising, thorough-going, whole-hearted, fervent in spirit. He only sees one thing, he cares for one thing, he lives for one thing, he is swallowed up in one thing; and that one thing is to please God. Whether he lives, or whether he dies—whether he has health, or whether he has sickness—whether he is rich or whether he is poor—whether he pleases man, or whether he gives offense—whether he is thought wise, or whether he is thought foolish—whether he gets blame, or whether he gets praise—whether he gets honour, or whether he gets shame—for all this the zealous man cares nothing at all. He burns for one thing; and that one thing is to please God, and to advance God's glory. If he is consumed in the very burning, he cares not for it—he is content. He feels that, like a lamp, he is made to burn; and if consumed in burning, he has done the work for which God appointed him. Such a one will always find a sphere for his zeal. If he cannot preach, work, and give money, he will cry, and sigh, and pray. . . . If he cannot fight in the valley with Joshua, he will do the work of Moses, Aaron, and Hur, on the hill [Ex 17:9-13]. If he is cut off from working himself, he will give the Lord no rest till help is raised up from another quarter, and the work is done. This is what I mean when I speak of "zeal" in religion.[5]

The supreme exemplar of this overmastering passion for the glory of God is the Lord Jesus himself. His whole life was marked by rejection of the glory of the crowd and devotion to the glory of God. Watching him cleanse his Father's house of the abuses of the religiously and economically powerful, his disciples remembered that it was written, "Zeal for your house will consume me" (see Jn 2:13-17). In dialogue with his theological opponents he declared, "I do not accept praise [glory] from men" (Jn 5:41). Describing his teaching, he remarked, "My teaching is not my own. It comes from him who sent me. . . . He who speaks on his own does so to gain honor [glory] for himself, but he who works for the honor [glory] of the one who sent him is a man of truth; there is nothing false about him" (Jn 7:16, 18). Defending himself from attack, he asserted, "I am not possessed by a demon, . . . but I honor [glorify] my Father and you dishonor me. I am not seeking glory for myself; but there is one who seeks it, and he is the judge" (Jn 8:49-50). Praying about his approaching passion, he cried out to the Father, "Now my heart is troubled, and what shall I say? 'Father, save me from this hour?' No, it was for this very reason I came to this hour. Father, glorify your name!" (Jn 12:27-28). And summarizing his whole incarnate life, he said to the Father without a trace of dishonesty, immodesty or self-consciousness, "I have brought you glory on earth by completing the work you gave me to do" (Jn 17:4).

Now what of us? How does the quality of our discipleship to the Lord Jesus compare to the example of the Master? His is the example of perfect humanity to which we must aspire. As James Packer notes, "Have we not need to pray, with that flaming evangelist, George Whitefield—a man as humble as he was zealous—'Lord help me to begin to begin'?"[6]

Turning from the Self

How, more precisely, do we "begin to begin"? Two passages of Scripture, one from each testament, help to answer this question. Consider, again, Psalm 115, where the more inward and spiritual aspects of our quest are taken up. The psalmist begins emphatically (note the repetition) where we too must begin: "Not to us, O LORD, not to us but to your name be the glory" (v. 1). Passion for the glory of God begins, and is only possible, when we consciously choose to reject our own honor, reputation and self-gratification.

Now this is no easy thing for fallen humans under the best of circumstances, for egocentricity plagues our human condition. The human heart is turned in upon itself. This "incurvation" makes us strangers to a thankful spirit, so that we use God's good gifts for selfishness and arrogant ends. Of course this does not make us irreligious, but we do not want God for his own sake but for our own ends.

Yet in our determinedly secular and individualistic society we do not live in the best of circumstances. The pervasive presence of individualism has resulted in the triumph of the therapeutic. In our culture, life's highest calling is the fulfillment of our individual needs, the exploration and realization of our individual potential and the satisfaction of our individual aspirations. Advertisers exhort us, "You owe it to yourself!" as the irrefutable sanction for a mindless participation in a decadent consumer economy. Many therapists, high priests of individualism, are necessary and available for hire not so much to cure new mental ills as to help us face the unprecedented demands placed on the isolated individual cut off from the more traditional ties of kinship, religious commitment, civic tradition and friendship.[7] "Community under these social arrangements becomes a 'community of interest' where self-interested individuals join together to maximize individual good."[8] So the message we hear and delight in with our turned-in hearts is "To me, to me . . ." As P. T. Forsyth wisely observes, "To make the development of man the supreme interest of God, as popular Christianity sometimes tends to do, instead of making the glory of God the supreme interest of man, is a moral error which invites the only treatment that can cure a civilization whose religion has become so false—public judgement."[9]

But when the Holy One draws near, and we are granted even the slightest perception of his towering, blazing glory, the lie is given to both our proud hearts and our sick social order. Then we can take our repentant stand with Jesus, the Lord of glory. We can say of ourselves, "I do not accept glory from human beings." Our deepest desire will be "Father, glorify your name."

Make no mistake, however. Fail to begin decisively here ("not to us, O LORD, not to us"), and you will never genuinely honor the Holy One, not even when you externally conform to his revealed will. You may develop quite a reputation for religion, but you will remain a stranger to his glory.

A Life of Trust

Psalm 115 also points us to the life of trust that brings glory to the name of the Holy One. Unlike the idolaters, who trust the works of their own imaginations and hands, the psalmist encourages us:

> O house of Israel, trust in the LORD—
>   he is their help and shield.
> O house of Aaron, trust in the LORD—
>   he is their help and shield.
> You who fear him, trust in the LORD—
>   he is their help and shield.
>
> The LORD remembers us and will bless us:
>   He will bless the house of Israel,
>   he will bless the house of Aaron,
> he will bless those who fear the LORD—
>   small and great alike.
>
> May the LORD make you increase,
>   both you and your children.
> May you be blessed by the LORD,
>   the Maker of heaven and earth.
>
> The highest heavens belong to the LORD,
>   but the earth he has given to man.
> It is not the dead who praise the LORD,
>   those who go down to silence;
> it is we who extol the LORD,
>   both now and forevermore.
>
> Praise the LORD. (vv. 9-18)

This appeal to trust is based on the goodness of the Lord. He has power to save (he is help and shield, vv. 9-11) and power to enrich (*bless* is repeated five times, vv. 12-15). Kidner goes to the heart of the psalmist's concerns when he comments, "The insistent repetition of the word 'bless' drives home the point that all of us alike—every group (12,13a), every type of person (13b), and every generation (14)—must have the smile and creative touch [of God] on us if we are to thrive."[10]

God is glorified when we consciously acknowledge our dependence on him for all good things. Our joy and enjoyment are thus bound up with the priority of his glory; our chief end is "to glorify God [by trusting dependence] and [thus to] enjoy him forever."

The life of dependent faith in Psalm 115 is expressed in three ways. First is prayer; the psalmist asks God to give the blessing (vv. 14-15) that he has already promised (vv. 12-13). Prayer is invariably a hallmark of the life of faith. Where we are not consciously trusting God, we will be found to be trusting ourselves. Self-trust is invariably self-glorifying. Believing prayer, on the other hand, glorifies the Holy One by expressing our neediness and inability to achieve the good we can envision. It claims his power and goodness as our only hope. So the truth stands in sharp relief: conscious dependence entails much prayer; little prayer entails unconscious dependence on ourselves.

Second, trust in the Holy One is expressed in the dedication of our lives (vv. 16-18). The psalmist identifies the earth as the arena that the Creator has given us for his glory. There is generosity in this gift but also responsibility. The earth belongs to him. It is not there as meaningless matter to be exploited, but as a trust to be committed to God's purpose and used to his advantage. We are thus stewards of ourselves and our whole environment.

Verses 17-18 add the thought that our time on this earth is another good gift from the Holy One to be used to his glory. The psalmist's intent here is not to deny the hope of life after death. As in other clearer psalm texts (11:7; 16:8-11; 17:15; 23:6; 49:15; 73:23-24; 139:18), he looks forward to extolling the Lord "both now and forevermore." Here his view is that thoughts of the alien realm of death and silence provide us a fresh stimulus to make the most of our lifetime for the honor of God (compare Jn 9:4). So all of the earth's resources and all of our time are to be dedicated to the glory of the Holy One.

Third, these activities of trust take place with the whole people of God. Because of our instinctive individualism, we are apt to think of prayer and dedication as private and individual. But here it is among all of God's people—house of Israel, house of Aaron (priests), God-fearers "small and great alike"—that we trust and pray and commit ourselves to stewardship of the earth. And note, there is no clerical or lay specialization. Prayer is not the exclusive concern of a priestly elite, nor is work the exclusive concern of laypeople. The community of God's people together are called to make visible the holy nearness of the Lord by a life of trusting prayer and dedication.

Knowledge, Freedom and Obedience

The second passage that will help us make a beginning in living for the glory of God is Paul's discussion of the first-century church's problem of meat offered to idols in 1 Corinthians 8—10. The problem was that most of the meat available in the ancient marketplace had some association with idolatrous worship. Some, particularly recent converts from paganism, had tender consciences about idolatry and argued that such meat should be completely avoided. Others argued that idols were not gods, only a figment of their human creators' imagination. So "a steak is a steak" and should be eaten with no pangs of conscience. Still others who followed this general line of thought became completely indifferent to the problem of idolatry and were participating in feasts in the temples of pagan gods.

Concluding his discussion of this situation, Paul says, "So whether you eat or drink or whatever you do, do it all for the glory of God" (1 Cor 10:31). In the midst of a situation of some moral uncertainty, the dominant aspiration and concern of believers is to be the glory of God.

Paul's own view of the morality of eating food offered to idols is clear: neither food nor abstinence from it brings us any nearer to God. To eat it makes us no better, to abstain makes us no worse (8:8). Food, even if offered to idols, has no moral or spiritual significance in and of itself. Theologians call this sort of thing, about which God has given us no direct revelation of his will, an *adiaphoron*. The Greek plural form *adiaphora* is often translated "things indifferent," referring to the absence of direct biblical statements about them and the resulting differences in the behavior of sincere believers.

This does not mean we can be indifferent in our attitudes about these matters, though. How they are handled makes all the difference. Even in ambiguous areas of life, where differences of opinion are inevitable, God is to be glorified. Paul's view is that every inch of life ("whatever you do, do it all") is to be claimed for the glory of the Holy One.

In developing his discussion, Paul raises three basic issues of great importance to glorifying God: the proper place of knowledge (8:1-8), the nature of true freedom (8:9—9:23) and the foundation of disciplined obedience to God's commands (9:24—10:22). Knowledge of God and his will clearly is important to the apostle Paul. Notice his repetition of the phrases "Don't you know..." (1 Cor 5:6; 6:2, 9, 16) and "I do not want you to be ignorant" (10:1; 12:1). An ignorant Christian is in no position to live to the glory of God.

But here Paul faces another problem, for as he says, "knowledge puffs up" (8:1). Some of the Corinthians boasted, "We all possess knowledge." Knowledge can become a source of pride, which inclines us to lord it over our Christian brother or sister who is weaker or knows less. If God is to be glorified, this pride must be renounced ("not unto us . . .") and our knowledge made an occasion for the sacrificial love that builds up others.

Next Paul discusses freedom. Freedom was a treasured possession of Paul and is of all believers under the grace of God. "It is for freedom that Christ has set us free. Stand firm, then, and do not let yourselves be burdened again by a yoke of slavery" (Gal 5:1). But if freedom is our birthright in Christ, it can also be misunderstood and expressed in ways that do not honor God. So Paul hastens to add to his ringing affirmation of the liberty found in Jesus, "You, my brothers, were called to be free. But do not use your freedom to indulge the sinful nature; rather, serve one another in love. The entire law is summed up in a single command: 'Love your neighbor as yourself' " (Gal 5:13-14).

So the bondage we are rescued from is not the moral demand of God's law, but the mistaken notion that our personal accomplishments in keeping God's law will restore us to God's favor. And the liberty we are to enjoy is not the liberty of lawlessness and self-satisfaction. It is the liberty under God's Spirit to fulfill the law's demands by a life of loving service to our neighbor.

This is precisely the issue Paul raises with the wayward Corinthians. They are free in Christ, but this freedom requires loving care, especially for those among the fellowship of believers of a sensitive conscience (8:9-23) and for outsiders who raise serious questions about their behavior (10:27-30). Both of these kinds of neighbor-love entail real personal sacrifice of "rights." The apostle's point is that true freedom includes the ability *not* to exercise my freedom for the sake of others. This freedom to love is seen most clearly in the cross of Jesus Christ. Indeed, the way of the cross is supremely the way in which God is glorified.

Finally Paul turns to address the issue of disciplined obedience, thinking particularly of the folk in Corinth whose "knowledge" and "freedom" have led to their participation in idolatrous feasts and practices. Here the foundation of his argument is the second commandment ("flee from idolatry," 10:14) and the experience of the Israelites when they broke this commandment in the wilderness (10:1-13). Any so-called knowledge that leads us to violate God's moral law turns out to be an expression of human ignorance ("I do not want you to be ignorant," 10:1), just as so-called freedom that ignores God's law is another name for rebellion that enslaves ("setting our hearts on evil things," 10:6). Such disobedience arouses the wrath of the Holy One: "Are we trying to arouse the Lord's jealousy? Are we stronger than he?" (10:22).

Against the life of self-serving ease, Paul sets the life of rigorous, purposeful self-discipline according to the standard of God's law (9:24-27). Like athletes in training, we are called to practice spiritual self-control, to avoid disqualification and to win an imperishable prize from the Lord, our Judge. The only way to glorify God is through thoughtful spiritual discipline and obedience to God's moral law.

Glorifying by Bearing Witness

Paul's own disciplined freedom was centrally focused on the calling to bear witness to the reality of the Lord Jesus Christ. He says, speaking of his sacrifices and exercise of personal discipline, "I do all of this for the sake of the gospel" (9:23). "For I am not seeking my own good but the good of many, so that they may be saved" (10:33). He does not hesitate to call us to the same focus. "Follow my example, as I follow the example of Christ" (11:1) are his concluding words.

This is not to say that the whole duty, or even the central duty, of every Christian is to witness to friends and neighbors. But it does press on us all the place of evangelism in the larger question of living to the glory of God. If we desire to manifest the excellence and the nearness of the Holy One in all of life, then the advancement of the Christian gospel, the message of the coming of the Lord of glory, will have a significant place in our concerns.

The challenge of evangelism in the glorification of God is particularly acute in any pluralistic pagan culture. Love, service, justice and beauty are all applauded so long as they are not too distinctively tied to the name of the Holy One. But when the name of God is announced not as some abstract, faceless deity but in all its majestic particularity, controversy and opposition are inevitable. So it is harder for us to speak of "the Lord" than of "God," and hardest of all to speak of "Jesus the Lord," if we speak of theological things at all.

Evangelism keeps the cutting edge of God's holiness in our lives when we are in danger of having it dulled and blunted. Without a passionate involvement in distinctively Christian witness, our passion for the glory of the one God will evaporate. Indeed, the profoundest motivation for the proclamation of the gospel is the desire to see men and women come to glorify God in all his majesty, authority and goodness.

Renunciation and Aspiration

To summarize: to glorify God is to desire to make clear and visible to all people the nearness and the overwhelming power, authority and goodness of the Holy One. This desire is the most basic and important ambition of those who have been restored to the friendship and fellowship of the Holy One by the priesthood and sacrifice of Jesus. His approval (glory *from* God) and his pleasure and reputation (glory *to* God) become more and more dominant in our lives. At every stage of the pilgrimage of our faith under grace, "we make it our aim to please him."

To accomplish this aim involves both renunciation and aspiration. Fundamentally we renounce our own glory and the idolatries of mind, worship and life that grow from it. Only then can we truly aspire to glorify the Holy One. Specifically Paul mentions the renunciation of pride (especially in our knowledge), rights and privileges, and moral autonomy, so that we may aspire to a life of love, sacrificial service and disciplined obedience.

Aspiration is equally important, for our focus must shift from ourselves to the nearness and excellence of the Holy One. More specifically this involves the disciplined practices of prayer, loving service, obedience and community. These constitute the inward dimension of a life lived to manifest the excellence of the Holy One. We also must recall the outward dimension.

All of life is the arena in which the glory of the Holy One is to be manifested. No part of life can be a matter of indifference or unconcern. No radical separation between "the secular" and "the sacred" is possible where the glory of the Lord is our concern. All of creation is full of his glory, so our handling of everything and everyone can display that glory for all to see. And the proclaiming of the gospel of the Lord Jesus Christ, which calls and enables sinners to bow before the glory of God, will be a passionate concern and a nonnegotiable part of our lives.

Dedication to God's Glory: Two Case Studies

This call to live all of life to the glory of God is not beyond Christian people like you and me. Consider two examples.

William Wilberforce was a nineteenth-century British Parliament leader who led the struggle to abolish the slave trade. He was a Christian man of deep personal faith. His abolitionist work was consciously motivated by obedience and love for the Lord Jesus Christ. So he launched the abolitionist cause in Parliament and persevered through what was to be a long and bitter struggle. Not only did Wilberforce sacrificially invest his time and personal fortune in the cause, but he also withstood biting criticism from his aristocratic social peers.

Certainly there was no glory for Wilberforce in the early days of the struggle. What kept him working away at such personal cost? At root it was a deep conviction that slavery was anti-God and that the Lord would see to the vindication of the truth. In addition a group of Christian brothers, derisively called the Clapham Sect, grew up to support one another in this worthy cause.

Among them was John Newton, a sea captain converted from the slave trade who became a prominent evangelical pastor, and the Earl of Shaftesbury, who later led the struggle for the rights of working women and children trapped in inhumane conditions in the early Industrial Revolution.

Perhaps the deepest insight into the heart and mind of this godly layman can be found in his journal, where he reports that he marked the passage of his bill to abolish the slave trade, his victory by normal human standards, by meditating on Psalm 115:1, "Not to us, O Lord, not to us, but to thy name be glory."[11] Here is a man who knew what it means to live for the glory of God alone.

Or consider the life of contemporary classical-guitar virtuoso Christopher Parkening. In an interview Parkening has recounted something of his spiritual pilgrimage. Having made it to the top of the performance world, he "retired" to a Montana farm to fish for trout. He'd done all he wanted to do and thought he would never play again. In the interview he went on to describe what then happened:

> Something was missing. Although I would have described myself as a Christian, I was not living the Christian life. I was also uneasy, embarrassed to be thought of as a Christian. On a visit to Los Angeles, a friend invited me to attend Grace Church. There I heard John MacArthur preach on Matthew 7, "Examine yourselves whether you be in the faith." That seemed aimed right at me.
>
> It was at that point, as I really started the Christian life, that I had a great hunger for the Word of God. I read I Corinthians, "Whatever you do, do all to the glory of God," and I thought, "Well, there are only two things that I know how to do: flyfish for trout or play the guitar." And the guitar seemed like the best option. This gave me a whole new perspective on playing the instrument.

Speaking of his repertoire, Parkening observed, "These are just pieces that I love. I find that I need to love a piece of music in order to play it well, to make music and not merely play notes. I am seeking to follow Bach, who wrote on his music 'To the glory of God.' The better I like a selection the more I can play to God's glory." Parkening spoke of the privilege it had been to study with the great master Andrés Segovia and added that he and Segovia "now have a very close relationship. I saw him recently in Spain, and I usually see him when he comes to L.A. We have also talked about the faith at times. I have shared with him my new commitment to Jesus, how I want to play everything to the glory of God."[12] (Segovia died in 1987, near the time this interview was published.)

Begin to Begin

Few of us will accomplish all that Parkening or Wilberforce were able to. We have neither their special abilities nor their unique opportunities. But all of us in our own situations can marshal our abilities and seize our opportunities to practice and display the nearness of the Holy One.

Have you begun to begin? Will you make the great Pauline doxology the prayer of your life?

Now to him who is able to do immeasurably more than all we ask or imagine, according to his power that is at work within us, to him be glory in the church and in Christ Jesus throughout all generations, for ever and ever! Amen. (Eph 3:20-21)

13

WORSHIP

T

HE AWESOME REALITY OF THE HOLINESS OF GOD IS AT THE VERY HEART OF WOR-
ship. Realization of the Lord's holiness always moves people to worship him.
When a sense of God's holiness is bright and clear, joyful worship flourishes.
When a sense of the holiness of the Lord declines or is lost, on the other hand,
worship becomes drudgery, and it too declines. It is trivialized into entertainment or a formula for self-help, or transformed into a merely aesthetic experience, or demonized into an anti-God exaltation of God's creatures.

Beauty and joy and blessing are all hallmarks of true worship. But they arise
as byproducts of worship. Worship is focused in a God-given response to the
majesty and sovereignty and goodness of our God himself.

What Is Worship?

To see how this is so, we need to understand what worship is. The Bible's
words for worship mean literally "bow down" or "lie prostrate." In the Old
Testament this word is used for bowing down in reverence and submission
both to men of superior position or power (2 Sam 18:21, for example) and
to God (Ex 12:27-28, for example). Three aspects are involved in both cases:
honor is shown to the greatness and goodness of the one bowed to, submis-

sion is given to his authority, and commitment is offered to his will.

The Old Testament also, however, makes a very clear distinction between bowing down to a powerful leader and bowing down to worship the Holy One. Respect, homage, submission and commitment may legitimately be offered to another human being. But here reserve is necessary. For example, Mordecai places himself in real jeopardy by refusing to kneel before the Persian leader Haman, even though no direct or obvious worship is involved. This refusal stems from Mordecai's loyalty to the Lord (Esther 3:2, 5).

When human monarchs or rulers exalt themselves to godlike status, those who are faithful to the Lord adamantly refuse to bend the knee. Under these circumstances, and despite the threat of death, even the meaningless formality of ritual prostration is rejected. So Daniel and his three friends must repeatedly resist bowing down to deified kings and their false national gods. As Psalm 146 puts it,

> Praise the LORD.
> Praise the LORD, O my soul. . . .
>
> Do not put your trust in princes,
>   in mortal men, who cannot save.
> When their spirit departs, they return to the ground;
>   on that very day their plans come to nothing. (vv. 1, 3-4)

Clearly, the meaning and significance of bowing down is completely determined by the object before which we bow. The Lord alone is God, the Holy One, the majestic, and mighty Creator and King of all. The quality of honor required by his matchless greatness and goodness, the submission due his sovereign authority, the commitment properly given to his righteous will must be utterly unique. His alone is worship, rightly so called. Consider these calls to worship in the psalms, which identify the holiness of the Holy One as both the reason for and the object of worship:

> Exalt the LORD our God
>   and worship at his holy mountain,
>   for the LORD our God is holy. (99:9)
>
> Worship the LORD in the splendor of his holiness;
>   tremble before him, all the earth. (96:9)

Come, let us bow down in worship,
    let us kneel before the LORD our Maker;
for he is our God
    and we are the people of his pasture,
    the flock under his care. (95:6)

Each of the three aspects of bowing down in true worship plays a part in the worship called for by the Psalter. The greatness and goodness of the Holy One move us to call forth to honor and exalt the Lord our God.

Zion hears and rejoices. . . .
For you, O LORD, are the Most High over all the earth;
    you are exalted far above all gods. (97:8-9)

Come, let us sing for joy to the LORD. . . .
For the LORD is the great God,
    the great King above all gods.
In his hand are the depths of the earth,
    and the mountains peaks belong to him. (95:1, 3-4)

Shout for joy to the LORD, all the earth.
    Worship the LORD with gladness. . . .
For the LORD is good and his love endures forever;
    his faithfulness continues through all generations. (100:1, 5)

The majestic sovereignty of the Holy One calls forth glad submission to his rule:

The LORD reigns,
    let the nations tremble;
he sits enthroned between the cherubim,
    let the earth shake. (99:1)

The LORD reigns, let the earth be glad;
    let the distant shores rejoice. (97:1)

Sing praises to God, sing praises;
    sing praises to our King, sing praises.
For God is the King of all the earth;

> sing to him a psalm of praise. (47:6-7)

And the awesome righteousness of the Holy One compels us to devote ourselves to keeping his will:

> Let those who love the LORD hate evil,
>> for he guards the lives of his faithful ones
>> and delivers them from the hand of the wicked.
> Light is shed upon the righteous
>> and joy on the upright in heart.
> Rejoice in the LORD, you who are righteous,
>> and praise his holy name. (97:10-12)

In the Old Testament, then, worship is utterly theocentric. What matters not just most, but completely and finally, is God, who he is and the sort of relationship he establishes with women and men. The response of worship is not just any response. Worship is controlled by its object, the Holy One himself. Because he is holy, his holiness becomes the center and circumference of worship.

The God-Centeredness of Worship

This principle of radical theocentricity stands on its head the anthropocentric (human-centered) categories normally employed in our thinking about worship. For example, from this biblical perspective the common question whether the origin of worship is to be found in such human emotions as fear, awe, thankfulness or love is quite beside the point. Such a question presupposes that worship is subjective, that it arises inherently from within human beings. Not so: worship is *objective*. All turns on the majesty, sovereignty and goodness of the Holy One.

Turning to the New Testament we find an intensification of this Old Testament theocentricity. Here "to bow down" denotes exclusive worship addressed to God. No book of the New Testament is more taken up with a concern for worship than Revelation. In the course of his visions, John is twice confronted with a wonderfully powerful angel. His first impulse is to fall at the angel's feet in worship. Immediately the angel responds, "Do not do it! I am a fellow servant with you. . . . Worship God!" (Rev 19:10; 22:8-9). Similarly, both Peter (Acts 10:25-26) and Paul (Acts 14:11-18) are horrified when well-meaning, ignorant pagans bow down before them. Says Peter when confronted with the prostrate Cornelius, "Stand up. . . . I am only a man myself."

That human emotions and reactions are involved in worship is, of course, significant and undeniable. Fear, awe, gratitude and love all should be experienced in worship. However, none of these subjective factors is basic. If there is awe in worship, it is awe of God; if there is love, it is the love of God; if worship is a human response, it is the response of the human subject to the Holy One who is beyond our knowing, but who has made himself known in sovereign, overflowing goodness.

Similarly, the forms of worship are not in the first instance matters of human invention. Worship is controlled by its object. It is not left to the caprice of men and women. It does not ask what things will be most helpful or meaningful or relevant from a human standpoint. And it certainly does not receive its shape from culture or social convention. We learn how to worship from the God who is the object of our worship.

All that is distinctive in the worship of the Old Testament is rooted in revelation. On the eve of the Israelites' entry into the Promised Land, the Lord warned them specifically about their worship practices: "See that you do all I command you; do not add to it or take away from it" (Deut 12:32). Many of these commands the people had no real instinct or desire to obey. They found the rituals and practices of the alien gods of Canaan closer to their instinct and taste. So the biblical lesson surely is clear: in worship the worshipers are not to trust their own instincts. They know neither what is best for themselves nor what is pleasing to the Holy One. We must learn to worship according to the way that the Holy One has himself appointed.

Much could be said about the particular forms of worship commanded by the Lord.[1] But it is this principle of obedient theocentricity that takes us to the heart and soul of biblical worship. True worship is first a matter of obedience and faithfulness.

The Worship of Christ

The New Testament deepens this exclusively God-centered pattern. It also reorients worship in a way that corresponds to its advance in the knowledge of the Holy One and its fulfillment of the Old Testament promises. Consider Revelation again. In the assembled court of heaven described in Revelation 4—5, the offering of worship begins with a glad recognition of the Lord's holiness.

> Holy, holy, holy
> is the Lord God Almighty,
> who was, and is, and is to come. (4:8)

But at the center of the worship of the court of heaven stands not only the Almighty Creator (4:9-11) but also the slain Lamb who is the triumphant Lion of the tribe of Judah (5:5-14). There can be no mistaking that the crucified and risen Jesus is the proper object of the worship of heaven. He receives worship in terms identical to those offered to the Creator:

You are worthy, our Lord and God,
 to receive glory and honor and power. (4:11)

Worthy is the Lamb, who was slain,
 to receive power and wealth and wisdom and strength
 and honor and glory and praise! (5:12)

And at the conclusion of this wonderful vision of the worship of heaven, worship that must be faithful and true, the Almighty and the Lamb receive worship from all of the creation as equals:
 Then I heard every creature in heaven and on earth and under the earth
 and on the sea, and all that is in them, singing:
  "To him who sits on the throne and to the Lamb
  be praise and honor and glory and power,
   forever and ever!" (5:13)
No clearer testimony could be offered to the New Testament conviction that in Jesus we meet the Holy One himself.

We see the same conviction at work in the story of the man born blind (Jn 9). After Jesus gives him his physical sight, the Pharisees examine and reject him because they have already rejected Jesus. So Jesus seeks the formerly blind man and reveals himself as the Son of Man. His spiritual eyes now fully opened, the man responds, "Lord, I believe," and worships Jesus (v. 38). This climactic response is true and proper worship, the response of every person whose spiritual vision is restored to see Jesus for who he truly is. Worship in the New Testament, then, is not just theocentric (worship of God the Father) but also christological (worship through and to God the Son).

This Christward orientation accounts for all that is distinctive in the worship of the New Testament as compared to the Old. The new impulse to simplicity arises because in Jesus we find the fulfillment of Old Testament priesthood and sacrifice. God has come in person and fulfilled his work of grace. As God's people gather around the Lord's Table, Jesus' priesthood and sacrifice in their fulfilled New Testament form are both the supreme theme of worship and that which makes possible the offering of acceptable service and praise. The way has been opened for sinners to freely and even boldly approach the Holy One. With this focus, worship gains both a depth and a spiritual simplicity that it could hardly have achieved under the revelation of the Old Testament.

Worship in the New Testament displays a new, more vital spirituality. It is worship of God the Father through God the Son in and by God the Holy Spirit. Now, it is possible to overstate this reorientation of worship. True worship has *always* been spiritual and in the Spirit. It is a glad, wholehearted bowing down to the Lord under the powerful working of the Spirit. How else could we interpret the impassioned, powerful, Spirit-filled denunciation of dead formalism by the Old Testament prophets? Or how are we to understand the deep, heart-based outpouring of the psalmists? They know an intimacy and intensity of encounter with the Holy One that we admire and long for. And not infrequently they mention the Holy Spirit by name (for example, see Ps 4:6; 51:4).

What is new is that Jesus, as he promised (see John 7:37-39; 13:20; 14:16-18; 15:26; 16:7-16), brought a specific coming of the Spirit that enables a new breadth, depth and permanence of experienced spirituality in all believers. As Jesus said to the Samaritan woman, in what is perhaps the most penetrating teaching in Scripture on the nature of worship, "A time is coming and has now come when the true worshipers will worship the Father in spirit and truth, for they are the kind of worshipers the Father seeks. God is spirit, and his worshipers must worship in spirit and in truth" (Jn 4:23-24). Or as the apostle Paul put it, characteristically echoing the Lord Jesus in his own style, "For it is we who are the circumcision, we who worship by the Spirit of God, who glory in Christ Jesus, and who put no confidence in the flesh" (Phil 3:3).

Often spiritual worship is viewed as a purely inward reality that bypasses all consideration of external forms. Such a contrast is quite misguided. The Holy Spirit gives the forms in the commandments of Scripture. Obedient (not merely traditional), thoughtful (not slapdash) ordering of worship (liturgy) plays a significant role. In addition the Holy Spirit touches and enlivens each of the God-given forms (prayer, praise, singing and musical praise, confession of sin, confession of faith, baptism, the Lord's Supper, Scripture reading and expository preaching, the collection) by working in the depths of our beings. We see and know the new covenant's inner ministry of the Holy Spirit in making us alive to God and giving us sanctifying power. The person who is born of the Spirit and led by the Spirit is the one who in obedient outward expression offers fitting and acceptable worship to the Father through the Lord Jesus. So acceptable worship is worship in spirit and in truth, worship by the Spirit of Truth.

Here, then, are the main aspects of the New Testament's christological reorientation of Old Testament worship. But it is most crucial that we see the fundamental similarity between Old Testament and New Testament worship. Throughout the Bible, worship is radically and thoroughly theocentric. It is rooted in who God is, in the holiness of the Holy One, and is ordered and shaped by his word of command and power.

Here, then, is a definition of worship: Worship is the glad and wholehearted offering of the honor, submission and commitment due to the Holy One— Father, Son and Holy Spirit—according to the means that the LORD both commands and empowers.

Because the controlling center of worship is thus radically theocentric, the overwhelming significance of worship is clear. What could be more important, invigorating or wonderful than to freely, obediently and self-forgetfully exult in the majesty and sovereignty and goodness of the Holy One? Is any higher calling conceivable? As Karl Barth so rightly says, "Christian worship is the most momentous, the most urgent, the most glorious action that can take place in human life."[2]

Extravagant Worship

Christian worship is wonderful, but it is also controversial. Something of both the controversy and the wonder stand out in the Gospel story of Mary of Bethany and her anointing of Jesus in the week before his passion. This act of devotion to the Lord Jesus opened her to withering criticism by some of the disciples. But of this act of worship, and only this act, Jesus said, "I tell you the truth [amen!], wherever the gospel is preached throughout the world, what she has done will also be told, in memory of her" (Mk 14:9). Clearly there is much here for us to learn about worship, this most urgent, glorious, momentous and controversial of human acts.

Jesus and his entourage paused in Bethany on their way toward the Passover celebration in Jerusalem. Jesus was fully conscious of his coming passion, while the disciples traveled with him in a self-imposed shroud of ignorance. Mary and her older sister Martha lived in their own home along with their brother Lazarus, whom Jesus had recently raised from the dead. They were obviously close friends of Jesus, and their home apparently offered him a refuge from his public ministry on numerous occasions.

On this last visit to Bethany, a dinner was given in honor of Jesus. Martha, the freeborn mistress of her own home, served the table. As the guests were reclining around the table (the normal posture for meals in New Testament times), Mary took a very large quantity—a pint—of nard, a fragrant and expensive perfume, and anointed Jesus' feet. The smell of the perfume, which was normally reserved either for burial rites or, in small doses, for cosmetic or romantic purposes, filled the whole house. Mary then loosened her hair, an act considered scandalous in her society,[3] and wiped Jesus' feet with it.

Such an act had to spark a reaction among the onlookers. Doubtless most were just embarrassed by this extravagant and "inappropriate" display of emotion. Reserved silence would have been their immediate response, with much subsequent scandalized clucking about socially appropriate behavior. Others, however, were not silent. They were morally outraged. Led by Judas, they objected, "Why wasn't this perfume sold and the money given to the poor? It was worth a year's wages [three hundred denarii]" (Jn 12:5).

This objection has a familiar ring to our ears. To the secular mind no act seems more pointless than worship, especially costly, devoted worship. It does no good in the world, and it actually distracts us from doing good. Religion is an opiate that blinds us to the crushing need around us and keeps the poor contented with daydreams of another world. Why not close down all religious activity and use those resources and personal energy to do something worthwhile? Christian believers do not exactly adopt this outlook, but they are deeply affected by it. So some make service to the poor the top priority of life (the most momentous and glorious action). Others "spiritualize" service and make evangelism, aid to the spiritually poor, life's highest calling. In either case, this world is what really counts, and meeting the needs of people around us is assumed to be our highest calling. Subtly we side with Mary's critics.

But Jesus said, "Leave her alone." He chides us, defending and honoring Mary, and challenges us to consider whether we have our priorities straight. Mary's understanding of his situation (she had anointed him for his burial) and her devotion to him will stand as an example of true worship wherever the gospel is proclaimed.

Jesus' next assertion grates on our ears: "You will always have the poor among you" (Jn 12:8). Many hear this as an expression of unconcern for the needs of the poor, an insensitive denial of the hurts and injustices of this world in favor of the claims of heaven or life after death. Is Jesus actually calling us to deny compassion and assistance to the poor because of the priority of "spiritual realities"?

Jesus' own ministry helps us to see that this outlook is a serious misunderstanding of his words. First, Jesus oriented his whole ministry around a compassionate identification with the poor. Jesus was poor at his birth. Remember that Mary and Joseph sacrificed a pair of doves or pigeons when Jesus was presented for circumcision (Lk 2:22-24). This was the offering allowed for those who could not afford the usual, more expensive offering of a sheep.

And the manifesto of Jesus' public ministry, announced in the synagogue of Nazareth, was

> The Spirit of the Lord is on me,
>> because he has anointed me
>> to preach good news to the poor.
> He has sent me to proclaim freedom for the prisoners
>> and recovery of sight for the blind,
> to release the oppressed,
>> to proclaim the year of the Lord's favor. (Lk 4:18-19)

Jesus went about serving the poor and the socially marginalized throughout the course of his ministry. That he would callously ignore the needs of the poor in the last week of his life seems very unlikely. Indeed, after this act of worship by Mary, he will summarize his life of service by taking on the social role of a household slave, washing the feet of his disciples and calling them to equivalent forms of service.

Second, in this saying about the poor Jesus is quoting Deuteronomy 15:11. Indeed, throughout his ministry Jesus pointed to the Old Testament as the final authority for all that he did and said. Further, his use of the Old Testament was distinctive. Jesus saw the whole Old Testament text as fulfilled in his person and work. So when he pointed to a particular text, he characteristically called attention to its whole context.[4]

Viewed in this way, Jesus' use of Deuteronomy 15:11 is anything but a calloused slighting of the needs of the poor. The context of the text is a ringing call for all debts to be canceled once every seven years, so that there will be no permanently impoverished class among God's people (Deut 15:1-11), and a demand from the LORD that all slaves or indentured servants be released from bondage on the same seven-year cycle (Deut 15:12-18). So the point is not self-centered unconcern but a command from the Lord to be generous and compassionate. Here is the full text of Deuteronomy 15:11: "There will always be poor people in the land. Therefore I command you to be openhanded toward your brothers and toward the poor and needy in your land."

Jesus' assertion of the perpetual presence of the poor should never be read as insensitivity to their plight or as a mandate for a passive acceptance and complicity in their grinding need.

What, then, was Jesus' point to Mary's critics? He goes on to say, "But you will not always have me" (Jn 12:8). All of this discussion takes place under the shadow of the cross. His physical presence and imminent movement toward the cross (he says Mary has anointed him for his burial) are matters of transcendent importance. When he is lifted up (on the cross and in glory), he will draw all people to himself. His act of sacrifice and atonement is the pivotal point of all human experience, because it sets men and women right with the Holy One and thereby empowers them to keep God's commands, to live in Jesus' way of self-sacrificing service. More good for the poor has come from this sacrifice of the incarnate God than from any other act in history. By restoring us to our God, it restores us to our right mind and empowers us to walk in God's way. And the heart and soul of God's way is revealed as the way of costly service.

Notice, Jesus' physical presence is temporary. His body will require no mausoleum where lines of people will shuffle by in morose reverence. The place of worship will not be a magnificent building built by human hands but a community of people, rich and poor alike. They will be the place of his risen spiritual presence. Resources are freed for service to a poor and needy world *because* Jesus himself in his resurrection glory is the focus of worship in spirit and in truth.

The Overflow of Worship

What the secularist critic of worship misses is not only the transcendent worth of the Holy One but also the fact that true spiritual worship, the worship of people like Mary, ignites zeal and power that leads to compassionate service to the poor. Worship, because it involves the uncompromised devotion of our will to the purpose of the Holy One, must always overflow in service to all sorts of people in every sphere of life.

This point is made repeatedly in Scripture. It is the essence of the prophets' critique of Israel's worship. For example, Isaiah makes this point when he indicts the supposedly orthodox worship of Judah:

"Stop bringing meaningless offerings!
    Your incense is detestable to me.
New Moons, Sabbaths and convocations—
    I cannot bear your evil assemblies.
Your New Moon festivals and your appointed feasts
    my soul hates.
They have become a burden to me;
    I am weary of bearing them.
When you spread out your hands in prayer,
    I will hide my eyes from you;
even if you offer many prayers,
    I will not listen.

Your hands are full of blood;
   wash and make yourselves clean.
Take your evil deeds
   out of my sight!
Stop doing wrong,
   learn to do right!
Seek justice,
   encourage the oppressed.
Defend the cause of the fatherless,
   plead the case of the widow. (Is 1:13-17)

His point is that true worship must be judged by the moral standard of God's commandments, and that the best litmus test of our obedience is not the formal observance of ritual but our treatment of the weak and marginalized. We think we can get away with injustice and unconcern, and we are right if we take only our social order as our judge. But when the Holy One is our Judge, the hollowness of worship without justice and love for the needy becomes quite clear.

In the New Testament, Paul similarly insists that true and spiritual worship must and will overflow in service. In his letter to the Romans (12:1) he defines spiritual worship as the offering of our whole selves to God in response to the riches of God's mercy. Notice, then, what follows inevitably: moral transformation of our minds, so that we are no longer captive to the dictates of the society around us and thus are able to discern God's will (12:2); humility (12:3); service to God's people according to the gifts God provides (12:4-8, 10, 13); loving service to enemies (12:14, 17-21); identification with the lowly (12:15-16); fruitful involvement in the public life of the state (13:1-7); obedient love to our neighbor (13:8-14); loving acceptance of all God's people, even those who disagree and are disagreeable (14:1—15:7); and vigorous, God-honoring, prayerful involvement in evangelism (15:8-33).

Quite an impressive list, isn't it? All of these things are very desirable. Why then are they so difficult and rare in our experience? Mark it well, all of this is the overflow of true and spiritual worship. Perhaps the reason these wonderful realities are so rare in our day is that we have lost the foundational reality that creates and invigorates all Christian service.

Radical Listening to God

As a step toward the recovery of true and spiritual worship, let's return to Mary of Bethany and seek to discover what made her worship of the Lord a model for all believers in all times. Two massively important aspects of Mary's worship cry out to us across the years: her thoughtful understanding of Jesus and his teaching and her uninhibited totality of response to the Lord.

We meet Mary for the first time, along with her older sister Martha, in Luke 10:38-42. Martha had opened their home to Jesus and was busily engaged in providing for his hospitality. The sheer volume of work involved (she was apparently entertaining not only Jesus but also his band of disciples) caused her great distraction and led her to resent Mary, who sat at Jesus' feet (the stylized posture of a pupil and disciple), listening to his teaching. Martha expressed her frustration by pointing out what she believed was Mary's thoughtlessness and asking Jesus to tell Mary to help.

In this scene Martha comes off in a poor light. But consider, as sympathetically as you can, what formed her reaction. In the Gospel accounts she appears quite an admirable person—resolute, energetic, willing to serve, ready of tongue, used to giving orders, as eager to make suggestions as to reprove. (see Lk 10:38, 40-41; Jn 11:20-21, 28, 39-40; 12:2). Further, she was seeking to fulfill a woman's traditional role in her culture—providing hospitality for her guest. Everything in her experience told her she was doing what was right. Beyond this, there was probably an element of humble sacrifice in what she did. In her Jewish context women were not allowed to serve at meals if men were in attendance, unless there were no servants to perform the task.[5] Since her household was obviously a prosperous one that almost certainly employed servants, her labors were atypical and reflected a personal desire and willingness to serve Jesus. When we notice that later she served Jesus and his disciples quietly and without complaint in another household (Jn 12:2), we get some insight into her genuine spirituality and devotion to the Lord. We see the liberty that Jesus seeks to form in us, freedom from hallowed social customs that restrict love but also freedom to serve, to take the lower place.

But in this instance, in her own home, there was something more basic than service, something she needed to learn. And Mary already knew what that was: to sit undistractedly at Jesus' feet in order to learn from him. True worship requires understanding of the Lord and his teaching. Perhaps Mary's character and temperament drew her in this direction. She was hesitant, quiet, easily moved, obedient, devoted (see Mk 14:3-4; Lk 10:39, 42; Jn 11:20, 29, 32). To be sure, Mary was not perfect. Sometimes her emotional makeup led her astray; in the emotionally trying circumstance of her brother Lazarus's death, she understood less about Jesus than did the steadier Martha (see Jn 11:17-37). But still Mary consciously chose "the one thing that is necessary," to learn from Jesus. Understanding and obeying Jesus would be the foundation of her life.

Sometimes this story is interpreted as urging the superiority of the contemplative life over the active life. But this is a misunderstanding. Jesus said it was a matter of *one thing.* The importance of listening to and learning his teaching was contrasted to everything else. His teaching is the foundation of both contemplation and action. In this Mary is a model for us: she responded to the teaching of Jesus by placing it first, ahead of tradition, social convention or personal preference.

This incident helps us see the socially radical character of the gospel and its liberating force for women in the time of Jesus. We see Jesus rearranging traditional roles and priorities in light of the dawning reality of the kingdom of God. Among Mary's contemporaries, it was very unusual for women to be taught. And it was unheard-of for a rabbi to come into a woman's house and teach her. Jesus' initiative and Mary's response have a revolutionary quality. Martha's service, the traditionally proper place for a woman, is not demeaned, denigrated or rejected, but it cannot come first. Appeals to a woman's traditional role, here voiced by Martha, do not take precedence. Women (like men) are called first to hear and obey Jesus' word. We must reorient our way of life according to what Jesus concludes is "best" (Lk 10:42).

The absolute, universal priority of responsive, obedient listening to Jesus gives women a new and equal place. Here is the egalitarian seed that dramatically bore fruit in transforming the status of women among the followers of Jesus. Given the low regard for women in the cultures of Jesus' time, is it not a wonderful and amazing mark of the goodness of the Holy One that Mary of Bethany, a woman, is the worldwide exemplar of worship? Worship is thus freed from traditional social conventions that have no foundation in God's revealed truth.

The Importance of Understanding

Mary's story also makes it plain that worship depends on understanding the word of God, on listening and obeying. Mary quietly, devotedly and thoughtfully attended to the teaching of Jesus. Small wonder that she alone seems to have had some sense of his impending passion (Jn 12:7). She took the perfume and anointed his body for burial, while the male disciples squabbled among themselves about places of preference right up to the very foot of the cross.

Indeed, what we do not understand can destroy worship, leaving us absorbed in ourselves in the very presence of the Lord. Conversely, the fire of worship is fueled when, like Mary, we grasp the truth of God in a profound and committed way. Understanding is indispensable to true worship.

Understanding is no less foundational for corporate worship than for a life of personal devotion. We see something of its fundamental importance in the wonderful account of the great revival and reformation of God's people in Nehemiah 8. All of the people who were capable of understanding (vv. 2-3) were assembled to hear a reading of "the Law of Moses, which the LORD had commanded for Israel" (v. 1). Because the law was already an ancient book by the time of Nehemiah (nearly one thousand years old) and was written in another language (Hebrew instead of the normally spoken Aramaic), it was necessary to translate and explain it. So Ezra, the priest, and several Levites (v. 7) not only read the law but also explained its meaning "so that the people could understand what was being read" (v. 8). This experience of expository preaching moved the assembled people to deeply felt worship. They "celebrated with great joy, because they now understood the words that had been made known to them" (v. 12).

The same foundational importance of understanding is expressed in Paul's instructions to the church in Corinth in 1 Corinthians 14. This richly gifted congregation apparently had drifted into a form of worship that overemphasized speaking in tongues and disorderly, ecstatic frenzy. The pagan worship they were familiar with proceeded along these lines, so they doubtless viewed their practice as normal and spiritual. Without rejecting any of their spiritual gifts, Paul reminded them of the importance of understanding to true spirituality and worship. At the heart of his instruction is his statement "If I pray in a tongue, my spirit prays, but my mind is unfruitful. So what shall I do? I will pray with my spirit, but I will also pray with my mind; I will sing with my spirit, but I will also sing with my mind" (vv. 14-15). Clear instruction, an active mind, and understanding are indispensable if the church as a body is to worship the Lord and be built up (vv. 1-12). So Paul urged them, "Brothers, stop thinking like children. In regard to evil be infants, but in your thinking be adults" (v. 20).

Each of the specific practical steps Paul instructed the Corinthians to take follows from the foundational importance of understanding. Speech that instructs, strengthens, encourages and comforts as from the Lord (that is, prophecy as speaking forth the word of God) is given first place in gatherings for worship (vv. 3-5, 39). Order, not chaotic frenzy, was to characterize Christian worship (v. 40). Even the seemingly more ecstatic gifts, like prophecy and tongues-speaking, can and must be controlled by those who receive these gifts for the sake of corporate order and understanding (vv. 32-33). People are to speak one at a time (v. 27 for tongues, v. 30 for prophecy). Only two or three messages in tongues and a similar number of prophecies are to be given (vv. 27, 29), and all messages or prayers in tongues must be accompanied by interpretation (vv. 27-28). The litmus test of these gatherings for worship is to be the response of an outsider (vv. 23-25). Unless strangers can understand and sense the Lord's presence and so be led to faith in the Lord, the gathering for worship misses the mark and displeases the Lord.

Worship without a deep understanding of the Lord and his Word degenerates into a parody of its true self. It becomes a cultured but dead ritual we mumble our way through (as in the time of Nehemiah) or a mindless exercise in ecstatic experience (as in Corinth). Always it falls prey to the spirit of the age. It thoughtlessly adopts the dominant religious forms of the surrounding culture (high ritual in the case of Israel, uncontrolled frenzied ecstasy in Corinth). And it drifts into false beliefs. Israel was prepared to admit idolatry and many gods into its "worship" life, and the cry "Jesus be cursed" found its way into Corinthian worship (1 Cor 12:3).

What of us? Do we come to worship with a desire to understand, to sit with Mary at Jesus' feet and have our minds enriched with his truth? Are we willing to engage in the hard work of thoughtfulness? If understanding is foundational to true worship, preaching and teaching will always have an important role to play. Do we insist on preaching that provides food for the mind, or do we settle for an uplift of our feelings? Do we hunger for the Word of God and expect preaching that makes clear the message of the biblical text? Do we come to listen to preaching with an eagerness to learn, a willingness to think deeply and obediently about the truth of God? Do we tolerate falsehood or half-truths in the name of tradition or relevance? Do we insist that what happens in the whole service, in word, song and gesture, find its roots in the teaching of Scripture? Do we bring active and obedient minds to all aspects of worship, so that our response to the Lord, like Mary's, is fitting and pleasing to him?

Mary's example of worship calls us to deeper and active understanding of God's truth. Have you heard the call? Will you "sit at Jesus' feet" so that you can truly worship?

An Unrestrained Response to God

Mary's anointing of Jesus, based as it was in a deep understanding, expressed what we may best call a thoroughgoing and uninhibited totality of response to Jesus and the grace of God.[6] Her bold and believing act of worship comes as a much-needed challenge to our muddle-headed ideals of restraint and respectability, our distrust of deep spiritual and emotional experiences. How far our conventional, lifeless, partial response of worship seems from worship that the New Testament characterizes as "unutterable and exalted joy" (1 Pet 1:8 RSV). Our worship practices seem to have bogged us down in a sort of conscientious halfheartedness. The challenge of Mary's "totality" must be received as from God.

But what more precisely did this "totality" in worship entail? First, Mary's act of anointing expressed an eagerness, an exuberance, a gladness of heart toward the Lord which could be best summed up in the word *delight*. Mary's focus was not on the crowd at the dinner but on the Lord Jesus, who was headed to the cross for her. She was not just discharging a religious duty at some minimally required level of involvement. Her response to him was an act of profound joy.

Surely this delight in the Lord was one of the principal fruits of her sitting undistracted at Jesus' feet. When we listen carefully, ponder deeply and understand truly who the Holy One is, who we are, how amazing his overflowing goodness is, how wonderful is his gracious initiative in coming among us to die for us, intimate love and sheer delight are the invariable result. Such delight demands some concrete expression. It bursts out in song or in tears or in both, because it is the deepest wellspring of our hearts.

Second, Mary's worship expressed a profound humility. Not only did she wash and perfume Jesus' feet, an act normally reserved for a household servant, but she then wiped his feet with her hair. This act, which risked scandal in her culture, was a statement of utter self-abasement and submission to the majesty and sovereignty of Jesus. Her worship was not basically a matter of happy celebration. She anointed him for his impending passion; the circumstances were anything but happy. But her delight in the Lord led her to utterly disregard her social circumstances and unreservedly bow before the Lord to honor and magnify him. This wonderful capacity of self-forgetfulness and submission is at the very heart of worship, inspired as it is by a delight in the greatness, sovereignty and goodness of the One at whose feet we fall.

Third, Mary's worship expressed an unrestrained generosity. Remember, even some of the disciples were scandalized by the quantity and expense of the perfume she lavished so freely on Jesus. There is something quite wonderfully extravagant in her offering of adoration to the Lord. Like the widow in Jesus' parable, Mary had obviously given her whole being to the Lord Jesus. How then could her last or her most precious possession be withheld? She gladly offered the very costly perfume as a token of the fact that the only fitting gift to Jesus is everything. Totality in worship involves exactly this sort of cheerful giving.

Fourth, Mary's worship expressed both simplicity and beauty. There is no elaborate liturgy in her service, no hint of any contrived complexity. She simply took something precious that was at hand and seized the opportunity of the dinner party to respond to the greatness and goodness of the Lord. Jesus silenced her critics with the retort, "She has done a beautiful thing to me" (Mk 14:6). Her simple act of total devotion was also a thing of beauty.

Worship does not focus on the creation of beauty. That would be mere aestheticism, the worship of beauty itself and so a form of idolatry. Worship focuses totally on the Lord. But as a result of a heart desire to offer the best, total worship always produces something of real beauty. After all, praise to the Holy One could be expressed only in prose. But we sense something of the poverty in this. Praise bursts forth naturally in poetry and song, forms of artistically enhanced speech. No divorce of art and worship is possible. Indeed, worship requires artistic elements to express the depths of intensity and delight involved in what I have called "totality." Worship properly involves an artistic dimension, where art is pressed into the service of the truth of God and devotion to God.

Examples of this aesthetic aspect of totality before the Holy One can be found in all eras of the life of the people of God. Consider Bezalel and Oholiab, the designers and master craftsmen who directed the construction and decoration of the tabernacle and its furnishings. For this important task, the Lord filled these craftsmen with "skill, ability and knowledge" ("natural" ability enhanced by training) and with the Holy Spirit (Ex 35:30-33). Part of their assigned task was to instruct others for this holy artistic calling of serving the worship of God (Ex 35:34-35). The Lord's approval of their work was evident when the Holy One himself came to fill the tabernacle with his cloud of glory (Ex 40:34-35).

Later in Old Testament history, David organized a levitical guild of temple musicians who served the worship of God. These men were priests, but their function is described as prophetic; they "prophesied, using the harp [and other instruments] in thanking and praising the LORD" (1 Chron 25:3). All members of this guild of 288 musicians were "trained and skilled in music for the LORD" (25:7). To them we doubtless owe the collection, and in some cases the composition, of the Psalms (the titles on Ps 50 and 73—83 attribute these psalms to Asaph, the leader appointed by David).

Great artistic servants of worship can be identified in every era of the postapostolic church. Perhaps the greatest in Western church history is Johann Sebastian Bach. Bach's name is synonymous with musical creativity and excellence. What is not so well known is his lifelong commitment to church music, to the service of musical praise. He suffered considerable resistance and opposition in this calling and was never well compensated or widely renowned during his lifetime. But his life's work is an incredible monument of musical excellence in the worship of God. Indeed, many of his manuscripts are marked "S.D.G.," the great Reformation watchword, "Soli Deo Gloria." Next to his over two hundred church cantatas, the most eloquent preacher seems tongue-tied.

Even Bach's purely instrumental music is beautifully expressive of the glory of God. Consider his justly famous trio sonatas for organ. These pieces are very demanding technically. They include melodies for the right hand, the left hand and the pedal, all sounding at once, each retaining its own identity, yet together forming a beautiful harmony. The result can best be described as a tonal picture of the Holy Trinity, of the eternal mystery of the Godhead—difficult, glorious, beautiful, majestic. Here, then, is great art consciously offered in the service of an even greater God, demanding that all of our technical, artistic and intellectual capacities be consecrated to the service and praise of the Holy One. And so it will ever be when we are moved to seek "totality" in our worship of the Holy One.

When we turn to the accounts of corporate worship in Nehemiah and 1 Corinthians, we find the same "totality" that Mary of Bethany demonstrated. Delight, humility, generosity and a beautiful simplicity are written all over these gatherings for worship. For example, in Nehemiah 8 the people eagerly attend a six-hour service of Bible exposition, responding with great enthusiasm and humility to the Word of God. One receives the impression not of carefully rehearsed liturgical responses but of a spontaneous outpouring of devotion to the Lord. The people used familiar liturgical practices (lifting hands, bowing down, prostrating themselves and shouting "Amen! Amen!") with great freedom and sincerity.

In 1 Corinthians 14:24-25, Paul observes that because of the evident reality and presence of the Lord in the worship of the Corinthians, an unbeliever will be led to acknowledge "God is really among you!" The casual way he refers to this sort of conversion suggests that such an experience was not at all unusual among the earliest Christians. Their totality in worship was unmistakably and wonderfully evident, and therefore was frequently used by the Lord to transform lives.

But perhaps the thing that most strongly marks these gatherings as total worship is the unusually wide degree of participation by the people. These accounts show every-member worship, totality for the whole people of God. In Nehemiah 8, "all the people assembled as one man" (v. 1), and "all the people" responded to the reading and exposition of Scripture in praise and self-abasement (v. 6). Later they all gathered in small groups to pore over the law and, as a result, were willing to reform centuries-old worship practices on the spot. Leaders, most notably the priest Ezra, had an important role to play, but the mass of people were anything but passive.

If the major shortcoming of the gathering for worship described in 1 Corinthians 14 was a lack of order, it certainly didn't lack eager, even exuberant, participation. "When you come together, everyone has a hymn, or a word of instruction, a revelation, a tongue or an interpretation" (v. 26). Order is easy to maintain in a cemetery, but the Corinthians' gathering was anything but a cemetery. Life abounded, overflowing in a vital quest for totality before the Lord in both private and public ways. Paul responded not by discouraging total participation but by providing instructions to make for an order that would strengthen and serve all.

Often our problems in worship are exactly opposite the ones faced by Ezra and Paul. When was the last time an overexuberant response had to be restrained in a worship gathering at your church? What are we to make of the tightly controlled performance—clergy and choir entertaining a passive congregation—that is worship for so many churches? How do we react to singing in whispers, chilly, routine formalities, closed-off lives that merit the derisive description "God's frozen chosen"? And what of the sermonette that tips its cap to a Scripture text, then launches into pop psychology, contemporary political issues or maudlin sentimentality, all justified because the people won't tolerate longer, more serious grappling with Scripture? None of this is total worship, and it must not be accepted as spiritually adequate or edifying.

May we be granted some renewed acquaintance with the majesty and sovereignty and goodness of our God. May the holiness of the Holy One shatter our complacency, so that worship is restored and renewed as "the most momentous, the most urgent, the most glorious action that can take place in human life."

14

Rend the Heavens
and Come Down

T HE MAJESTY, SOVEREIGNTY AND GOODNESS OF THE HOLY ONE DEMAND THAT WE
think great thoughts. Such thoughts about God are important and necessary
and wonderful. This book argues for, insists on and rejoices in the understanding of the Holy One that he has given us in his Word.

But here we need to pause and be reminded that *thinking* about God
clearly, truly and majestically is only a sort of preliminary. The Holy One is
not a set of exceedingly great and wonderful ideas. He is the real and living
Person described by these ideas.

So don't let these wonderful truths be mere notions running around in your
brain. Stop and confront the reality of this living Person. Thoughts about the
Holy One must be turned into prayer to the Holy One and friendship with
the Holy One.

The Holy One of Israel
Perhaps the most profound example of this movement from conscious meditation (head) to personal communion (heart) is found in the majestic prayer
near the end of the prophecy of Isaiah. In the course of this prayer the prophet
concisely reviews much of the truth about the holiness of God we have been

considering and instructs us in the way to personal communion with the Holy
One himself.

> Look down from heaven and see
>> from your lofty throne, holy and glorious.
> Where are your zeal and your might?
>> Your tenderness and compassion are withheld from us.
> But you are our Father,
>> though Abraham does not know us
>> or Israel acknowledge us;
> you, O LORD, are our Father,
>> our Redeemer from of old is your name.
> Why, O LORD, do you make us wander from your ways
>> and harden our hearts so we do not revere you?
> Return for the sake of your servants,
>> the tribes that are your inheritance.
> For a little while your people possessed your holy place,
>> but now our enemies have trampled down your sanctuary.
> We are yours from of old;
>> but you have not ruled over them,
>> they have not been called by your name.
>
> Oh, that you would rend the heavens and come down,
>> that the mountains would tremble before you!
> As when fire sets twigs ablaze
>> and causes water to boil,
> come down to make your name known to your enemies
>> and cause the nations to quake before you!
> For when you did awesome things that we did not expect,
>> you came down, and the mountains trembled before you.
> Since ancient times no one has heard,
>> no ear has perceived,
> no eye has seen any God besides you,
>> who acts on behalf of those who wait for him.
> You come to the help of those who gladly do right,
>> who remember your ways.
> But when we continued to sin against them,
>> you were angry.
>> How then can we be saved?

All of us have become like one who is unclean,
  and all our righteous acts are like filthy rags;
we all shrivel up like a leaf,
  and like the wind our sins sweep us away.
No one calls on your name
  or strives to lay hold of you;
for you have hidden your face from us
  and made us waste away because of our sins.

Yet, O LORD, you are our Father.
  We are the clay, you are the potter;
  we are all the work of your hand.
Do not be angry beyond measure, O LORD;
  do not remember our sins forever.
Oh, look upon us, we pray,
  for we are all your people.
Your sacred cities have become a desert;
  even Zion is a desert, Jerusalem a desolation.
Our holy and glorious temple, where our fathers praised you,
  has been burned with fire,
  and all that we treasured lies in ruins.
After all this, O LORD, will you hold yourself back?
  Will you keep silent and punish us beyond measure? (Is 63:15—64:12)

Isaiah's prayer begins with the reality of God's holiness. The Lord is addressed as transcendent (he must look down from heaven), sovereignly great (from his lofty throne) and ravishingly beautiful (this is the sense of the Hebrew words for "holy and glorious"; see 63:15). Make no mistake, it is the Holy One in his uncreated grandeur and power whom we address here.

Indeed, Isaiah could rightly be called "the prophet of God's holiness." Statistically, this great prophetic book contains over one-third of the ascriptions of holiness to God in the Old Testament. The most emphatic emphasis on divine holiness comes with Isaiah's use of the title "the Holy One of Israel," which occurs twenty-five times in Isaiah and only seven times in the remainder of the Old Testament. This title for the living God is distributed throughout the sixty-six chapters of Isaiah's prophecy and may well have been coined by the prophet himself. As a name for God it is full of majesty and wonder: the transcendent and majestic Lord has brought himself into close relationship with a particular people, unworthy and wayward as they are, in an act of sovereign goodness.

Isaiah's whole prophecy could rightly be viewed as a meditation on the implications of this title of majesty and goodness and the prophet's confrontation with the glory and purity of the Holy One in the temple (see Is 6).[1] What results is a marvelous vista of God's plan of salvation. Chapters 1—39 recount the awesome threat of judgment that holiness constitutes to a wayward, careless and unresponsive people. Chapters 40—55 reveal the lengths to which the Holy One will go in sovereign goodness to deal with sin, reclaim sinners for himself and thus bring glory to his own great name. And chapters 56—66 disclose the eternal state of holiness that he will prepare and in which his people will enjoy him forever. The scope, character and intensity of the prophetic vision, turning as it does on the majesty, sovereignty and goodness of the Holy One, are breathtakingly wonderful.

So this great prophet leads us to pray in response to wonderful realities and truths about God. He invites us and guides us from meditating on the truth of God's holiness to confronting the Holy One in all his majesty and goodness. Isaiah's prayer takes up three concerns that we, as much as his original readers, need to raise up to the One seated on the lofty, holy, beautiful throne in heaven. We can best conceive of these concerns as arranged in three concentric circles and see the prayer moving toward the circle's center.

A Call for Renewal

The first circle of concern and petition is a *call for renewal.* Isaiah's prayer is set against the background of the military defeat, deportation and material desecration of Israel at the hands of the Babylonians. The temple lies in ruins, the monarchy is effectively destroyed, the cities have become a desert. This picture of weakness and defeat is intensified in contrast to the glorious heritage of Israel. The Lord, after all, had defeated their enemies and delivered them in fulfillment of his promises to Abraham. He had led them and lived among them by his Holy Spirit (for all of this see Is 63:7-14). All of this grace had been good for Israel and had glorified the name of God. Now the nation's reduction to defeat, impotence and captivity weighs like a heavy burden. Not only is it painful to God's people, but it is also theologically wrong. How can the wasted condition of God's people be squared with the majesty and beauty of the Holy One? So the prophet leads us to pray, "Return for the sake of your servants. . . . Oh, look upon us, we pray, for we are all your people" (63:17; 64:9).

Now, we clearly are not facing Isaiah's situation of national disgrace, defeat and exile. For one thing, the coming of the Lord Jesus has dramatically altered the external character and social organization of the people of God. We are no longer a small nation-state but an intentional, multicultural fellowship. Yet the inward and spiritual realities are not so different. Today Christians in the West face a powerful set of spiritual and cultural foes, and it is not at all clear what the outcome of this struggle will be. As Robert Wilken, professor at the University of Virginia (and no friend of fundamentalist culture warriors), comments,

> The ferocity of the current assault on the legacy of Christian culture, however, has brought a new clarity of vision. The alternatives are set before us with unusual starkness; either there will be a genuine renewal of Christian culture—there is no serious alternative—or we will be enveloped by the darkness of paganism in which the worship of the true God is abandoned and forgotten. The sources of the cultural crisis, it turns out, are theological.[2]

As we look around ourselves and at ourselves in the culture of the postmodern West, what do we find? Some take heart from the relatively high rate of church attendance and substantial number of professing believers in the United States. But the problem of Isaiah's time and of our own is not in the measurable level of religious activity. Doubtless in Isaiah's day *all* people were more "religious" than we are. Certainly signs of decline and weakness are found in the combination of prevalent religious practice and moral and spiritual powerlessness. By this standard we are not far different from Israel in the time of Isaiah.

As an illustration of our own spiritually weak and needy state, consider the advance of the homosexual lobby. Not very long ago our culture was marked by a moral consensus that rejected homosexual behavior. In this it followed the moral understanding of the Judeo-Christian heritage, though this consensus also gave tacit (and often explicit) approval to the persecution of homosexuals in an open breach with biblical standards. In the last few years this consensus has almost entirely disappeared and has been replaced with a public morality of approval and even promotion of homosexuality. Basing its appeal on the language of personal rights (including the right to privacy), on inadequate sociological survey research (notably the methodologically flawed Kinsey reports) and ultimately on the foundation of moral relativism, the gay lobby has been spectacularly successful. It has completely won its struggle for acceptance and approval in the public worlds of education, government, communications and entertainment.

In the academic community the gay lobby has become the darling minority, deeply infiltrating the liberal arts and even establishing gay and lesbian studies as formal academic disciplines. As one professor notes, the gay community is "coming out ahead."[3] Not only have university administrators actively sought to create a climate of nondiscrimination toward homosexuals, but they have actually moved into advocacy. Homosexual couples now are housed in university-subsidized married-student apartments, and homosexual partners receive full spousal benefits. Active hostility is expressed toward anyone who dares to disapprove of these moves, especially biblically based Christians.

Christians' responses to these developments have been revealing of our moral and spiritual weakness. Even in Christian colleges, dispute has arisen about the compatibility of Christian faith and homosexual practice. Some faculty have been quietly supportive of "gay Christianity," while homosexual students have appealed for full acceptance in these biblically based institutions. Formal public discussion has been sponsored by some colleges. While administrations have consistently and rightly rejected both homosexual practices and gay-bashing, all of the discussion has been a great stride forward in the homosexual struggle for legitimacy and acceptance. "Gay Christianity" has been placed within the legitimate spectrum of topics for discussion. Might this not be the very thin edge of a very thick wedge being driven into these Christian institutions?

Meanwhile on secular campuses, biblically faithful Christians find themselves in a struggle for the right to continue to exist as a minority of conscience. In many places nondiscrimination policies have been applied in such a way that all campus groups must agree to accept practicing homosexuals as leaders and members in good standing. That such a procedure is a violation of First Amendment rights of religious practice is obvious, and legal proceedings have tended to vindicate dissenting religious groups. Characteristically, legally sophisticated evangelicals have argued for a religious exemption from these antidiscrimination policies and have been grudgingly granted it. But again, note the moral and spiritual impotence of this "victory." The people who seek to speak for God are granted the right to go on living as a fraternity of bigots, as long as they keep their "bigotry" private and quiet. And no effective voice is raised in the public academic arena for the standards of God's holiness.

This unseemly state of affairs is repeated in several other cultural and political arenas. The remorseless advance of secularism (well analyzed by Os Guinness[4]) with its marginalization of the church and any religiously based moral reasoning, the deadly rise of violence fueled by a voyeuristic entertainment industry, the dehumanizing filth of pornography masquerading as freedom of speech in "progressive" circles, the silent holocaust of abortion and euthanasia abetted by a greedy medical establishment, the well-publicized AIDS epidemic driven largely by an insatiable sexual promiscuity, and the steady erosion of the family through degrading poverty and sexual infidelity all point in the same direction. Our culture is without either moral direction or moral self-discipline.

And the people of God, living in the midst of the wreckage, have no more credibility or spiritual energy than any other social group. As Isaiah so poignantly says, "all that we treasured lies in ruins." Indeed, many have described our culture as a "cut-flower" culture. We seem capable of some genuine beauty, but the beauty we produce is cut off from its nourishing roots. It cannot last, because it is cut off from the source of its life. Again, as Isaiah says, "we all shrivel up like a leaf, and like the wind our sins sweep us away." When we ask whether current states of affairs in our churches and nations measure up to the greatness and goodness of our God, we feel with crushing intensity the weight of Isaiah's call for renewal.

Oddly enough, however, we find prayer for renewal difficult. In our technologically sophisticated world we are more inclined to turn to some program and method, some technique, some managerial derring-do to address our weakness. The list of such programs from my adult lifetime is impressive: small groups, spiritual gifts, liturgical renewal, contemporary music, drama, seeker-sensitive meetings, signs and wonders, revival of evangelical scholarship and culture formation, political and social action, church growth. Each item on this list is good and important. A case can be made from Scripture for each. But none has produced quite the earth-shaking result it promised at first. Such a list should not breed cynicism about the concerns it reflects. We ought to be concerned about these matters. But what matters most, indeed supremely, is the renewing power of the Holy One. These good things must not become substitutes for disciplined, passionate prayer for renewal.

A Cry of Repentance

This thought brings us to the second circle of Isaiah's prayer. Well might we ask, Why does such passionate, committed prayer seem so rare? For it seems characteristic of our time that gatherings for prayer are the worst attended in our churches, and prayer is either perfunctory (a bland invocation to begin and a benediction to close our meetings) or optional.

Isaiah's answer to our question is, in a word, "sin" (64:5), which corrupts even our good deeds, causes us to disintegrate like the shriveled leaves of a parched plant and takes away our appetite for seeking God in prayer (64:6-7). Notice the horrible and fearful conclusion we must draw: *prayerlessness is Godlessness.* And this godlessness is the Holy One's judgment on us, hardening our hearts, dulling our consciences and making us wander from his ways.

So Isaiah's second circle of prayer is a *cry of repentance,* a sober recognition that our prayerlessness, waywardness and Godlessness stand in desperate need of the Holy One's free and full forgiveness. He leads us to pray, "Yet, O LORD, you are our Father. We are the clay, you are the potter; we are all the work of your hand. Do not be angry beyond measure, O LORD; do not remember our sins forever" (64:8-9).

The two essential elements of true repentance are visible in this petition. First, we cast ourselves on God's free mercy, acknowledging our guilt and utter dependence on him. We deserve his anger but call on him to avert it lest we perish. A clarifying comment on the phrase "beyond measure" (64:9, 12) may be helpful. This NIV translation suggests that perhaps the Holy One might be angry beyond just and permissible limits and that we are asking only that he pull back from that dangerously intolerant level of wrath. Such a view is, of course, unworthy of the majesty and justice of the Holy One, and not surprisingly, it is not required by the Hebrew text. Literally it should be translated "unto muchness," and it carries the meaning of "with all its inherent force." So we cry out to our holy God, "Do not let us feel the full weight of your anger."

As Isaiah well knew, the Holy One would raise up a Servant to bear the full weight of this righteous judgment in our place (Is 53). So it is that living this side of Jesus' cross, resurrection and ascension, we pray this prayer in Jesus' name and for his sake, trusting the overflowing goodness of the Holy One in his Son's cross to have quenched the wrath we deserve.

Second, true repentance turns from sin and places our very selves in God's hands. Repentance includes an irreducible dimension of submission to the Holy One. So we gladly abandon ourselves to the shaping plan and power of the Potter, our heavenly Father. The cry of repentance directs us into the glorious gospel paradox that we save our life only by emphatically and intentionally losing it in a joyful and thoroughgoing submission to the Holy One.

A Plea for Spiritual Reality

This brings us to our central circle of prayer concern, for Isaiah's prayer and ours is a *plea for spiritual reality.* At its center this great model prayer is a heartfelt petition for God to manifest himself, to press in on us in all his matchless sovereignty and goodness. The prayer is framed with a request to the Holy One not to hold back from us. At its beginning it is a cry to our heavenly Father to not withhold his tenderness and compassion (63:15), and the conclusion comes full circle with its plea to the Lord not to withhold himself. Tenderness and compassion mean little apart from the presence of a person. We yearn for his nearness. So in the most graphic of requests, we plead, "Rend the heavens and come down!" (64:1, 3).

This centripetal movement is not only a matter of literary structure in Isaiah's beautiful poem. It is also basic to its thought. Where will the power come from to renew God's people and extend God's kingdom? Certainly it does not reside within the creation, with the capabilities and schemes of even the greatest of God's servants individually or collectively. And what hope is there in the face of our sin—hope that we will even recognize our true spiritual condition, to say nothing of hope for the forgiveness and moral re-creation we so desperately need?

We long for this power and this grace. But as a consequence we must long, and are led to long, for something greater, for the personal glory of the Holy One to shatter the barriers erected by our hardness and waywardness. We long for him to stoop to give himself to us. So it is that the heart of all our praying and seeking is the passionate plea, "Oh, that you would rend the heavens and come down."

Have you learned to pray like this, believingly and persistently? Often we simply have not learned to pray at all. We need to recall, then, that prayerlessness is Godlessness. Stripped of our excuses and rationalizations, we can own our real situation and be led to cry out to the Holy One.

But even when we do pray, there appears to me too little of the God-centered passion we see in Isaiah's prayer. Characteristically we ask God to make life easy and comfortable. His goodness is such that the Holy One hears us for the sake of his Son. But if we would move from the great thoughts of God's holy majesty and goodness to a personal realization of these awesome realities, we must learn to pray like Isaiah.

May none of these wonderful truths be mere notions that delight our minds. May great thoughts of God lead to a life of personal conversation and communion with the Holy One.

No Eye Has Seen

And what of the effect of such praying? Says Isaiah, echoing similar thoughts throughout Scripture (see, for example, Ps 116; Jer 33:3; Ezek 36; Mt 6; Lk 11; Phil 4; Jas 5): "Since ancient times no one has heard, no ear has perceived, no eye has seen any God besides you, who acts on behalf of those who wait for him" (64:4).

Two stories illustrate this great truth, one contemporary and the other from the mid-eighteenth century. The contemporary tale is a small manifestation of the wonderful advance of the kingdom of God among Koreans. The churches of Korea have known amazing growth. In fact, there are more Presbyterians in Korea than in Scotland or the United States (the Presbyterian churches of these countries sent the first missionaries to Korea). The growth of God's people in Korea is fueled by the prodigious Korean commitment to daily prayer—prodigious by our decadent Western standards, but just normal for Korean Christians.

A Korean colleague of mine is the son of one of the patriarchs of the Korean Presbyterian Churches of the USA. His father's practice was to spend considerable time at his church each Saturday evening. In seminary my friend learned that it is best for preachers to rest well on Saturday evening, so he passed this advice along to his father, urging him to stay at home and rest. His father made no reply, though he was clearly unhappy with the suggestion. Instead he invited my friend to come with him the next Saturday.

That night my friend stood in shamed amazement as he watched his father walk through the sanctuary, praying for each member of the congregation at the place where he or she habitually sat during services. The prayer time consumed three hours, which passed away like minutes. Small wonder the hand of God was manifested among these people.

Thank God for a pastor who resisted theologians' worldly-wise advice and chose instead to lay hold on the Holy One for the sake of his people. We need not necessarily adopt his particular Saturday-evening prayer practice. But his passion and persistence in prayer stand as a wonderful model. Who would not want such a pastor? May God multiply his number.

The eighteenth-century story begins in 1746, with certain Scottish pastors' calls to English-speaking Christians for special prayer for the conversion of the world. They proposed special prayer gatherings on Saturday evenings, Sunday mornings and the first Thursday of each quarter over a period of seven years. The great American theologian Jonathan Edwards wrote a treatise in support of this proposal, *A Humble Attempt to Promote Explicit Agreement and Visible Union of God's People in Extraordinary Prayer for the Revival of Religion.* (Incidentally, this treatise has been resurrected as the mandate for the current movement for concerts of prayer.) Edwards argued from Scripture that God's promises give Christians a strong incentive to pray for such revival and that believers also have a positive duty so to pray.

It is natural to wonder what resulted from this 1746 call to prayer. There is no way to determine how well the call was heeded during the seven years.

The awakening Edwards himself was a part of in New England had petered out in 1742, so there was no merely emotional energy to fuel participation. And we also have no way of knowing whether the special prayer gatherings continued after 1753 among those who had learned the habit of praying according to the call.

Nothing very startling happened at first. Indeed, revival fires cooled notably in both Old and New England. Yet the Holy One calls us to *wait* for him. To quote Edwards,

> It is very apparent from the word of God, that he is wont often to try the faith and patience of his people, when crying to him for some great and important mercy, by withholding the mercy sought for a season. And yet he, without fail, at last succeeds those who continue instant in prayer, with all perseverance. . . . Whatever our hopes may be, we must be content to be ignorant of the times and seasons, which the Father hath put in his power, and must be willing that God should answer prayer, and fulfill his own glorious promises, in his own time.[5]

Edwards died in 1758, having seen little of the divine answer. But from 1770 onward Methodist preachers in Britain and North America saw great growth and occasional revival conditions. The Second Great Awakening burst into full flame in the 1790s, along with revival in Norway under Hans Nielsen Hauge and in Finland under Paavo Ruotsalainen. Furthermore, the Protestant missionary movement was born, which gave biblical Christianity a toehold in all parts of the world within a generation. No one but the Holy One knows how this amazing outburst of spiritual energy was related to the prayer movement of several decades before. But it seems clear that the two were bound together in the sovereign plan of the Holy One. They encourage us to think great thoughts of God and his ways with us and to turn those thoughts into fervent and disciplined prayer.

*　　*　　*

Some conclusions conclude. Others, the best sort, are a kind of preface for better things. May this conclusion be among the latter. And it will be if the Holy One himself meets us and moves us to believing and persistent prayer along the model of Isaiah's great prayer. *Oh, that you would rend the heavens and come down!*

Notes

Preface
[1]Richard F. Lovelace, *Dynamics of Spiritual Life: An Evangelical Theology of Renewal* (Downers Grove, Ill.: InterVarsity Press, 1979), pp. 81-82.
[2]Ibid., pp. 84-85.
[3]J. I. Packer, *Knowing God* (Downers Grove, Ill.: InterVarsity Press, 1973), p. 5.
[4]Quoted in ibid., p. 7

Chapter 1: The Meaning of *Holy*
[1]T. Jacobson, *The Treasures of Darkness* (New Haven, Conn.: Yale University Press, 1976), pp. 102-3.
[2]Ibid., p. 8.
[3]Ibid., p. 9.
[4]Quoted in Robert Alter, *The Art of Biblical Narrative* (New York: Basic Books, 1981), p. 25. Alter's keen and sensitive treatment of Old Testament narrative is a helpful and necessary corrective to more standard treatments of the Old Testament, which depend on the development of a highly speculative prehistory of the text and which arbitrarily dismember and thus misconstrue the text as we have received it.
[5]Christopher J. H. Wright, *An Eye for an Eye: The Place of Old Testament Ethics Today* (Downers Grove, Ill.: InterVarsity Press, 1983), p. 112.
[6]William F. Albright, *Yahweh and the Gods of Canaan* (New York: Doubleday, 1969), p. 185.
[7]C. S. Lewis, *Miracles* (London: Collins, 1947), p. 98.

Chapter 2: The Majesty of God
[1]A. W. Pink, *Sovereignty of God* (London: Banner of Truth, 1961), pp. 12-14, 111-13.
[2]Emil Brunner, *Our Faith* (Philadelphia: Westminster Press, 1949), p. 12.

Chapter 3: God the Creator
[1]Quoted in James Houston, *I Believe in the Creator* (Grand Rapids, Mich.: Eerdmans, 1980), pp. 35-37.

[2]Ibid., p. 36.

[3]These thoughts are freely adapted from Louis Berkhof, *Systematic Theology* (Grand Rapids, Mich.: Eerdmans, 1939), p. 126.

[4]Luci Shaw, "Getting Inside the Miracle." From *Polishing the Petoskey Stone,* © 1990 Luci Shaw, Harold Shaw Publishers, Wheaton, IL 60189. Used by permission.

[5]For this discussion I draw on Gerhard Hasel, "The Polemic Nature of the Genesis Cosmology," *Evangelical Quarterly* 46 (1974): 81-102.

[6]John Calvin, *Commentary on Psalms* (Grand Rapids, Mich.: Eerdmans, 1981), 5:184-88.

[7]Charles E. Hummel, *The Galileo Connection: Resolving Conflicts Between Science and the Bible* (Downers Grove, Ill.: InterVarsity Press, 1989), p. 176.

[8]Donald M. McKay, *The Clockwork Image: A Christian Perspective on Science* (Downers Grove, Ill.: InterVarsity Press, 1974), pp. 42-44.

[9]Robert Jastrow, *God and the Astronomers* (New York: Norton, 1978), pp. 115-16.

[10]Several scholars, notably Reijer Hooykaas and Stanley Jaki, have sketched out historically the fruitfulness of Christian theism for the use of modern sciences. See Reijer Hooykaas, *Religion and the Rise of Modern Science* (Grand Rapids, Mich.: Eerdmans, 1972), and Stanley Jaki, *Cosmos and Creator* (Chicago: Regnery, 1980).

[11]Jonathan Edwards, *The Nature of True Virtue,* quoted in Leland Ryken, *Triumphs of the Imagination: Literature in Christian Perspective* (Downers Grove, Ill.: InterVarsity Press, 1979), p. 36.

Chapter 4: Our God Reigns

[1]J. I. Packer, *Knowing God* (Downers Grove, Ill.: InterVarsity Press, 1973), p. 6.

[2]Paul Jacobs and Hartmut Krienke, "Foreknowledge, Providence, Predestination," in *The New International Dictionary of New Testament Theology,* ed. Colin Brown, 3 vols. (Grand Rapids, Mich.: Zondervan, 1975-78), 1:693.

Chapter 5: The Goodness of God

[1]Alasdair MacIntyre, *After Virtue: A Study in Moral Theory,* 2nd ed. (Notre Dame, Ind.: University of Notre Dame Press, 1984), pp. 22-34.

[2]J. I. Packer, in *Law, Morality and the Bible,* ed. Bruce Kaye and Gordon Wenham (Downers Grove, Ill.: InterVarsity Press, 1978), p. 184.

[3]Ibid., pp. 185-87.

[4]See S. Motyer, "Righteousness by Faith in the New Testament," in *Here We Stand* (London: Hodder & Stoughton, 1986), p. 35.

Chapter 6: God the Judge

[1]John Hick, *Death and Eternal Life* (London: Gollias, 1976).

[2]Leon Morris, *Testaments of Love* (Grand Rapids, Mich.· Eerdmans, 1981), p. 167.

[3]Steven Travis, *I Believe in the Second Coming of Jesus* (Grand Rapids, Mich.: Eerdmans, 1982), p. 204.

Chapter 7: God the Warrior

[1]Aldous Huxley, *Ends and Means* (New York: Harper, 1937), pp. 270-71.

[2]Langston Hughes, *The Best of Simple* (New York: Hill & Wang, 1961), p. 10.

[3]Many more examples could be mentioned. See Christopher J. H. Wright, *An Eye for an Eye: The Place of Old Testament Ethics Today* (Downers Grove, Ill.: InterVarsity Press, 1983).

[4]Quoted in John W. Wenham, *The Goodness of God* (Downers Grove, Ill.: InterVarsity Press, 1974), pp. 167-68.

[5]G. E. Wright and F. V. Filson, *The Westminster Historical Atlas to the Bible* (Philadelphia: Westminster Press, 1948), p. 36.

Chapter 8: The Devastation of Sin

[1]Mary Douglas, *Purity and Danger* (London: Routledge and Kegan Paul, 1966), p. 51, cited in Gordon Wenham, *Leviticus* (Grand Rapids, Mich.: Eerdmans, 1979), pp. 23-24.

[2]This figure is taken from Wenham, *Leviticus,* p. 19. Used by permission.

[3]This figure is taken from ibid., p. 177. Used by permission.

[4]Douglas, *Purity and Danger,* p. 57; quoted in Wenham, *Leviticus,* p. 184.

Chapter 9: The Necessity of Sacrifice

[1]Gordon Wenham, *Leviticus* (Grand Rapids, Mich: Eerdmans, 1979), p. 56.

[2]Gordon Wenham, *Numbers* (Downers Grove, Ill.: InterVarsity Press, 1981), pp. 29-30.

[3]See ibid., pp. 25-26.

[4]This figure is taken from Wenham, *Leviticus,* p. 53. Used by permission.

[5]This figure is taken from R. K. Harrison, *Leviticus* (Downers Grove, Ill.: InterVarsity Press, 1980), p. 38. Used by permission.

[6]P. T. Forsyth, *The Work of Christ* (London: Independent Press, 1948), p. 90.

[7]See Leon Morris, *Testaments of Love* (Grand Rapids, Mich.: Eerdmans, 1981), pp. 142-60.

Chapter 10: The Majesty of the Cross

[1]Rodney Clapp, personal communication, September 16, 1992.

Chapter 11: The Fear of the Lord

[1]David Myers, *The Inflated Self* (New York: Seabury, 1980).

[2]Martin Bolt and David G. Myers, *The Human Connection: How People Change People* (Downers Grove, Ill.: InterVarsity Press, 1984), p. 30.

[3]Ibid., p. 33.

[4]C. S. Lewis, *Mere Christianity* (New York: Macmillan, 1960), p. 99; quoted in Bolt and Myers, *Human Connection,* p. 36.

[5]To see this claim demonstrated through a careful study of the entire text of Ecclesiastes, see Stafford Wright, "The Interpretation of Ecclesiastes," in *Classical Evangelical Essays on Old Testament Interpretation,* ed. Walter C. Kaiser (Grand Rapids, Mich.: Baker Book House, 1972), pp, 133-50; and Walter C. Kaiser, *Total Life* (Chicago: Moody Press, 1978).

Chapter 12: Glory

[1]Robert N. Bellah et al., *Habits of the Heart: Individualism and Commitment in*

American Life (New York: Harper & Row, 1985), p. 14.

[2]Derek Kidner, *Psalms 73—150: A Commentary,* Tyndale Old Testament Commentaries (Leicester, U.K.: Inter-Varsity Press, 1973), p. 405.

[3]Frank M. Cross Jr., "The Priestly Tabernacle," in *The Biblical Archaeologist Reader,* ed. D. N. Freedman and G. E. Wright (Garden City, N.Y.: Anchor Books, 1961), pp. 225-27.

[4]Ibid., p. 226. See also R. E. Clements, *God and Temple: The Presence of God in Israel's Worship* (Philadelphia: Fortress, 1965), pp. 35-57.

[5]J. C. Ryle, *Practical Religion* (Edinburgh: Banner of Truth, 1959), p. 130.

[6]J. I. Packer, *Knowing God* (Downers Grove, Ill.: InterVarsity Press, 1973), p. 158.

[7]Bellah et al., *Habits of the Heart,* pp. 118-19.

[8]Ibid., pp. 133-34.

[9]P. T. Forsyth, *The Justification of God* (London: Independent, 1948), p. 117.

[10]Kidner, *Psalms 73-150,* p. 406.

[11]See ibid., p. 404.

[12]"Christopher Parkening: Guitarist with a Mission," *Eternity* 38 (March 1987): 77

Chapter 13: Worship
[1]For an excellent summary, see G. W. Bromiley, "Worship," in *Zondervan Pictorial Encyclopedia of the Bible,* edited by Merrill C. Tenney (Grand Rapids, Mich.: Zondervan, 1978), pp. 969-90, especially 976-82.

[2]Quoted in J. J. von Allmen, *Worship: Its Theology and Practice* (New York: Oxford University Press, 1965), p. 13.

[3]Ben Witherington III, *Women in the Ministry of Jesus* (Cambridge: Cambridge University Press, 1987), p. 113.

[4]See C. H. Dodd, *According to the Scriptures* (London: Nisbet, 1952), and R. T. France, *Jesus and the Old Testament* (London: Tyndale, 1971).

[5]Witherington, *Women in the Ministry,* p. 101.

[6]I owe this expression to J. I. Packer, *Keep in Step with the Spirit* (New York: Revell, 1987), pp. 231-32.

Chapter 14: Rend the Heavens and Come Down
[1]For a deepening of this analysis, see the wonderful commentary of Alec Motyer, *The Prophecy of Isaiah* (Downers Grove, Ill.: InterVarsity Press, 1993), pp. 17-19.

[2]Robert Wilken, "No Other Gods," *First Things,* November 1993, p. 14.

[3]Jerry Z. Muller, "Coming Out Ahead: The Homosexual in the Academy," *First Things,* October 1993, pp. 7-24.

[4]Os Guinness, *The Gravedigger File: Papers on the Subversion of the Modern Church* (Downers Grove, Ill.: InterVarsity Press, 1983).

[5]Jonathan Edwards, in *The Works of Jonathan Edwards,* rev. and ed. Edward Hukman (original 1834; London: Banner of Truth, 1974), 2:312.